C0-DVI-220

THE FAITH OF QUMRAN

THE FAITH OF
QUMRAN

THEOLOGY OF THE DEAD SEA SCROLLS

EXPANDED EDITION

Helmer Ringgren

Translated by Emilie T. Sander

Edited with a New Introduction
by James H. Charlesworth

GRADUATE THEOLOGICAL UNION LIBRARY 1962

Christian Origins Library

Crossroad • New York

BM
487
R513
1995

G

1995

The Crossroad Publishing Company
370 Lexington Avenue, New York, NY 10017

Copyright © 1963 by Fortress Press
New Foreword Copyright © 1995 by James H. Charlesworth

This book is a translation of *Tro och liv enligt Döda-havsrullarna* by Helmer Ringgren, published by Diakonistyrelsens Bokförlag, Stockholm, in 1961.

All rights reserved. No part of this book may be reproduced, stored in a retrieval system, or transmitted, in any form or by any means, electronic, mechanical, photocopying, recording, or otherwise, without the written permission of The Crossroad Publishing Company.

Printed in the United States of America

Library of Congress Catalog Card Number: 95-067351

ISBN: 0-8245-1258-8

Preface

This book was written in the conviction that before
we start comparing isolated beliefs and practices of the
Qumran community with those of the New Testament
church, we should establish their meaning in their original context. For this purpose there is need of a systematic account of the doctrines and practices of the
Qumran community as set forth in the Dead Sea Scrolls.
It is true that we do not yet have access to the complete
bulk of material from the caves, but it seems likely that
what we have enables us to draw a fairly correct picture
of the community and its beliefs. The documents that
are still to be published might modify our views in
certain questions of detail, but their publication will
probably not necessitate any fundamental change of the
total picture.

I cannot present this book to the American public
without expressing my deep gratitude to my excellent
translator, Miss Emilie T. Sander. She has done exceptionally good work, much more than is usually expected
of a translator. Besides rendering the Swedish text
correctly and readably in English she has also checked
all the references to the texts as well as to books and
periodicals, noting English editions now available and

correcting several mistakes. She has adapted my Swedish version of biblical and Scrolls citations with constant attention to the usage of the RSV, while at the same time retaining my independent interpretations of the Hebrew where I differ from other translators. It is hard to find adequate expression for my appreciation of her work.

My own contribution to the American edition is limited to the rewriting of a couple of passages and a few additions to bring the text up to date. Some recent publications have been added in the footnotes and the bibliography.

Turku, Finland   H.R.
January, 1963

It is a venture to republish a book unchanged after thirty years. In this case, however, it seems justified. The texts that have been published since 1963 might have enabled me to make a few additions, especially on the Songs of the Sabbath Sacrifices. The recently published Dead Sea Scrolls would obviously enable me to add interesting details, but they would not change my basic ideas substantially. It is only to be hoped that future publications will make a second, revised edition necessary.

Uppsala, Sweden   H.R.
July 21, 1993

Translator's Note

The abbreviations used for designating the manuscripts of Qumran follow those of Barthélemy-Milik (eds.) in *DJD:* the small number indicates the number of the Cave in which the manuscript was found. "Q" stands for "Qumran," and the letters following are usually the first letters of the Hebrew title of the manuscript. Thus:

> $_1$QS = $_1$Q *sérek hay-yáḥad* (order of the community) = The Manual of Discipline (found in Cave 1)
>
> $_1$QH = $_1$Q *hôdāyôt* (thanksgivings) = The Thanksgiving Psalms
>
> $_1$QM = $_1$Q *milḥāmāh* (war) = The War Scroll
>
> $_1$QpHab. = $_1$Q *pešer* Habakkuk (interpretation of Habakkuk) = The Habakkuk Commentary
>
> $_4$QpPs.37 = $_4$Q *pešer* on canonical Psalm 37 = Commentary on Psalm 37 (found in Cave 4)
>
> CD = The Cairo Damascus Document

Small Roman numerals indicate columns and are followed by the number of the line in Arabic numerals. Thus: $_1$QS xi.12 = The Manual of Discipline, column xi, line 12. Arabic numbers are used for division into chapter and verse, as with biblical quotations—Ps. 94:18. It

should be noted that The Fragments of a Zadokite Work
(= The Damascus Document) as edited by Charles
(*Apocrypha and Pseudepigrapha of the Old Testament*)
is divided into chapters and verses while Rabin (*The
Zadokite Documents*) uses column and line indications;
the latter system of notation has been used here.

Brackets in the text citations indicate that the translator or editor of the original text made a conjecture as
to the reconstruction of a lacuna in the manuscript.

In my work on this translation, which was done con-
currently with my doctoral studies at the Harvard
Divinity School, I profited greatly from the resources of
that institution. I wish especially to express my appreciation for the generous help and advice given by my
teachers, Professor Frank Moore Cross, Jr. and Professor
Krister Stendahl.

E.T.S.

Foreword

While preparing courses on the Dead Sea Scrolls for undergraduates, seminary students, or doctoral candidates I have lamented that Helmer Ringgren's *The Faith of Qumran* was out of print. While writing selected bibliographies on Qumran theological concepts I almost always stressed the importance of Ringgren's excellent study. Recently I discussed the need to reprint some major Qumran books with Magen Broshi, the Curator of the Shrine of the Book, in which the Dead Sea Scrolls are exhibited to the public. I brought up the need to reissue Ringgren's book. He urged me to do so. He emphasized that no other book on the Dead Sea Scrolls seemed so important for a wide audience.

Most scholars interested in Qumran have been attracted by the thoughts, or theologies, presented and developed in the Dead Sea Scrolls. One would think that there are numerous books devoted to the theologies represented at Qumran. In fact, with the exception of F. Nötscher's *Zur* *theologischen Terminologie der Qumran-Texte,*1 Ringgren's book is the only one which attempts to present a synthesis of the theologies at Qumran.

It is now available again, thanks to the leadership and dedication of Crossroad Publishing Company of New York. It is another addition to an already distinguished series, Crossroad's Christian Origins Library.

Abiding contributions are found in Ringgren's book, notably the following:

1. a systematic presentation of the theologies at Qumran must follow a minute study of the content and literary character of each scroll (p. 1);

2. the Rule of the Community is not a unity; it is "a compilation of material" (p. 2; this suggestion is now confirmed by the study of the fragments of this scroll found in Cave IV);

3. the first person pronoun in the Thanksgiving Hymns (1QH) "must be an individual, since on several occasions the "I" is set in contrast to a plural designation, . . ." (p. 15);

4. it is certain that the Righteous Teacher was "a priest who was regarded as an inspired interpreter of the Scriptures," he certainly founded the Community, and was persecuted by his adversary, the Wicked Priest, but he was not crucified (p. 35);

5. the Qumranites usually used the arachic *'ēl* for God, greatly revered the divine name, and emphasized God's transcendence (p. 48);

6. God acts "for his own sake," and not because of human plight (p. 51);

[1] F. Nötscher, *Zur theologischen Terminologie der Qumran-Texte* (Bonner Biblische Beiträge 10; Bonn: Peter Hanstein Verlag, 1956).

7. God is the sole Creator (p. 52);

8. "the course of the world and of history" is determined according to "divine predestination" (p. 60);

9. from the beginning God has determined each human's "lot" (p. 72);

10. the cosmic dualism is evident in that the struggle between the two heavenly spirits is not only centered in the human heart, it is "also a world-wide battle between" the Angel of Light and the Angel of Darkness (p. 76);

11. one of the leading Qumran motifs is the human's nothingness in face of God's omnipotence (pp. 94–95);

12. as David Flusser pointed out, there is at Qumran a dualism between flesh and spirit in the sense that the opposition is between the human as flesh and the divine spirit as the means for salvation (p. 100);

13. some passages in the Thanksgiving Hymns imply "a double predestination" (p. 107);

14. the Qumranites claimed to experience "fellowship with the heavenly world" (p. 128, cf. p. 149);

15. the "key note" in Qumran piety is jubilation (p. 132);

16. many ideas in the Qumran Scrolls indicate that the Qumran Community was an Essene community (*passim*, pp. 151, 241);

17. the Qumranites hoped for a new earth and a new Jerusalem, but at the same time "experienced a union with God" in the present (p. 151);

18. the Qumranites perceived that the Endtime was near, but also experienced their own deliverance as a Community of the eschatological age (p. 154);

19. while it is not necessary that messianic ideas are intended each time a scribe used the word "anointed," and while we must be careful not to read meanings into texts,

yet it seems many at Qumran would have believed that when God renews his covenant "two anointed ones shall arise" (p. 171 [the rest of the paragraph needs revision today]);

20. the task of the Righteous Teacher was to instruct and especially "to make known" God's mysteries (p. 185);

21. although the Righteous Teacher was not portrayed as the Messiah, he was most likely conceived as "a prophetic forerunner to the two Anointed Ones" (p. 198);

22. *rabbîm* is "the term for the fully initiated members" (p. 212);

23. the exclusion of the Qumranites from the Jerusalem cult "necessitated a spiritualization of the sacrifical cult" (p. 215);

24. most likely "a purifying bath was a prerequisite condition for participation in the common meal" (p. 220);

25. S. Talmon rightly pointed out that the confession of sin associated with the covenant renewal suggests the hypothesis that this ritual occurred on the Day of Atonement (p. 226).

Obviously, there are other important points to be found in this book. The above list may stimulate many to read through the chapters, which may be studied successively or as self-contained presentations.

I wish to express my appreciation to Fortress Press, which published this book in 1961, thirty years ago, for the permission to reissue this work. I am also grateful to Professor Ringgren who has added to his preface. With the help of Henry W. L. Rietz I compiled a selected and annotated bibliography. Along with this bibliography, my introduction "The Theologies in the Dead Sea Scrolls" intends to

bridge the gap between 1963 and 1993 and to draw attention
to the major developments in the field of Qumran Studies.

Princeton Theological Seminary

James H. Charlesworth

Princeton, NJ
July 30, 1993

Introduction to the Expanded Edition

The Theologies in the Dead Sea Scrolls

James H. Charlesworth

The study of the Dead Sea Scrolls was significantly advanced when Ringgren's *The Faith of Qumran* appeared in 1963. Major volumes had appeared and been widely influential; among these are classic studies by N. Avigad, W. H. Brownlee, F. F. Bruce, M. Burrows, J. Carmignac, F. M. Cross, A. Dupont-Sommer, S. Holm-Nielsen, H. W. Huppenbauer, J. Licht, J. T. Milik, C. Rabin, H. H. Rowley, K. Schubert, K. Stendahl, R. de Vaux, E. L. Sukenik, P. Wernberg-Møller, Y. Yadin, and the first three volumes of Discoveries in the Judaean Desert.

Now, thirty years later, one has to be extremely cautious in attempting to write a definitive study of what has been called "Qumran theology." We are constantly enriched by the fresh information pouring from the fragments being published, or being prepared for publication. Two examples make this point in a poignant way. When the Princeton Theological Seminary Dead Sea Scrolls Project was launched in 1985, about 80 documents were to be included in the first "comprehensive" edition of the sectarian Dead Sea Scrolls. Scholars often expressed astonishment that so many documents were to be included. Now, the list has swelled to well over 400.

The second example is also instructive. Professor Jacob Milgrom significantly changed his introduction to the "Purification Rule" (4Q514), because of the assignment to him of another virtually unknown document; fortunately this major change was possible, even though we were at the galley stage of proofs. Qumran research is moving at an unprecedented pace. It is simply not possible to assess the data and to attempt a "theology" of these documents; but an assessment of the theological contributions of the Scrolls is indispensable. Hence, Ringgren's work is reissued in the endeavor to stimulate more theological reflections on the thoughts present at Qumran.

I shall try now only to present seven caveats that have helped me in thinking about the theologies at Qumran. These should help make Ringgren's important study of the "Theology of the Dead Sea Scrolls" more valuable today, and will help pave the way for such a book on the theologies at Qumran.

1. Old Testament Pseudepigrapha not from Qumran. For at least a decade after the first discoveries in 1947 the documents contained in *The Old Testament Pseudepigrapha* (ed. J. H. Charlesworth),[1] were incorporated into an assessment

---

[1] See at the back of this book "Theologies at Qumran: Selected and Annotated Bibliography."

of "Qumran theology." That assessment is inaccurate. These documents were not composed at Qumran. Only a few of them were influential at Qumran; among these would be Jubilees, the Books of Enoch (1Enoch), and perhaps the earliest versions of the Testaments of the Twelve Patriarchs. These are not Qumran compositions; they reflect the theologies of other Jewish groups contemporaneous with the Dead Sea Scrolls.

2. Scrolls Originating Elsewhere And Perhaps Edited at Qumran. Some documents which probably did not originate at Qumran are often used to study "Qumran theology." These documents clearly belong to the narrow definition of "the Dead Sea Scrolls," but they should be used with extreme caution in assessing "Qumran theology." Among such documents are the Damascus Document and the Temple Scroll; both of these reached their final form at Qumran but probably reflect many ideas that antedate the founding of the Community at Qumran around 150 B.C.E.

3. Scrolls Originating Elsewhere And Not Apparently Altered at Qumran. It is imperative that Scrolls which were not composed at Qumran and do not represent Qumran theological reflections are not allowed to distort the attempts to understand and portray what was regnant at Qumran. Among these scrolls are the Qumran Pseudepigraphic Psalms (4Q380 and 4Q381), the Prayer of Joseph (4Q371–372), Second Ezekiel (4Q385–389), and the Copper Scroll (3Q15).

4. The Study of Qumran Theologies Must Be Focused on Scrolls Composed at Qumran. There is a consensus over the last thirty years that numerous documents were composed at Qumran. The Study of Qumran theology should be grounded in the ideas, concepts, and terms found in these scrolls. Most important among such scrolls are the following: The Rule of the Community (1QS), the Rule of the Congregation (1QSa), Blessings (1QSb), the War Scroll (1QM), the Thanksgiving Hymns (1QH), the Pesharim (esp. 1QpHab, 4QpNah, 1QpPs68), and the Angelic Liturgy (4Q400–407). Although, as already indicated, Ringgren's valuable study here reissued needs updating, its continuing importance is clear because he tended to base his work on many of these major Qumran compositions.

5. *There is no "Qumran Theology."* In the sixties scholars became disenchanted with a systematic presentation of "Old Testament" ideas into a grand schema labeled biblical theology, despite the attempts of W. Eichrodt and even G. von Rad; yet, at the same time specialists on Qumran spoke about "Qumran theology." If the presupposition that there was only one system of thought at Qumran was ever valid, it is now no longer warranted. There were different ideas of the human (see Lichtenberger), and different explanations of God's responsibility for sin and evil, and apparently different messianic ideas.

Let me focus on only the latter two. 1) The Rule of the Community presents a somewhat successful attempt to absolve God of the responsibility for sin by claiming that evil comes from the Angel of Darkness (1QS 3). This position is compromised by the idea in the War Scroll which states that God created the evil angel, Belial, for the pit: "And you, O God, made Belial, the angel of Hatred, to corrupt. . . ." (1QM 13.11). 2) It is no longer easy to report that the Qumranites believed in two Messiahs, the Messiah of Aaron and Israel, despite the reading in 1QS 9.11: "until the coming of the Messiahs of Aaron and Israel." This passage is missing in one of the witnesses to the Rule of the

Community from Cave IV, notably 4QS E (see Charlesworth and Qimron in the PTS DSS volume number 1).

Numerous theologies were found at Qumran. The calendars were all lunar–solar, and not simply lunar as in the Jerusalem cult; but these calendars were not identical. Varieties in theological reflection are demanded by the following: the longevity of the Qumran Community (it existed for three centuries from the middle of the second century B.C.E. to 68 C.E.); the expansion of the Community from a rather small group to well over 100 members; the death of its charismatic founder, the Righteous Teacher, to whom alone God revealed the mysteries of the prophets (cf. 1QpHab7); the demise of the first priests who created the Community and once were among the leaders in the Jerusalem cult; and their replacement by other Jews, some of whom were not priests.

6. *Trends of the Qumran Theologies.* Obviously, the theologies at Qumran, as those within the so-called Old Testament, were united by certain overriding convictions and affirmations. God was one, and not one of many gods to be worshipped; "el" alone was God (1QS 3.15). Under God were other heavenly beings, the archangels, the *elim*, angels, and the Holy Ones. A profound cosmic dualism tends to shape the documents composed at Qumran, and this was expressed in a definitive form in the Rule of the Community (1QS 3–4) and later developed in the War Scroll. Almost all thoughts and actions at Qumran were shaped by an "eschatological" fervor. The Qumranites yearned for the Judgment Day and the time when the angels of evil would be defeated (1QM).

Although dualistic thought at Qumran was profoundly influential, the Qumranites also affirmed that dichotomies were breaking down. Heaven was no longer only above the earth; it impinged on their earthly services so that their Community was like an antechamber of heaven. Indeed, the suggestion that the Qumran Community was occasionally portrayed as, or better functioned as, the Temple, which is developed by G. Klinzing, seems confirmed by the copy of the Rule of the Community which seems to depict the Community as *Miqdash*, "Temple"; contrast 4QS E Frg. 1 Col. 3 1-2 ("[. . .] a sanctuary *(miqdash)* in the midst of the Council of the me[n of the Community]") with 1QS 8.11 ("they shall be set apart (as) holy in the midst of the Council of the men of the Community"). The earthly services mirrored the singing of the heavenly ones; in fact the Angelic Liturgy describes the angels' worship of God in the heavenly Temple, but the Qumranites on earth participated in this worship (Schwemer). The difficulty of translating terms like *elim* and *qedhoshim*, especially attempting to discern when angels or Qumranites were meant, and the concept that the Qumran male could evolve into angelic status indicates that the categorical distinction between angels and humans had broken down. Finally, the "end of days" were not off in the distant; the Qumranites claimed that the New Age was sometimes being experienced as present in their Community (H.-W. Kuhn), especially during their worship services in which angels were present (1QSa 2.9). Hence, the categorical opposites of heaven and earth, human and angel, and the Endtime and the present, were no longer distinct.

Perhaps the most significantly unique feature of the theologies at Qumran is the belief in predestination (Broshi, cf. Merrill). A Son of Light and a Son of Darkness (1QS 3-4) is determined before birth; no action or belief on earth can alter this categorical foreordination. Each person has nine parts of light or darkness. Every individual has at least one portion of light or darkness. The most wretched Son of Darkness has eight parts from the House of Darkness but only one part from the House of Light (4Q186 1.3). The most glorious Son of Light has eight parts from the House of Light and only one part from the House of Darkness (4Q186 2.1). Hence, one is predestined before birth regarding not only his earthly thoughts and actions, but also his eternal destiny.

7. *Finally, the Coherence of Qumran Theologies Does not Lie in Disparate Concepts.* The key to understanding the theologies at Qumran is not via the study of individual concepts, like "Covenant," "Exile," "Community," "Purity," or even the ideas just enumerated. The foundational thought is apparent only in the way all such terms, concepts, perceptions, and hopes are expressed and related in these invaluable Scrolls. All concepts, in my judgment, need to be comprehended in terms of the overriding intentionality, spirit and setting *(Sitz im Leben)* which gave rise to each passage; most importantly among these are the belief that the Holy Spirit from God was present in their Community and only there, that angels were intermittently present with them, that the present was the Endtime, and that all prophecies were about the history and life of the Community, pointed directly to them as the Sons of Light, and are comprehensible only through the revelations delivered solely to their leader, the Righteous Teacher.

Contents

Abbreviations

AcOr	Acta Orientalia
BA	Biblical Archeologist
BASOR	Bulletin of the American Schools of Oriental Research
Bibl. Orient.	Bibliotheca Orientalis
Bibl. Res.	Biblical Research
BJRL	Bulletin of the John Rylands Library
BZ	Biblische Zeitschrift
CBQ	Catholic Biblical Quarterly
CQR	Church Quarterly Review
DJD	Discoveries in the Judean Desert (Barthélemy-Milik eds.)
DSS	The Dead Sea Scrolls (M. Burrows)
EphThLov	Ephemerides Theologicae Lovanienses
EvTh	Evangelische Theologie
EWQ	The Essene Writings from Qumran (Dupont-Sommer, Vermes trans.)
Exp. Times	The Expository Times
HS	Horae Soederblomianae
HTR	Harvard Theological Review
IEJ	Israel Exploration Journal
JBL	Journal of Biblical Literature
JJS	Journal of Jewish Studies

JNES	Journal of Near Eastern Studies
JQR	Jewish Quarterly Review
JR	Journal of Religion
JSS	Journal of Semitic Studies
MLS	More Light on the Dead Sea Scrolls (M. Burrows)
NRTh	Nouvelle Revue Théologique
NT	Novum Testamentum
NTS	New Testament Studies
PEQ	Palestine Exploration Quarterly
RB	Revue Biblique
RHPhR	Revue d'histoire et de philosophie religieuses
RHR	Revue d'histoire des religions
RoB	Religion och Bibel
RQ	Revue de Qumran
RScRel	Revue des sciences religieuses
RSPhTh	Revue des sciences philosophique et théologiques
ScJTh	Scottish Journal of Theology
SEA	Svensk exegetisk årsbok
SNT	The Scrolls and the New Testament (K. Stendahl ed.)
STDJ	Studies on the Texts of the Desert of Judah
StTh	Studia Theologica
TLZ	Theologische Literaturzeitung
ThZ	Theologische Zeitschrift
TWzNT	Theologisches Wörterbuch zum Neuen Testament (G. Kittel ed.)
VigChr	Vigiliae Christianae
VT	Vetus Testamentum

WdO	Die Welt des Orients
WZKM	Wiener Zeitschrift für die Kunde des Morgenlandes
ZAW	Zeitschrift für die alttestamentliche Wissenschaft
ZkathTheol	Zeitschrift für katholische Theologie
ZNW	Zeitschrift für die neutestamentliche Wissenschaft
ZRGG	Zeitschrift für Religions– und Geistesgeschichte
ZThK	Zeitschrift für Theologie und Kirche

Introduction

LITERARY QUESTIONS

Before an analysis of the theology of the Dead Sea
Scrolls can be pursued, the content and literary character
of the Scrolls themselves must be noted.[1] Some of the
smaller text fragments found in the caves at Qumran
will be included, as well as the so-called Damascus Document, fragments of which were also discovered at
Qumran. The biblical manuscripts, however, will not
be considered since their significance is primarily connected with the establishment of the biblical text and
only to a very small extent with the theology of the
sect.[2]

[1] For such a survey see: O. Eissfeldt, *Einleitung in das Alte
Testament* (2nd ed.; 1956), pp. 788 ff.

[2] The attempt of Brownlee and others to find messianic theology
in certain variant readings in the Isaiah Scroll (W. H. Brownlee
and J. Reider, "On *MŠḤTY* in the Qumran Scrolls," *BASOR*
134 [1954], 27-28; and Brownlee, "Messianic Motifs of Qumran
and the New Testament, Part II," *NTS* 3 [1956/57], 195-210)
appears debatable; cf. D. Barthélemy, "Le Grand Rouleau d'Isaïe
trouvé près de la Mer Morte," *RB* 57 (1950), 546-549; and J. V.
Chamberlain, "The Functions of God as Messianic Titles in the
Complete Qumran Isaiah Scroll," *VT* 5 (1955), 366-372. The
same also applies more or less to F. F. Bruce, *Biblical Exegesis in
the Qumran Texts* (1959).

1

The Manual of Discipline (₁QS)[3]

When this scroll was found, Millar Burrows called it "The Manual of Discipline," since its content reminded him of the manual of discipline of the Methodist Church. "The Rule of the Congregation" or "The Order of the Community" would, perhaps, be more adequate titles; but the designation "The Manual of Discipline" has won such widespread use that there seems to be no point in introducing another name. In Hebrew it is called *sérek hay-yáḥad*, i.e., the order of the community, although the title page which was found later seems to have had the text, *ḥoq hay-yáḥad*, "the rule of the community."[4] The word *sérek* occurs several times in the text itself with the meaning "order," "rule."

The Manual of Discipline is not a literary unit. Rather, it appears to be a compilation of material from different sources.[5] Its main divisions are as follows:

[3] For the text, see: M. Burrows (ed.), *The Dead Sea Scrolls of St. Mark's Monastery*, Vol. II:2, *Plates and Transcription of the Manual of Discipline* (1951). For English translations with commentary see: Brownlee, *The Dead Sea Manual of Discipline.* ("*BASOR* Suppl. Studies 10-12.") (1951); P. Wernberg-Møller, *The Manual of Discipline (STDJ I)* (1957); and A. Dupont-Sommer, *The Essene Writings from Qumran* (hereafter referred to as *EWQ*), trans. G. Vermes (1961), pp. 68-103. There is also a translation in Burrows, *The Dead Sea Scrolls* (hereafter referred to as *DSS*) (1955), pp. 371-389. Concerning the arrangement and literary form see: P. Guilbert, "Le Plan de la 'Règle de la Communauté,'" *RQ* 1 (1958/59), 323-344.

[4] Y. Yadin, "Three Notes on the Dead Sea Scrolls," *IEJ* 6 (1956), 159 and Plate 28D (facing p. 201); D. Barthélemy, J. T. Milik, *et al.*, *Qumrân Cave 1, Discoveries in the Judaean Desert I* (hereafter referred to as *DJD I*) (1955), p. 107 and Plate 22, No. 28.

[5] Already noted by Burrows, *DSS*, p. 26.

1) i.1–iii.12. Entrance into the Covenant (i.e., the sect) and the yearly renewal of the covenant.
2) iii.13–iv.26. A short presentation of the theology of the sect.
3) v.1–vi.23. Regulations for the community.
4) vi.24–ix.25. On discipline and similar matters.
5) ix.26–xi.22. A hymn.

With the exception of the concluding hymn, the Manual of Discipline represents a literary type hitherto unknown in Jewish literature. It is in part a rule of the congregation comparable with Catholic monastic "rules," and in part what could be called a catechism. There are certain similarities to early Christian "church orders" and catechisms, especially to the *Didachē* (which contains: 1. The Teaching of the Two Ways; 2. Cultic Directions; 3. Rules for Life and Church Discipline) and the latter part of the Epistle of Barnabas.[6] The *Sitz im Leben* of the Manual of Discipline is probably to be found in the situation described in vi.13 ff.: he who wishes to enter into the community shall "be instructed in all the community's rules" (or "ordinances"; *kôl mišpᵉṭê hay-yáḥad*).

Two fragments which perhaps originally were sewed together with the Manual of Discipline belong in the same category.[7] One of them which is called The Rule

---

[6] J.-P. Audet, "Affinités littéraires et doctrinales du 'Manuel de Discipline'" (Part I), *RB* 59 (1952), 219-238; (Part II), *RB* 60 (1953), 41-82; cf. L. W. Barnard, "The Problem of the Epistle of Barnabas," *CQR* 159 (1958), 211-230.

[7] Milik, in *DJD I*, pp. 107 f.

of the Congregation (*sérek hā‘ēdāh*; ₁QSa)[8] consists of two fairly well preserved columns and is hence also called "The Two Column Fragment." It contains rules for "the congregation of Israel in the end of days," particularly with reference to the age when the members can be considered qualified for various tasks and for the common meal in the presence of the royal Messiah.

The other fragment (₁QSb)[9] consists of five columns, all in very bad condition, and contains a collection of blessing-formulas directed to various groups and individuals: "those who fear God," the high priest, the priests, "The Prince of the Congregation" (*neśî' hā‘ēdāh*). This fragment may be called The Blessings (*b͑erākôt*). In the perspective of form-criticism, they appear to be a continuation of the formulas of blessing in the Old Testament.

The Damascus Document (CD)

This document was found in 1896-97 in a genizah—a storeroom or repository for old and discarded manuscripts—in the Karaite Synagogue in old Cairo, and was published by Schechter in 1910.[10] It is preserved in two fragments, which partly overlap;[11] the smaller (B, cols.

---

[8] For the text see: *DJD I*, No. 28a., pp. 108 ff.; for English translations: Burrows, *More Light on the Dead Sea Scrolls* (hereafter referred to as *MLS*) (1958), pp. 393-395; and *EWQ*, pp. 104-109.

[9] For the text see: *DJD I*, No. 28b., pp. 118-130; for English translations: *EWQ*, pp. 110-113, *MLS*, pp. 396-398.

[10] S. Schechter, *Fragments of a Zadokite Work* (1910); see also new editions: L. Rost, *Die Damaskusschrift* (1933); C. Rabin, *The Zadokite Documents* (2nd ed.; 1958); also *DSS*, pp. 349-364; *EWQ*, pp. 114-163.

[11] Rabin establishes a compromise text for which he has received

xix-xx) being a more detailed version than the larger (A).

The manuscripts date from the tenth and the eleventh centuries, but the document itself must be considerably older—although it has not been possible to reach a consensus as to its age and place of origin. Since fragments have now turned up in the caves at Qumran,[12] there is proof that it belonged to the writings of the Qumran community; hence in all probability it must have originated in the first or second century B.C.

The document begins with a paraenetic-didactic section (i-viii and xx), in which the author seeks to derive lessons from biblical history and reflects upon various aspects of the community of "the new covenant." In this section a rather free interpretation of certain biblical passages plays a large role. Certain similarities between this paraenetic section and Stephen's speech in Acts 7 have been noted.[13]

much criticism (among others from H. Huppenbauer, *Der Mensch zwischen zwei Welten* [1959], p. 54. On the other hand, J. Carmignac, "Camparaison entre les manuscrits 'A' et 'B' du Document de Damas," *RQ* 2 (1959/60), 53-67, finds that both versions may very well derive from a common original.

[12] The fragments are from Cave 6; see: M. Baillet, "Fragments du Document de Damas. Qumrân, Grotte 6," *RB* 63 (1956), 514-523. According to Milik in P. Benoit, *et al.*, "Editing the Manuscript Fragments from Qumran," trans. J. L. Moreau, *BA* 19 (1956), 89, there are also fragments which were found in Cave 4. They are also reported to have been found in Cave 5 by Milik in "Le travail d'édition des manuscrits du Désert de Juda," *VT Suppl.* 4 (1956), 22.

[13] J. Daniélou, *The Dead Sea Scrolls and Primitive Christianity*, trans. S. Attanasio (1958), pp. 93 ff.; cf. O. Cullmann, "The Significance of the Qumran Texts for Research into the Beginnings of Christianity," in K. Stendahl (ed.), *The Scrolls and the New Testament* (hereafter referred to as *SNT*) (1957), p. 26, (originally published in *JBL* 74 [1955], 221); and S. E. Johnson,

The second portion of the document (ix-xvi) contains a collection of regulations concerning oaths, the giving of testimony, judges, "the overseer for the camps," the Sabbath, etc. These rules are probably regarded as explanations and applications of the Law of Moses, since it is repeated several times that this Law should be observed (xv.12; xvi.1, 4 f.; cf. ₁QS v.8); and the Manual of Discipline gives directions for the study of the Law (v.11; vi.6; viii.15) and says that those concealed things which are found by him who seeks in the Law shall be communicated to the members of the community (viii.11 f.).[14]

The end of the document is lost. Molin assumes that, like the Manual of Discipline, it originally concluded with a hymn, (and that the Manual of Discipline once started with a paraenetic section).[15] But considering the composite character of the Manual of Discipline, this is a highly uncertain theory.

It has usually been supposed that the Damascus Document is considerably later than the Manual of Discipline. There are also advocates of the reverse order,[16] however, and it is possible that they are correct.

"The Dead Sea Manual of Discipline and the Jerusalem Church of Acts," in *SNT*, p. 136 (originally published in *ZAW* 66 [1954], 113).

[14] Cf. M. Delcor, "Contribution à l'étude de la législation des sectaires de Damas et de Qumrân," (Part I), *RB* 61 (1954), 533-553; (Part II), *RB* 62 (1955), 60-75.

[15] G. Molin, *Die Söhne des Lichtes* (1954), p. 109.

[16] B. Otzen, "Die neugefundenen hebräischen Sektenschriften und die Testamente der zwölf Patriarchen," *StTh* 7(1953), 141; H. H. Rowley, "Some Traces of the History of the Qumran Sect," *ThZ* 13 (1957), 539 f.

The Commentaries (pešārîm)

A literary genre which seeems to have enjoyed great popularity at Qumran was that of the Bible commentary. Thus far a complete commentary on the first two chapters of Habakkuk (₁QpHab)[17] has been found, and also fragments of commentaries on Isaiah,[18] Hosea,[19] Nahum,[20] Micah,[21] Zephaniah,[22] and the canonical Psalter.[23]

All these commentaries are so arranged that the biblical text has been divided up into sections of one or two verses and each section is followed by an explanation

[17] For the text see: Burrows (ed.), *The Dead Sea Scrolls of St. Mark's Monastery*, Vol. I, *The Isaiah Manuscript and the Habakkuk Commentary* (1951). For a detailed study: K. Elliger, *Studien zum Habakuk-Kommentar vom Toten Meer*. ("Beitr. zur hist. theol., 15.") (1953). For English translations: Brownlee, "The Jerusalem Habakkuk Scroll," *BASOR* 112 (1948), 8-18; Brownlee, "Further Light on Habakkuk," *ibid*. 114 (1949), 9-10; and *DSS*, pp. 365-370; *EWQ*, pp. 255-268.

[18] Preliminary publication by J. M. Allegro, "Further Messianic References in Qumran Literature," *JBL* 75 (1956), 177 ff. and Allegro, "More Isaiah Commentaries from Qumran's Fourth Cave," *JBL* 77 (1958), 215-221; see also: *MLS*, pp. 403-404; *EWQ*, pp. 274-276.

[19] Allegro, "A Recently Discovered Fragment of a Commentary on Hosea from Qumran's Fourth Cave," *JBL* 78 (1959), 142-147; see also: *EWQ*, pp. 276-278.

[20] Allegro, "Further Light on the History of the Qumran Sect," *JBL* 75 (1956), 89-93; see also: *MLS*, p. 404; *EWQ*, pp. 268-270.

[21] For text see: *DJD I*, pp. 77 ff. (No. 14); for English translation: *MLS*, p. 404; *EWQ*, pp. 276-278.

[22] *DJD I*, p. 80 (No. 15); for English translation: *EWQ*, pp. 276-278.

[23] For commentary on Psalm 37 see: Allegro, "Further Light . . . ," *op. cit.*, pp. 94 f.; Allegro, "A Newly-Discovered Fragment of a Commentary on Psalm XXXVII from Qumran," *PEQ* 86 (1954), 69-75; *MLS*, pp. 401-403; *EWQ*, pp. 270-273. For other psalm fragments see: *DJD I*, pp. 81 f. (No. 16).

which refers it to the events of the writer's own time, so that contemporary history appears as fulfilment of biblical prophecy. These interpretations are generally introduced with the word *pišrô*, "its explanation (or interpretation) is . . . (or concerns . . .)." The word *pêšer* is therefore used sometimes as a designation for the whole genre, which should be distinguished from the midrash and from the commentary proper.[24]

What then is a *pêšer?*[25] The word itself—cognate with the Arabic *tafsîr* (a Koran commentary)—occurs in Daniel 5:7, 12, 15 with reference to the "interpretation" or "decipherment" of the writing on the wall at Belshazzar's feast, and in Ecclesiastes 8:1: "the wise man" who understands the *interpretation* of a thing (or, of a word: *pêšer dābār*). In rabbinic exegesis *pêšer* designates the explanation of a difficult passage in the Bible or in the Mishnah.

Two passages in the Habakkuk Commentary provide further information. In ii.6-9 a priest is mentioned whom God has given to the house of Judah to interpret (*LPŠR*) all the words of his servants the prophets; and in vii.4-5 this priest is identified with "the Teacher of Righteousness (*môrēh haṣ-ṣédeq*) . . . to whom God has made

[24] One of Zeitlin's principal arguments against the usual dating of the Dead Sea Scrolls is that commentaries did not come into use before the Middle Ages. But if the *pêšer* is a technique of interpretation other than that of the commentary proper as known from the Middle Ages, that argument falls.

[25] What follows here is based for the most part on G. Vermès, "A propos des commentaires bibliques découverts à Qumrân," *RHPhR* 25 (1955), 95-102. See also: L. H. Silberman, "Unriddling the Riddle. A Study in the Structure and Language of the Habakkuk Pesher," *RQ* 3 (1961/62), 323-364.

known all the mysteries of the words of His servants the prophets."

A *pêšer* is therefore an interpretation or explanation of the words of the prophets based upon divine revelation.

According to the Manual of Discipline, wherever ten members of the community are present there shall be a "man who studies (searches in) the Law" (*dôrēš hat-tôrāh*) (vi.6-7) and this interpreter of the Law is to inform the members concerning what he has found in Scripture (viii.11-12, cf. ix.12-14). Nightly meetings for the study of "the Book" are also mentioned (vi.7-8). This could suggest the function and place of the commentaries in the life of the sect.[26] It is most probable that on such occasions the text was read section by section and each section was immediately explained and discussed.[27] This is reminiscent of the way in which the Law and the prophets were read and "interpreted" into Aramaic in the synagogues;[28] which, as is well known, gave rise to the Targums.

It is worth noting that according to the Talmud (b Meg 3a) the Targum Jonathan reveals mysteries which Jonathan had learned from the prophets Haggai, Zechariah, and Malachi, and which are so remarkable that the earth shook when it heard them. According to this

---

[26] Cf. Milik, "Fragments d'un Midrash de Michée dans les Manuscrits de Qumrân," *RB* 59 (1952), 418.

[27] F. M. Cross, Jr., *The Ancient Library of Qumran* (2nd ed.; 1961), pp. 93 f. shows that according to Philo (*Quod omnis probus liber sit*, 82) the Essenes acted in this way.

[28] Cf. Neh. 8:8: They read from the Book of the Law of God *mᵉpōrāš*, i.e., with interpretation.

theory, the Targum is thus more than simply an Aramaic paraphrase of the words of the prophet; it is a revelation of mysteries, precisely like the *pēšer* literature.

In this connection it is also significant, as Brownlee has shown, that the Habakkuk Commentary is at several points dependent on or at least in agreement with the Targum Jonathan to the prophets.[29] In another case, however, the Targum seems to have known but misunderstood the exegesis of the commentary.[30] It is therefore likely that the commentary and the Targum are simply manifestations of one and the same exegetical tradition.

Milik wants to distinguish three types of *pēšer* according to whether the biblical passage is interpreted in relation to the history of the sect, contemporary political history, or eschatological events.[31] In principle, however, there is no profound difference between the three, and in such a text as the Habakkuk Commentary all three occur together.[32]

This method of interpretation is reminiscent of that which is used in certain late Targums (e.g., to the Song of Songs) and in the *Midrashîm*: the interpretations are based on single words lifted out of their context, on paronomasia, on the assumption of a double meaning in certain expressions, and on small emendations of the text

[29] Brownlee, "The Habakkuk Midrash and the Targum of Jonathan," *JJS* 7 (1956), 169 f.; cf. also N. Wieder; "The Habakkuk Scroll and the Targum," *JJS* 4 (1953), 14–18.

[30] Rabin, "Notes on the Habakkuk Scroll and the Zadokite Documents," *VT* 5 (1955), 156 ff.

[31] Milik, *Ten Years of Discovery in the Wilderness of Judaea*, trans. J. Strugnell (1959), p. 40.

[32] Cf. Burrows' views in *MLS*, p. 167.

to make it fit the view of the interpreter.[33] Thus, for example, the *kaśdîm*, "the Chaldeans," of Habakkuk are interpreted as the *kittîyîm*, "the Kittaeans (Kittim)" who were of the writer's own time; "the righteous one(s)" of Habakkuk is taken to refer to the Teacher of Righteousness and "the wicked one(s)" to "the Wicked Priest." The clause, "the righteous shall live by his faith" serves as a reminder concerning certain persons who showed faith(fulness) to the Teacher of Righteousness, etc. (The Hebrew *'emûnāh* can mean both faith and faithfulness.)

Rabin has called attention to an Egyptian parallel to the *pēšer* literature, namely, the so-called Demotic Chronicle,[34] which contains a series of enigmatic oracles which are applied to contemporary events.[35] It seems doubtful, however, that there is any literary connection, as Rabin thinks, between the chronicle and *pēšer*. Above all, it is difficult to understand how the contact would have taken place.

The Genesis Apocryphon (₁Q Gen. Apoc.)

This text, which as yet has only been published in part,[36] differs from most of the other Qumran texts by

[33] Cf. I. L. Seeligmann's account concerning midrash exegesis: "Voraussetzungen der Midraschexegese," *V. T. Suppl. 1* (1953), 150-181; Bruce, *Biblical Exegesis . . . , op. cit.;* O. Betz, *Offenbarung und Schriftforschung in der Qumransekte* (1960).

[34] See: *Handbuch der Orientalistik* I:2, pp. 118 f.

[35] Rabin, "Notes on the Habakkuk Scroll . . . ," *op. cit.,* pp. 148 ff.

[36] For text and translation see: N. Avigad and Y. Yadin, *A Genesis Apocryphon* (1956); English translations are also found in *MLS*, pp. 387-393, and *EWQ*, pp. 284-294.

being written in Aramaic and not in Hebrew. It contains a paraphrase of Genesis with numerous digressions, and is reminiscent in many respects of the so-called Book of Jubilees.

Sometimes, as for example in Genesis 14, the Aramaic text follows the biblical original quite faithfully, but in other cases it contains long additions of a legendary nature. A part of the material which has thus been added is completely or partially known from other Jewish sources, as for example, the legend concerning the birth of Noah and Methuselah's prophecy concerning his future (col. ii);[37] other sections, on the other hand, are entirely new to us, e.g., the legend linked to Abraham's visit in Egypt (xix.10 ff.) which, among other things, contains the praise of Sarah's beauty, spoken by the Egyptian princes (xx.2-8) and is in form a typical *waṣf* (descriptive song) reminiscent of those found in the Song of Songs.[38]

The part of the scroll which is preserved ends in the middle of the story which corresponds to Genesis 15. The text is theologically unrewarding, but from a linguistic point of view it is very important since it provides extremely valuable material for the study of Palestinian Aramaic.[39]

---

[37] Avigad and Yadin, *op. cit.*, pp. 16 f.

[38] Cf. M. H. Goshen-Gottstein, "Philologische Miszellen zu den Qumrantexten," *RQ* 2 (1959/60), 46 ff.

[39] Concerning this see: E. Y. Kutscher, "The Language of the Genesis Apocryphon: A Preliminary Study," *Scripta Hierosoly-mitana* 4 (1958), 1-35.

The Thanksgiving Psalms (*Hôdāyôt;* ₁*QH*)

The manuscript [40] consists of four parts each with four columns, two separate columns in fairly well preserved condition and a large number of fragments. It contains a collection of poems or psalms, but the exact number cannot be established because of the fragmentary condition of the scroll. There are fourteen clear examples of the introductory phrase, *'ôdᵉkāh 'ᵃdônāy*, "I thank Thee, O Lord"; and one hymn which begins with *bārûk 'attāh 'ᵃdônāy*, "Praised (blessed) be Thou, O Lord." But the number of hymns certainly must have been considerably larger. The manuscript is written in two different hands with the change taking place at xi.22. Nevertheless columns xiii-xvii are written by the first hand, and only columns xii and xviii and some fragments show the second; this indicates that the editors did not retain the original sequence.

Sukenik, who prepared a preliminary edition of certain portions of the scroll, gave it the title *Hôdāyôt* or The Thanksgivings, because of the introductory words of the psalms. The question could be raised, however, as to whether this title really represents the actual content and function of the scroll. (In the War Scroll xv.5

[40] See the text in E. L. Sukenik and N. Avigad, *The Dead Sea Scrolls of the Hebrew University* (1956, Hebrew Edition 1955); and J. Licht, *Megillat hahôdāyôt* (*The Thanksgiving Scroll*) (1957, with commentary in Hebrew). For English translations with commentary see: M. Mansoor, *The Thanksgiving Hymns* (*STDJ III* [1961]); S. Holm-Nielsen, *Hodayot, Psalms from Qumran* (1960); and *EWQ*, pp. 198-254. Selections from the Thanksgiving Psalms are found in *DSS*, pp. 400-415. On the text see: Carmignac, "Compléments au texte des Hymnes de Qumrân," Part I, *RQ* 2 (1959/60), 267-276; Part II, 549-558.

mention is made of "their thanksgiving," *hôdôtām*, but it is not certain that this is to be understood as a technical term.)

Despite the fact that the language of the scroll is strongly influenced by biblical Hebrew, particularly the language of the Psalter,[41] it is difficult to refer the *Hôdāyôt* to any of the categories or *Gattungen* of the psalm literature. There are elements which belong to the category of the thanksgiving psalm, others to the hymn of praise or the psalm of lamentation; but these elements are intermingled with each other and with a certain didactic element in a way which Ludin-Jansen has shown to be typical of late Jewish psalms.[42] Regular metrical construction can hardly be demonstrated;[43] it should rather be called rhythmic prose. Furthermore, the

[41] Even the introductory phrase: "I thank Thee, O Lord," is taken from the canonical Psalter (52:11; 118:21; 139:14). For further material on the Old Testament quotations see: Carmignac, "Les citations de l'Ancien Testament, et spécialement des poèmes du serviteur, dans les hymnes de Qumrân," *RQ* 2 (1959/60), 357-394. Valuable references are also found in T. H. Gaster, *The Dead Sea Scriptures* (1956); see also: Holm-Nielsen, *op. cit.*, pp. 301-315 and his commentary on each psalm.

[42] H. Bardtke, "Considérations sur les cantiques de Qumrân," *RB* 63 (1956), 220-233; cf. H. Ludin-Jansen, *Die spätjüdische Psalmendichtung* (1937).

[43] Molin, "Die Hymnen von Chirbet Qumran, (1QT)," in *Festschrift für Prof. Dr. Viktor Christian: Vorderasiatische Studien* (1956), pp. 74-82, thinks that occasionally traces of the regular Old Testament metrical patterns can be found, but also points out that there is just as often no trace of metrical arrangement. In a detailed analysis C. F. Kraft, "Poetic Structure in the Qumran Thanksgiving Psalms," *Bibl. Res.* 2 (1957), 1-18 arrives at a similar conclusion. M. Wallenstein, "A Hymn from the Scrolls," *VT* 5 (1955), 277 discusses the relationship to other later Jewish poetry and demonstrates that with respect to form they have very little in common with liturgical poems from the third to the sixth

meditative style of the Thanksgiving Psalms is very striking with its preference for repetition.[44] This should also be considered when dealing with questions of authorship and *Sitz im Leben.*

The question of the identification of the "I" in the Thanksgiving Psalms is by no means simple. It is fairly sure that the subject of the psalms is not the community as a unit, i.e., a collective "I," but must be an individual, since on several occasions the "I" is set in contrast to a plural designation, e.g., ii.30: "I will praise Thy Name in the congregations";[45] xiv.18 "I was brought into community with all the men of Thy council." But who is this individual? Much of what is said could apply to any devout member of the community: sorrow over sin, help from God, grace and deeper insight.[46] But there are other sections which are unimaginable in the mouth of the average pious man. Therefore most investigators assume that the "I" in the *Hôdāyôt* must be a leading person within the sect. Such a person might say, for example, "Through me Thou hast illumined the faces of the many" (iv.27), or "Thou hast made me a father to the children of *ḥésed* (grace, mercy)" (vii.20), or "By my hand Thou hast opened their spring" (vii.21), or even ". . . to distinguish through me between the righteous and the wicked" (vii.12).

centuries and still less with the so-called *piyyuṭîm* which begin to make their appearance at the end of the sixth century.

[44] Licht, "The Doctrine of the Thanksgiving Scroll," *IEJ* 6 (1956), 1-13, 89-101; Molin, *op. cit.,* p. 74.

[45] Of course in this case we have to do with a quotation from Ps. 26:12.

[46] Molin, *op. cit.,* p. 75.

Here it is hardly possible to avoid thinking of the founder of the community, the so-called Teacher of Righteousness. This conclusion, from which Bardtke [47] and Licht [48] shy away, has been drawn by Dupont-Sommer,[49] Molin [50] and others; and there are actually no weighty arguments against it.

Concerning the function and purpose of the psalms there is as yet no consensus. Reicke considers them to be cult-hymns comparable with those which, according to Philo's statement, it was the custom of the Therapeutae to sing [51] (there are allusions to thanksgivings and songs of praise also in the Dead Sea Scrolls themselves: ₁QH xii.3 ff.; ₁QS x.1 f.; ₁QM xv.5). Bardtke and Molin, on the other hand, maintain that these psalms were used by the members of the community at their spiritual exercises as a basis for their meditation: "Thus the utterances of the Master become a means of educating his disciples, particularly the novices." [52] The choice between these two alternatives is difficult. It is almost necessary to assume that the sect had some sort of cult-hymns for its meetings, but the style and general

[47] Bardtke, *op. cit.*, pp. 229, 232; *ibid.*, "Das Ich des Meisters in den *Hodajoth* von Qumran," *Wissenschaftliche Zeitschrift d. Universität Leipzig* 6 (1956/57), 93 ff.

[48] Licht, "The Doctrine . . . ," *op. cit.*, p. 2.

[49] For example, Dupont-Sommer, "Les manuscrits de la Mer Morte; leur importance pour l'histoire des religions," *Numen* 2 (1955), 184.

[50] Molin, *op. cit.*

[51] B. Reicke, "Remarques sur l'histoire de la forme (Formgeschichte) des textes de Qumran," in *Les manuscrits de la Mer Morte* (Colloque de Strasbourg, 1955) (1957), pp. 38 ff. The Therapeutae were a Jewish sect in Egypt, who were described by Philo.

[52] Molin, *op. cit.*, p. 75.

character of the Thanksgiving Psalms seem to speak for the latter alternatives.

The concluding psalm in the Manual of Discipline and some hymnic sections of the War Scroll belong to the same category.

The War Scroll (Milḥāmāh; $_1QM$)

This manuscript [53] which, when it first became known received the name, "The War between the Children of Light and the Children of Darkness," consists of nineteen columns, of which the last is so very badly damaged that it is impossible to determine whether or not it is the last in the scroll. The content of the document is evident from the title: it deals with a war between the tribes of Levi, Judah, and Benjamin—the children of light—on the one hand; and the Edomites, Ammonites, Philistines, Greeks, and other peoples—the children of darkness—on the other. First a general plan for the war is presented: it is to last for forty years, and each year one particular people will be defeated (i.1–ii.14).[54] Then follows a detailed description of the organization of the army, weapons, banners, trumpets, and the formation of the troops; and detailed descriptions are given of what the priests are to do and say before and after the battle, which hymns are to be sung, etc.

[53]For the text see: Sukenik and Avigad, *The Dead Sea Scrolls . . .* , *op. cit.;* French translation with commentary: Carmignac, *La règle de la guerre . . .* (1958); J. van der Ploeg, *Le Rouleau de la Guerre [STDJ II]* (1959). For a detailed study see: Yadin, *The Scroll of the War of the Sons of Light against the Sons of Darkness,* trans. B. and C. Rabin (1962). See also: *EWQ,* pp. 164-197 and selections in *DSS,* pp. 390-399.

[54]For further details, see below, pp. 161 ff.

From a literary point of view, the Scroll is perhaps not a unit.[55] In xii.10-15 a hymnic section is found which recurs almost word for word in column xix. It is quite obvious that a new section begins after xii.15, and the latter part of the book repeats in many respects what was already said in the former. It can not be said, how-ever, that the two parts are two recensions of the same text; they are, rather, two works with similar content and similar aim. A newly-published fragment [56] consti-tutes, apparently, an older form of the book, or perhaps a third document in the same category.

Thereby the question of the literary character and purpose of the War Scroll is immediately raised. Is it a description of an actual war, and was the Qumran community organized as a military entity with a mission —when the time came—to fight all the Gentiles with the sword? Or is the book an allegory or still something else?

Three points are fairly clear. First of all, the enumer-ation of the enemies (ii.10 f.) consists of so many peoples that an actual war is completely out of the question. The list is, further, so stereotyped and obviously based on the list of peoples in Genesis 10 (and other similar lists in the Old Testament), that it must be viewed as the result of purely theoretical speculations.

Second, the mottoes to be written on banners and

---

[55] Cf. Rabin, "Literary Structure of the War Scroll" in *Essays on the Dead Sea Scrolls in Memory of E. L. Sukenik* (1961), pp. 31-41 (in Hebrew).

[56] C.-H. Hunzinger, "Fragmente einer älteren Fassung des Buches Milhamā aus Höhle 4 von Qumran," *ZAW* 69 (1957), 131-151.

weapons are throughout of a symbolic and religious nature. While this is not a decisive argument for an allegorical interpretation, it must, nevertheless, be said to point in this direction.

Third, the very designation of the fighting parties, "children of light" and "children of darkness" is an intimation that the war belongs on the religious plane.

It is fairly clear that the war in question must be the eschatological final battle and that the Scroll must be considered as a sort of apocalypse. The estimates of the duration of the war also argue for this hypothesis, since speculations concerning God's plan for history and the time for his intervention are typical of apocalyptic literature. On the other hand, the accurate directions for the battle itself, i.e., for the behavior of the pious in the final conflict against the evil powers, is a hitherto unknown motif in Jewish literature.

The style of the War Scroll exhibits certain liturgical features:[57] prayers and hymns before and after the battle, exhortations by the priests, etc. The whole book has even been called "a liturgy for the Holy War" and this designation is actually well grounded.

The criteria for the dating of the War Scroll are somewhat vague. Avi-Yonah[58] and Février[59] have inde-

---

[57] R. North, " 'Kittim' War or 'Sectarian' Liturgy?" *Biblica* 39 (1958), 84-93.

[58] M. Avi-Yonah, "The 'War of the Sons of Light and the Sons of Darkness' and Maccabean Warfare," *IEJ* 2 (1952), 1-5.

[59] J. G. Février, "Tactique héllénistique dans un texte de 'Ayin Fashkha," *Semitica* 3 (1950), 53-59; cf. also: K. M. T. Atkinson, "The Historical Setting of the 'War of the Sons of Light and the Sons of Darkness'," *BJRL* 40 (1957/58), 272-297; M. H. Segal, "The Qumran War Scroll and the Date of its Composition,"

pendently sought to determine the military tactics reflected by the Scroll, but the results are somewhat uncertain. The former decides on a late Maccabean or early Roman date, while the latter prefers Hellenistic tactics of the third century B.C. The difference is probably of minor significance. If the new fragment of the Scroll is older than the text in question, it must be surmised that the original text arose in Maccabean times.

Miscellaneous Fragments

Besides the fairly well-preserved documents and some fragments belonging to the same literary categories which we have included in our discussion above, there are a large number of more or less fragmentary works with varied form and content, most of which are as yet unpublished.[60] Some of the most important will be mentioned.

"The Patriarchal Blessings" (4Q Patr. Blessings)[61] constitutes an elaboration of the blessings of Jacob in Genesis 49. From the point of view of form, this fragment stands somewhere between the commentaries and the Genesis Apocryphon (the term *pišrô* is not used).

The messianic Florilegium (4Q Flor.)[62] emphasizes

Scripta Hierosolymitana 4 (1958), 138-143; Yadin, *The Scroll of the War . . .* , *op. cit.*, chaps. 6 and 7.

[60] See the report in *BA* 19 (1956), 75-96; and later communications in Milik, "Le travail d'édition . . . ," *op. cit.*; J. Strugnell, "The Angelic Liturgy at Qumrân—4Q *Sérek Širòt 'òlat Haššabbāt*," *VT Suppl.* 7 (1960), 318-345.

[61] See: Allegro, "Further Messianic References . . . ," *op. cit.*, pp. 174-176; and *EWQ*, pp. 314 f.

[62] Allegro, "Further Messianic References . . . ," *op. cit.*, pp. 176-177; Allegro, "Fragments of a Qumran Scroll of Eschatologi-

the re-establishment of the Davidic line in the messianic age by citing several biblical passages, particularly Nathan's prophecy to David in II Samuel 7:11-14.

The so-called Testimonia Document (4Q Testi monia)[63] consists of a collection of biblical passages which refer to the messianic hope of the community: Deuteronomy 5:28-29; 18:18-19; 33:8-11; Numbers 24: 15-17; followed by a reference to Hiel's rebuilding of Jericho (I Kings 16:34)—probably with the purpose of showing that the words of Scripture always find their fulfillment (cf. Josh. 6:26), or possibly alluding to some current happening.

The so-called Book of Mysteries (1Q 27)[64] is preserved in a two-column fragment. It is an eschatological sermon which stresses the certainty of the victory of the good and refers to the decisive outcome as "the coming mystery (*rāz*)."

There are some fragments of an Aramaic version of the Testament of Levi (4QT Levi)[65] which prove that at least this part of the Testaments of the Twelve Patriarchs is not a Christian product. Some Hebrew fragments of the Testament of Naphtali[66] confirm this

cal Midrāšîm," *JBL* 77 (1958), 350-354; cf. Yadin, "A Midrash on 2 Sam. vii and Ps. i-ii (4Q Florilegium)," *IEJ* 9 (1959), 95-98; D. Flusser, "Two Notes on the Midrash on 2 Sam. vii," *IEJ* 9 (1959), 99-109, and *EWQ*, pp. 310-314.

[63] See: Allegro, "Further Messianic References . . . ," *op. cit.*, pp. 182-187; *EWQ*, pp. 315-319; *MLS*, p. 400.

[64] For English translations see: *EWQ*, pp. 326-328 and *MLS*, p. 398.

[65] Milik, "Le Testament de Lévi en Araméen," *RB* 62 (1955), 398-406.

[66] Milik, "Le travail d'édition . . . ," *op. cit.*, p. 24.

conclusion and demonstrate that the whole question of
the composition of the Testaments must be re-examined
in the light of the new finds.[67]

There are also many fragments of other writings, some
hitherto completely unknown, as e.g., a description of
the New Jerusalem (in Aramaic),[68] a prayer which is
ascribed to the Babylonian king Nabonidus (4Q Prayer
of Nabonidus)[69] (apparently belonging to the same cycle
of motifs as the Book of Daniel); and others known
only in translation, such as the Book of Jubilees [70] and
the (Ethiopic) Book of Enoch.[71]

A most interesting group of fragments are the so-called
mišmārôt,[72] which give a description of the duties of the
priests week by week according to the ordinary lunar

[67] See the discussion in Burrows, MLS, pp. 179 f. It is not
necessary to go as far as M. Philonenko, Les interpolations
chrétiennes des Testaments des douze patriarches et les manuscrits de Qoumran (1960) (also in two parts in RHPhR 38
[1958], 309-343, and 39 [1959], 14-28) and almost totally deny any
Christian reworking of the documents in question; cf. the review
of this problem by M. de Jonge, "Christian Influence in the
Testaments of the Twelve Patriarchs," NT 4 (1960), 182-235; also
E. Larsson, "Qumranlitteraturen och De tolv patriarkernas testamenten" (a review of Philonenko, op. cit.), SEÅ 25 (1960), 109-
118.

[68] DJD I, pp. 134 f. (No. 32); cf. M. Baillet, "Fragments
Araméens de Qumrân 2—Déscription de la Jérusalem nouvelle,"
RB 62 (1955), 222-245.

[69] Milik, "Prière de Nabonide et autres écrits d'un cycle de
Daniel—Fragments Araméens de Qumrân 4," RB 63 (1956), 407-
415; for English translations: MLS, p. 400 and EWQ, p. 321.

[70] DJD I, pp. 82 f. (Nos. 17-18).

[71] DJD I, pp. 84 f. (No. 19), many fragments in Caves 4 and 6;
cf. Milik, "Hénoch au pays des Aromates (chaps. xxvii à xxxii)—
Fragments Araméens de la Grotte 4 de Qumrân," RB 65 (1958),
70-77.

[72] Milik, "Le travail d'édition . . . ," op. cit., p. 25.

calendar and a solar calendar with a 364 day year. They are particularly important since they confirm the assumption that the Qumran sect had a calendar which differed from that of the rest of Judaism.

Another group of fragments comprise a Liturgy of the Sabbath Offering (*sérek šîrôt 'ôlat haš-šabbāt*).[73] This appears to have contained directions for all the Sabbaths of the year according to the calendar of the Qumran sect. A typical section begins: "For 'the man with insight' (*maśkîl*), Song for the Sabbath sacrifice for the seventh Sabbath, on the 16th day of the 2nd month. Praise God, all ye angels . . ." and then the man with insight exhorts the angels under their various names and designations to praise God. Since it is often said here that the angels "bless," this group of texts in certain respects forms a parallel to another group, the so-called *berākôt* (blessings), of which several fragments are also preserved.[74] They are most closely comparable with the blessings in ₁QSb mentioned above.

Some parts of a collection of liturgical prayers called *The Words of the Luminaries* have been published by Baillet.[75] They deal with the election of Israel, the faithlessness of the fathers and the ensuing punishment as well as God's forgiveness. Theologically, this document contains very few of the characteristic doctrines of the Qumran community.

The Copper Scroll [76] consists of three pieces of copper

[73] Strugnell, *op. cit.*

[74] *Ibid.*, p. 319.

[75] Baillet, "Un recueil liturgique de Qumrân, Grotte 4: 'Les paroles des luminaires,'" *RB* 68 (1961), 195-250.

[76] Text and translation with commentary by Allegro, *The*

sheet, 80 x 30 cm. each, bearing a Hebrew inscription on one side. The language is proto-Mishnaic Hebrew, and the text consists of an enumeration of sixty-two items of miscellaneous treasures—silver, censers, etc.— hidden in various places, the locations of which are described in very vague terms. It is uncertain whether these refer to real objects which had been the property of the Qumran sect or which had been rescued from the Temple of Jerusalem, or whether it is simply a collection of folkloristic traditions concerning hidden treasures. Milik [77] prefers the latter alternative; Allegro [78] considers them to be real treasures. The future will probably show who is correct.

HISTORICAL QUESTIONS

Many historical questions are associated with the manuscripts from Qumran. When and how were the scrolls placed in the caves? Where did they come from? What is "the community of the New Covenant" which is mentioned in one of the scrolls and what is its history? What historical events are those to which the scrolls allude? These are important questions but they are by no means easy to answer—especially since the documents themselves speak of them only enigmatically and by allusion.

It is generally assumed that there is a connection between the manuscripts in the caves and the building that

---

Treasure of the Copper Scroll (1960); French translation and commentary by Milik, "Le Rouleau de Cuivre de Qumrân (3Q 15)," *RB* 66 (1959), 321-357.

[77] Milik, "Le Rouleau . . . ," *op. cit.*, p. 322.

[78] Allegro, *The Treasure . . .* , *op. cit.*, chaps. 3 and 7.

has been excavated at Khirbet Qumran in the immediate vicinity of the caves and that is assumed to have been the "cloister" of the community. It is evident that the members of the sect had to abandon their quarters in great haste and at that time left their manuscripts behind in the caves.

This hypothesis has been disputed by del Medico,[79] who thinks that the scrolls came from a genizah and that there never had been any Qumran community. In one respect del Medico must be considered correct: there are many unclear points in the story of the first discovery of the scrolls, and the precise relationship between the building and the caves is not so easy to determine—it is worth noting that no manuscripts at all have been found in the building itself. But on the other hand, del Medico has presented no compelling arguments *against* the assumption of some sort of connection between the scrolls and the cloister. Even if this means a prejudgment of our identification of the Qumran community, it should be remembered that both the building and the contents of the scrolls seem to indicate some connection with the Essenes who are mentioned in other contemporary documents. It seems highly improbable that this double correspondence should be a mere coincidence.

If the building and the objects found in it be used as means of dating the scrolls, then the most valuable evidence would be coins. The oldest coins are from the reigns of John Hyrcanus I (135-104 B.C.), Alexander

[79] H. E. del Medico, *L'énigme des manuscrits de la Mer Morte* [1957], pp. 49 ff.

Jannaeus (103-76 B.C.) and Antiochus VII Sidetes (138-129 B.C.), while the latest came from A.D. 68.[80] It must therefore be considered certain that the buildings were abandoned at the approach of the Roman legion shortly before the destruction of Jerusalem. For the earliest dating of the construction of the building we can hardly go much further back than 130-120 B.C. or perhaps a little bit later. But in that case it is reasonable to assume that the community had already existed for some time, before a cloister of such size could have been built.

Concerning the history of the community, allusions in the scrolls themselves are the sole sources of evidence and these are purposely vague and open to several different interpretations. The historical allusions are most frequent in the Habakkuk Commentary, but the War Scroll and the Damascus Document also contain some relevant material.

The discussion at this point must be limited to three main problems: the Kittim, the Teacher of Righteousness and his time, and the migration to Damascus.

The Kittim

The Kittim (written *KTY'YM* = *kittī'īm* or *KTYYM* = *kittīyîm*) are chiefly known from the Habakkuk Commentary and the War Scroll. The word is biblical. According to Genesis 10:4, the Kittim are among the sons of Javan and must, therefore, have something to do with the Greeks, since the name Javan is related both in form

---

[80] See: R. de Vaux, "Fouilles de Khirbet Qumran: Rapport préliminaire sur les 3e, 4e, et 5e campagnes," *RB* 63 (1956), 565 f.

and association to "Ionian." In Isaiah 23:1, 12; Jeremiah
2:10; Ezekiel 27:6 the word rendered "Chittim" (another spelling of Kittim) in the King James Version
seems to refer to the people of Cyprus and is given as
"Cyprus" in these passages in the Revised Standard
Version. In Numbers 24:24, however, the reference is
enigmatic; the King James Version reads "Chittim"
while the Revised Standard Version reads "Kittim." In
Daniel 11:30, as also in the Targums, this passage is taken
as referring to the Romans. According to I Maccabees
1:1 Alexander the Great comes from the land of the
Kittim and in 8:5 Perseus, king of the Macedonians, is
called the king of the Kittim.

The following facts concerning the Kittim are found
in the Habakkuk Commentary: they are fleet and heroes
in warfare (ii.12 f.), feared by people whose cities they
plunder (iii.1 f., 4 f.); they are cunning and deceitful
(iii.5 f.) and do not believe in the statutes of God
(ii.14 f.). They come from afar from the isles in the
sea (or: the coastlands) (iii.10 f.); they scorn the
fortresses of the peoples (iv.5 f.) and their rulers
(môše̊lîm) come one after another to destroy the earth
(or: the country) (iv.12 f.). They gather wealth and
loot as abundant as the fish of the sea (vi.1 f.), and they
sacrifice to their standards and worship their weapons
(vi.3 f.). They are cruel and merciless and "destroy
many with the sword, youths, men and old men, women
and small children and toward the fruit of the womb
have they no compassion" (vi.10-12). And finally it is
said that "Jerusalem's last priests" with all their riches
and spoils shall be delivered into the hands of the Kittim

"because they are the 'remnant of the peoples' " (ix.4-7, commentary on Hab. 2:7 f.).

Almost all of these statements could refer to any enemy nation at all; in any case the description would fit both the Romans and the Seleucid Greeks. However, the worship of battle standards and weapons is considered to refer to the Romans, although there is not clear evidence of such practice among them before the time of Josephus;[81] and it is possible that the custom could already have existed in the Seleucid armies.[82] But there is yet another important point: the verbs which are used concerning the Kittim are throughout in the so-called imperfect and must consequently—according to the linguistic usage of the Hebrew of the time—refer to events that either are contemporaneous or are still in the future.[83] Therefore the Kittim are not yet in Palestine and "Jerusalem's last priests" have not yet fallen into their hands. If identification with the Romans is accepted—and an identification with the Seleucids would give too early a date—this would point to a date a year or so before Pompey's conquest of Palestine in 63 B.C.; while the Teacher of Righteousness, who is al-

[81] *DSS*, pp. 133 f.

[82] H. H. Rowley, *The Zadokite Fragments and The Dead Sea Scrolls* (1952), pp. 72 ff.; *ibid.*, "The Teacher of Righteousness and The Dead Sea Scrolls," *BJRL* 40 (1957/58), 131.

[83] J. van der Ploeg points this out in "Le Rouleau d'Habacuc de la Grotte de 'Ain Fešha," *Bibl. Orient.* 8 (1951), 10. It is more fully developed in van der Ploeg, "L'usage du parfait et de l'imparfait comme moyen de datation dans le commentaire d'Habacuc," in *Les Manuscrits de la Mer Morte, op. cit.,* pp. 25-35; see also: van der Ploeg, *The Excavations at Qumran,* trans. K. Smyth (1958), pp. 57 f., and Carmignac. "Notes sur les peshârîm," *RQ* 3 (1961/62), 533 ff.

ways mentioned in the so-called perfect must have lived earlier.

Against this identification of the Kittim there is, however, an important objection. The War Scroll (i.1 f.) speaks of "the Kittim of Assyria (*kittīyê 'aššûr*)" who together with Edom, Moab, Ammon, and the Philistines will fight against the sons of Levi, Judah, and Benjamin. This expression can be understood as referring to the Seleucids (Assyria = Syria). Further, a damaged passage two lines further down contains the word "Kittim in Egypt" which some scholars have taken as a designation for the Ptolemies. This expression, however, is in no way parallel with the genitive construction in "Kittim of Assyria," but since there is a lacuna in the text immediately before the words in question, the context can only be conjectured; it ought to have been something like: "[the kings] of the Kittim [will force their way into] Egypt," or "the Kittim [will attack] Egypt." Consequently, nothing directly indicates that "the Kittim in Egypt" should have been Ptolemies in distinction from "Kittim of Assyria," i.e., the Seleucids.

It is important to note the uses of the word Kittim in the War Scroll, where it occurs eighteen times in all. In one place there is a reference to the king of the Kittim, but otherwise Kittim are mentioned in very general terms. It seems probable that Kittim here is not an actual name of a particular people, but is a designation of all the peoples who are enemies of Israel, God's chosen people.[84] The Kittim and the children of dark-

---

[84] J. Carmignac, "Les Kittim dans la 'Guerre des fils de lumière contre les fils de ténèbres,'" *NRTh* 77 (1955), 737 ff.

ness are identical. In an unpublished fragment the Kittim are even the same as "the peoples" ('*ammîm*). Hence it would be possible to speak of the "Kittim of Assyria," while the actual name of a nation could not be put in such a double genitive construction in Hebrew. But precisely this expression refers in all probability to the Seleucids.

This identification seems to complicate the problem even more. But yet another factor must be taken into account. In the fragmentary Nahum Commentary the Kittim are connected for the first time with actual historical names. Nahum 2:11b "where the lion and the lioness had their path, where the lion cubs walked around without anyone frightening them away," is interpreted in the following way: "[This refers to Deme]trius, the king of Greece, who on the advice of the 'seekers of smooth things (flattery)' tried to force his way into Jerusalem. From the days of Antiochus until the days when the rulers of the Kittim arose [this city has never 'frightened away'] the kings of Greece; but at last it will be trampled down." Since "the rulers of the Kittim" are here distinguished from Antiochus, they cannot very well be Seleucids; they are also clearly distinguished from the kings of Greece and therefore may in all probability be identified with the Romans.

For "Demetrius, king of Greece," there are two alternatives: the first is Demetrius I, who ascended the throne two years after the death of Antiochus IV and who at the request of the high priest, Alcimus, sent his general, Nicanor, to take Jerusalem. The other is Demetrius III Eukairos, who in 88 B.C. at the request of the party rebelling against Alexander Jannaeus invaded Palestine and defeated Alexander at Shechem; although admittedly nothing about an attempt to take Jerusalem is known. The latter alternative seems preferable. This would also explain another section in the Nahum Commentary, which speaks of a lion of wrath, who hanged alive (i.e., crucified) those who sought "smooth things." For Josephus tells that after Demetrius had returned to his land Alexander crucified eight hundred of the rebels (*Antiquities* XIII, 14, 1-2).

With these assumptions the following solution of the Kittim problem suggests itself. The documents are of different ages and therefore do not all refer to the same events. In the War Scroll, which seems to be the oldest, the word "Kittim" taken from the Bible is used to designate all nations who are enemies of God's people, Israel, and the Kittim of Assyria are Seleucids. The Habakkuk Commentary [85] and Nahum Commentary belong to a later period—between 88 and 63 B.C., and the Kittim there are the Romans.

The Teacher of Righteousness

The identity and date of "the Teacher" is assuredly one of the most hotly debated historical questions in connection with the Dead Sea Scrolls. The title, in Hebrew *môrēh haṣ-ṣédeq*, occurs in the Damascus Document, the Habakkuk Commentary and the Commentary on Psalm 37. It was probably coined in contrast to the

---

[85] The passage in the Habakkuk Commentary, "when the final time delays" (vii.12) is also evidence of the relative lateness of this document.

Old Testament expression *môrēh šéqer*, "teacher of false-hood, false teacher" (Hab. 2:18; Isa. 9:15). There is probably also an allusion to Joel 2:23 where there is a promise of *ham-môrēh liṣdāqāh*. This expression is usually translated in accordance with the context as "early rain for your vindication" (RSV) but it may also be translated literally as "the teacher for (or: of) righteousness" since the Hebrew word for "teacher" is the same as that for "early rain." According to a fairly obvious reconstruction of a damaged place in the Commentary on Psalm 37, the Teacher of Righteousness has founded a community, i.e., in all probability the Qumran community.

The Habakkuk Commentary contains numerous allusions to the Teacher and his enemies. He is first mentioned in i.13 where "the righteous one" (Hab. 1:4b "the wicked snares the righteous") is said to be the Teacher of Righteousness, while "the wicked one" is the wicked priest, who is mentioned in several places in the commentary. In ii.1 f. certain people, who followed the Man of the Lie (*'îš hak-kāzāb*) did not listen to the Teacher's words, and further, they did not believe his interpretation of the prophets concerning the events of the end time (ii.6 ff. compared with vii.4 f.). From a comparison of both of these passages just noted it also appears that the Teacher was a priest, which is expressly stated in the Commentary on Psalm 37.

The Teacher met with strong opposition. In v.9 ff. there is mention of people ("the house of Absalom") who "remained silent when the Teacher of Righteousness was chastised,[86] and did not help him against the

[86] Lit.: "at the chastisement of the Teacher . . . ," which leaves

Man of the Lie who rejected the Law," while in viii.1 f. others are praised for their loyalty (or faithfulness, *ᵉmûnāh*) to the Teacher of Righteousness.

The chief opponent of the Teacher is called *hak-kôhēn hā-rāšāʻ* (probably an ironic allusion to *hak-kôhēn hā-rôʼš*, the chief priest, i.e., the high priest), "the wicked priest who was named for truth in the beginning of his appearance, but when he began to rule in Israel his heart became haughty and he forsook God" and plundered in order to obtain riches for himself in that he also took "the wealth of the peoples" and walked in abominations and impurity (viii.8 ff.). Since similar statements are made in ix.5 ff. concerning "the last priests of Jerusalem" who "gathered riches from the spoils of the peoples," it is probable, that the wicked priest was the high priest of that period. Another passage states that the wicked priest walked in the ways of drunkenness (xi.13 f.) and that he wrought works of abomination and defiled the temple (xii.8 f.).

Mention is also made of a "Preacher of the Lie" (*maṭṭîp* [87] *hak-kāzāb*) "who enticed many to build a city of falsehood through bloodshed and to establish a congregation (*ʻēdāh*) in lies (*šéqer*) . . . that he made many grow weary in the service of falsehood" (x.9 ff.), but we are not told whether this "preacher" or "prophet" is identical with the wicked priest, neither is it clear whether "city" and "congregation" refer to the same thing or not.

the question of the subject open. Carmignac, "Notes . . . ," *op. cit.*, pp. 507-510, thinks it was the Teacher who chastised somebody, probably the Man of the Lie.

[87] The word is used of (ecstatic) prophetic preaching.

The conflict between the priest and the Teacher is described as follows: ". . . the wicked priest who persecuted the Teacher of Righteousness in order to confound him (or: swallow him up) in the anger of his wrath even to the place of his exile;[88] and at the time of the festival of rest, the Day of Atonement he appeared to confound them and to make them stumble on the day of fasting, their Sabbath of rest" (xi.4-8 on Hab. 2:15). These words are certainly extremely unclear, but this much seems certain: that the Teacher was forced into exile—to Qumran?—and that the priest interrupted him and his followers while they were celebrating the Day of Atonement, which presumably means that they had a calendar which in some way was different from that of orthodox Judaism so that their festival did not coincide with the official one.

The wicked priest seems, however, to have received his punishment. Column viii ends with some words concerning "the priest who rebelled [against God's] statutes," and column ix begins: "his plague with judgments on the wickedness and horrors of sore diseases, and vengeance upon the body of his flesh." It is probable that these words refer to the priest, since some lines further down read "the wicked priest, whom, for an offense against the Teacher of Righteousness and his followers, God delivered into the hand of his enemies, in

---

[88] The Hebrew is: 'BYT GLWTW, a phrase which has given interpreters many headaches. Since it appears, however, that the first word is a contraction of 'el-bêt, "to the house, i.e., the place . . . ," there is no longer any doubt as to what the phrase means. Cf. DSS, pp. 154 ff.

that He humiliated him with a destroying plague in bitterness of soul, because he had done evil against His elect" (ix.9 ff.).[89]

In summary it should be recognized that actual information recorded concerning the Teacher of Righteousness is both scanty and vague. He was a priest who was regarded as an inspired interpreter of the Scriptures, and he founded a community. He was "chastised" (= brought before a court?) and on this occasion some of his followers failed to lend him support. His adversary, the wicked priest, persecuted him and forced him into exile; but nowhere is it said that he was killed, let alone crucified, as it has often been maintained.

Before discussing some of the identifications which have been proposed, some of the statements concerning the Teacher in the Damascus Document must be noted.

Two passages mention the death of "the Teacher of the community" (or: "the unique [90] Teacher") (xx.14 f.; xix.35-xx.1), and in one of them it is said that forty years will elapse after that event until the men of war who followed the Man of the Lie will be annihilated. A third passage (xx.32) which speaks of those who listen to the voice of the Teacher of Righteousness has been taken to indicate that the Teacher is still alive, but such a conclusion is by no means necessary.

The decisive passage is, however, i.3 ff.:

[89] The Hebrew word *BHYRW* appears to be in the singular; in other cases the word is clearly in the plural: "the elect ones." It is thus probable that this is also the case in this passage. See below, pp. 183 f.

[90] The text has *yāḥîd* "only, unique," but possibly it should be read *yaḥad*, "community."

For when those who deserted him acted disloyally, He hid His face from Israel and from its Temple and gave them over to the sword; but when He considered the covenant with the first (generations), he left a remnant for Israel and did not abandon them to destruction. And in the time of wrath, 390 years from the time when he gave them into the hand of Nebuchadnezzar, the King of Babylon, He afflicted (or: visited) them. And He caused a root of planting to shoot forth out of Israel and out of Aaron to inherit the land and to grow fat in his good earth. And they recognized their iniquity and knew that they were guilt-laden men. But they were like blind men and groped for the way for twenty years. And God observed their works how they sought Him with their whole heart and He raised up for them a Teacher of Righteousness to lead them in the way of His heart.

In this passage there are two indications of dates, which could shed light on the question concerning the Teacher of Righteousness: 1) the 390 years and 2) the twenty years after Israel "had inherited" the land or "had taken it into possession."

The 390 years are presumably derived from Ezekiel 4:5 where they may designate the period of the Israelite monarchy. But the expression here is ambiguous; it is not apparent from the Hebrew word order whether the 390 years should be counted before or after Nebuchadnezzar's conquest of Jerusalem in 586 B.C. Exact biblical parallels to the Hebrew expression (II Chron. 34:8, 36:22) indicate, however, that it cannot be translated "390 years after he gave them. . . ."[91] But if the 390 years fall before Nebuchadnezzar, they would lose their whole significance for establishing the time in which

[91] E. Wiesenberg, "Chronological Data in the Zadokite Fragments," *VT* 5 (1955), 284 ff.

the Teacher of Righteousness lived. Hence this biblical allusion is without any value for chronological assessment.

Thus the only information that remains is that the Teacher appeared twenty years after the people took the land in possession. If this "repossession" or "settlement" is identified with the recovery of national independence during the early Maccabean period, as Brownlee [92] postulates—the return from Babylon seems to be a little too early—the years 152, 143 or 140 B.C. may be considered as possible dates and the appearance would occur in 132, 123 or 120 B.C. All of these dates fall in the reign of John Hyrcanus, and this is also in accord with the distribution of coins at Qumran.

It should be added that a passage in the Damascus Document (viii.11) mentions "the head of the kings of Greece who comes to take vengeance," which shows that the document must have been composed in the Greek (Seleucid) period and before the appearance of the Romans.

This is all that the available material has to offer and it is evidently not a simple task to identify by means of this information the persons and events alluded to. Several different proposals have emerged, but none is convincing enough to exclude the possibility of other solutions. It must be remembered that our knowledge about this period of Jewish history is quite limited, so that it is both possible and probable for a religious teacher to have appeared and worked among the Jews without having left any trace in our sources. If the

[92] Brownlee, "Messianic Motifs of Qumran and the New Testament, Part I," *NTS* 3 (1956/57), 12 ff.

wicked priest is assumed to have been a high priest, then it would be expected that his identification could be more easily made than that of the Teacher. But even this question is complicated by the fact that it is not known whether the wicked priest is identical with the "Man of the Lie" and "The Preacher of the Lie" or not.

According to Gaster [93] the "Teacher of Righteousness" is not an individual but an office. But this does not seem to agree with statements in the Habakkuk Commentary; and in any case the wicked priest is an individual.

Roughly, there have been five (or six) different dates proposed for the appearance of the Teacher. Two of these can be eliminated without much discussion.

1) Zeitlin's theory [94] that the Scrolls are medieval, conflicts both with the archeological data and the contents of the Scrolls.

2) Del Medico's [95] and Roth's [96] theory, which dates the Teacher in A.D. 66, may also be eliminated. According to this theory, a certain Zealot named Menaḥem would have been the Teacher, and the high priest Anan or Ananias the wicked priest, while Agrippa II is identified with the Preacher of the Lie who built a city. On New Year's Day of A.D. 66 Menaḥem appeared in royal pomp in the temple "to worship God," but he was seized and executed, possibly on the "Day of Atonement." But

[93] T. H. Gaster, *The Dead Sea Scriptures* (1956), pp. 26 f.

[94] S. Zeitlin's theory has been presented in a large number of articles in *JQR*, of which he is the editor.

[95] H. E. del Medico, *L'énigme des manuscrits de la Mer Morte* (1957).

[96] C. Roth first presented this theory in *Commentary:* "A Solution to the Mystery of the Scrolls," *Commentary* 24 (1957), 317-324.

Menaḥem was not a priest, while it is explicitly said that the Teacher of Righteousness was a priest; and quite a number of details in the Habakkuk Commentary do not agree with Josephus' account concerning Menahem. In addition, this theory does not allow for sufficient time for the formation of the Qumran community and the writing of the Scrolls and is not consistent with archeological data.

3) A dating in the early Maccabean period (between 170 and 160 B.C.) is maintained by Rowley[97] and Stauffer.[98] According to the former, the wicked priest was the high priest Menelaus who was installed by Antiochus Epiphanes. According to I Maccabees 1:33, II Maccabees 5:23 Menelaus built up the city of David, and in connection with this I Maccabees 1:35 ff. tells of great bloodshed in the city and profanation of the temple and II Maccabees 5:24 of a bloody massacre on the Sabbath day. The Teacher would have been Onias IV, the high priest who was deposed by Antiochus. It is known that Menelaus had instigated the murder of Onias. The events alluded to would in this case have taken place about 170 B.C.

Stauffer identifies the Teacher with a certain teacher of the Torah (Law), Jose ben Joezer from Zeredah who belonged to the Ḥasidic movement. He is said to have had an opponent named Yakim, who is identified by

---

[97] Rowley's theory is presented in a number of his works as, for example: *The Zadokite Fragments, op. cit.*; "The Internal Dating of the Dead Sea Scrolls," *EphThLov* 28 (1952), 257-276; "The Covenanters of Damascus and the Dead Sea Scrolls," *BJRL* 35 (1952/53), 111-154.

[98] For a summary of Stauffer's theory see: E. Stauffer, *Jerusalem und Rom im Zeitalter Jesu Christi* (1957), pp. 128 ff.

Stauffer with Alcimus who was appointed by Demetrius I; there are intimations that Alcimus crucified his uncle (i.e., Jose ben Joezer) on a sabbath (*ca.* 162-160 B.C.). Stauffer also finds these events reflected in the Nahum Commentary (in which both Antiochus and Demetrius as well as the crucifixion terror are mentioned).

However, this theory leads to certain objections: too little is known of Jose ben Joezer to permit any sure conclusions and the Nahum Commentary does not actually contain the information which Stauffer finds in it. It is most improbable that the Teacher would have remained unmentioned, had he actually been among those crucified according to the Nahum Commentary. Stauffer's theory remains highly uncertain, yet there is some small possibility that it might be correct.

4) A view which makes Alexander Jannaeus (103-76 B.C.) the wicked priest is espoused by many scholars [99] and there is actually much that speaks in its favor. While it is not a decisive argument that the Nahum Commentary alludes to the events of 88 B.C., since the Teacher is not mentioned in it, still it must be granted that a part of what is told concerning the wicked priest fits Jannaeus very well. But in that case no identification of the Teacher is possible; no known historical figure fits the picture. On the other hand, this theory carries with it so many difficulties that it hardly can be accepted as a solution to the problem.[100]

[99] Among others there are: Allegro, *The Dead Sea Scrolls* (1956), pp. 94 ff.; Bruce, *Second Thoughts on the Dead Sea Scrolls* (2nd ed.; 1961), pp. 100 ff.

[100] See: *DSS*, pp. 175 ff.; Rowley, "The Covenanters of Damascus . . . ," *op. cit.*, pp. 133 f., 136.

5) Finally, there is the theory proposed by Dupont-Sommer [101] to the effect that the Teacher was murdered shortly before Pompey's conquest of Jerusalem in 63 B.C. In that case he must have begun his activity under Alexander Jannaeus, but the wicked priest who persecuted him would thus be Alexander's son, Hyrcanus II. Dupont-Sommer finds some support for his thesis in the Testament of Levi 17, which mentions seven priests whom he identifies with the Hasmonaeans; the last three of these, who are judged particularly severely are, Aristobulus, Alexander Jannaeus, and Hyrcanus II, all of whom assumed the royal title. Further, in the so-called Testimonia Fragment from Cave 4 there is an interpretation of Joshua 6:26 which is said to allude to "an accursed man, a tool of Belial" and his sons who will rebuild the city of Jerusalem and make it into a city of wickedness. According to Dupont-Sommer this refers to Alexander and his two sons, Hyrcanus II and Aristobulus II, and their restoration of Jerusalem's walls before the siege of 65-63 B.C. It may be recalled that the Habakkuk Commentary also mentions the building of a city of falsehood. But this theory also permits no sure identification of the Teacher of Righteousness.

It may be added that an unpublished fragment contains the name of Queen Šᵉlāmṣīyôn (Salome Alexandra), Alexander Jannaeus' widow, but no connection is established with the events here under discussion. We may note in passing that Hyrcanus (*HRQNWS*) and

---

[101] Dupont-Sommer, *The Dead Sea Scrolls, A Preliminary Survey*, trans. E. M. Rowley (1952); *The Jewish Sect of Qumran and the Essenes*, trans. R. D. Barnett (1954).

Aemilius (*'MYLYWS*) governors in Syria at about the time of the birth of Christ are also mentioned.[102]

From many points of view the last theory is attractive. But it should not be forgotten that the documents which can be dated approximately 65 B.C. do not mention the Teacher of Righteousness with the exception of the Habakkuk Commentary which speaks of him in the past tense, while the Kittim are spoken of in the Hebrew "imperfect," i.e., using the form of the verb which indicates something which is in the present or the future time. Further, as Rowley has quite correctly pointed out, this late dating of the Teacher leaves several important details unexplained. And finally, the manuscripts themselves and the archeological data seem to require a somewhat longer history of the sect.

For these reasons Brownlee's dating of the Teacher *circa* 130-120 B.C. seems more probable; his death would then fall in the reign of Alexander Jannaeus. But the religious and political situation in Palestine at that time does not seem to have been particularly conducive to the rise of a sect which laid particular emphasis on Zadokite descent in the priesthood. On the other hand, the required conditions could be better found if we were allowed an earlier dating, i.e., the time when the Hasmonaeans appropriated the priestly office (153 B.C.); although it is not completely impossible that the protest against this could have received its sharpest formulation somewhat later.

At present it seems impossible to reach any more exact

[102] See: Milik, "Le travail d'édition des manuscrits du Désert de Juda," *VT Suppl. 4* (1956), p. 26.

date for the Teacher of Righteousness. All that can be said is that he must have flourished some time between 170 and 63 B.C. and rather before than after 100 B.C.

The Migration to Damascus

Some passages in the Damascus Document speak of entering into the new covenant in the Land of Damascus (vi.19; viii.21; cf. xx.12); once it mentions an "interpreter of the law who came (comes) to Damascus" (vii.17 f.) and another time "those of Israel who repented and went out of the land of Judah and sojourned in the land of Damascus" (vi.5).

This seems to mean that the community on some occasion migrated to Damascus in order to settle there. It has been generally assumed that this happened after the destruction of Jerusalem. But after the discovery of fragments of the Damascus Document in Qumran this theory has become less probable. Since it is hardly likely that the sect first emigrated to Damascus and then afterward returned to Qumran, another explanation must be sought.

Now it is clear that the Damascus Document considers the migration to Damascus as the fulfillment of the prophecy in Amos 5:26 f., and it is therefore possible that Damascus be understood figuratively and simply refer to Qumran. North [103] even thinks that "the 'land of Damascus' may be considered an appellation of the Nabataean Kingdom . . . ," and that Qumran at that time at least was to a certain degree under Nabataean

[103] R. North, "The Damascus of Qumran Geography," *PEQ* 87 (1955), 48; see also the discussion in *MLS*, chap. 19, pp. 219-227.

rule. It is also possible that the Damascus Document could be older than, e.g., the Manual of Discipline, so that it could have been written before the settlement at Qumran; in that case "the land of Damascus" could indicate another of the areas in the vicinity of the Dead Sea which without doubt lay within the Nabataean realm. This solution seems very probable, although at present nothing can be considered to be definitive. The only thing that is certain is the allusion to the prophecy in Amos.

Part One

DOCTRINE

1

God

THE TRANSCENDENT ONE

There is a general tendency within post-exilic Judaism strongly to emphasize that God is exalted and transcendent. This tendency can already be seen in such an external phenomenon as the avoidance of pronouncing the name of God—Yahweh—and the substitution of circumlocutions such as the Lord (*'ᵃdônāy*), the Name (*haš-šēm*), the Presence (or "In-dwelling," *šᵉkīnāh*). This can also be seen in the Qumran writings.[1]

The divine name Yahweh does not occur in the extra-biblical texts. In one of the Isaiah scrolls there are readings which indicate that *'ᵃdônāy* was read instead of Yahweh. In the Habakkuk Commentary and the Micah Commentary the divine name *YHWH* is written with the old Semitic alphabet, and the same applies to El (God) in the Thanksgiving Psalms. This is apparently intended to emphasize the character of the divine name as being something particularly meaningful and totally different from all other names.

[1] M. Delcor, "Des diverses manières d'écrire le tétragramme sacré dans les anciens documents hébraïques," *RHR* 147 (1955), 145-173.

The attempt to avoid the name Yahweh can also be noted in quite a few quotations. Where, for example, Isaiah 40:3 is cited in the Manual of Discipline viii.14, the divine name is replaced by four dots, and in viii.13 the scribe has substituted the letters *HW'H'* (perhaps = *hû' 'elôhîm*, "he, God"). In ₁QS ii.15 there is a clear allusion to Deuteronomy 29:20, but the divine name Yahweh has been replaced with El (God), and the same phenomenon can be observed in the quotation from Psalm 106:25a, 40 in CD iii.8. ₁QM x.4 has "your God" in place of "Yahweh, your God" in a quotation from Deuteronomy 20:2-4; the same applies to x.7 in a citation from Numbers 10:9.

The usual designation for God is the archaic *'ēl* (only infrequently the normal *'elôhîm*); the word *'adônāy*, "the Lord," occurs mainly in the Thanksgiving Psalms' introductory phrase: "I thank Thee, Lord" (*'ôdekāh 'adônāy*). The epithet "God of the gods" (*'ēl 'ēlîm*) is also found (₁QM xiv.16, perhaps also xviii.7) "prince of the gods" (*śar 'ēlîm*) and "the Most High" (*'elyôn* ₁QS iv.22, etc.).[2]

This shows that the Qumran congregation shares contemporary Judaism's great reverence for the divine name, which in turn is connected with the emphasis on the transcendence of God. In agreement with this ₁QS vi.27 gives orders for punishment of him "who names anything with that name which is honored above everything."

[2] P. Boccaccio, "I manoscritti del Mar Morto e i Nomi di Dio *YHWH, 'EL*," *Biblica* 32 (1951), 90-96.

GOD'S MAJESTY AND GLORY

God's greatness and majesty are also very prominent features in the theology of the scrolls, and this expresses itself particularly in the Thanksgiving Psalms and the hymnic sections of the other scrolls. God is great, glorious, sublime; he is eternal, strong and powerful, wise and omniscient:

Who is like unto Thee, O God of Israel,
in heaven and on earth,
who doeth such mighty deeds as Thou
and hath such power as Thou?

—₁QM x.8 f.

Who can endure Thy glory? —₁QS xi.20

None is as Thy strength in power,
Thy glory hath no [equal],
Thy wisdom hath no measure,
[Thy truth] no boundary.

—₁QH ix.16 f.

I know that truth is (in) Thy mouth
and in Thine hand righteousness,
and in Thy thought all knowledge
and in Thy power all strength,
and all glory is with Thee.

—₁QH xi.7-8

Behold, Thou art prince of the gods
and king of the honored ones,
Lord of every spirit[3]
And ruler over all works.
Without Thee nothing is done,

[3] The title "Lord of spirits" occurs about fifty times in I Enoch.

And nothing can be known without Thy will.
There is none beside Thee,
And no one is like unto Thee in power,
Nothing compares to Thy glory,
And Thy strength is beyond price.

—₁QH x.8-11

Nothing happens in the world save by the will of God.
This is an axiom of faith which is repeated time after
time:

According to Thy will everything comes to pass
And without Thee nothing is done.[4]

—₁QH i.20

And again:
Through His knowledge everything comes to pass
And everything that is, He secureth through His plan,
And without Him nothing is done.

—₁QS xi.11

One finds here, as Licht correctly points out, "an honest
intellectual attempt to free the concept of deity from all
dependence on human will and action."[5] Man cannot
do anything to influence God's will, not even indirectly.
What God has ordained is absolute and cannot be
changed by the actions or qualities of created beings.

The goal and purpose of creation lies not with man
but with God, it is nothing other than God's glory.
God's glory is the only acceptable reason for his actions.[6]

[4] Cf. John 1:3.
[5] Licht, "The Doctrine of the Thanksgiving Scroll," *IEJ* 6
(1956), 9.
[6] F. Nötscher, "Schicksalsglaube in Qumrân und Umwelt," *BZ*
3 (1959), 229 f.

He has stretched out the heavens to his glory ($_1$QH i.10), and to his glory has he created all things (x.12), given the Law and founded his congregation (vi.10). It can also be said that he acts for the sake of his name ($_1$QM xviii.8), which in principle is the same thing.

Here the scrolls continue a line of thought that is found already in the Old Testament, in the canonical Psalter and, above all, in the prophet Ezekiel: God does not act because he is affected by man's fate but for his own sake, for the sake of his name or for the sake of his glory. "It is not for your sake, O house of Israel, . . . but for the sake of my holy name . . ." (Ezek. 36:22). And when he acts thus, "He shows His holiness," i.e., he upholds the inviolability of his nature, guards his honor. Similar expressions are very numerous in Qumran, particularly in the Thanksgiving Psalms.

Even the division of the generations of men into the righteous and the wicked with all its consequences is finally aimed at revealing God's glory and honor. His wonderful guidance shows forth in his gracious acts toward the elect; and the wicked were created so that God's might and wrath should be revealed upon them:

> . . . that Thou mayest be glorified[7] through the judgment of the wicked, and show Thyself mighty in me before the children of men.
>
> —$_1$QH ii.24

God's judgments befall the wicked as a warning, it is said, "in order that [all] shall know His glory and His great power" ($_1$QH xv.20); and when he "deals won-

[7] Or: Show Thyself glorious.

derfully with the many," he does so "for the sake of His glory and in order to make known His mighty acts before all the living" (iv.28).

THE CREATOR AND SOVEREIGN RULER

This mighty God is the Creator; he alone has created the world and all that is within it. There is no mythological creation story, neither is there any philosophical cosmogony. The biblical concept of creation is accepted without discussion: God created everything through an act of his absolute will. Therefore his sovereignty over the world is complete. He governs it since it is his creation:

> Praised be Thou, O Lord,
> Thou who hast fashioned [all things,
> mighty] in deeds,
> all things are Thy work.
>
> —₁QH xvi.8
>
> Through the thought of Thy heart
> [hast Thou made everything,
> and without Thee nothing is done][8]
> And without Thy will nothing exists,
> and no one understands [Thy counsel]
> or beholds [Thy mysteries].
>
> —₁QH x.1 f.

In this connection *rāṣôn* "(good) pleasure," "will," is a central concept. This is God's will, his counsel, without which nothing comes into being and nothing happens and through which everything is predestined but which nevertheless always remains the gracious will of God.

[8] Reconstructions are based on passages such as i.20, x.9. Cf. also ₁QS xi.11, 17.

Before Thou didst create them,
Thou knewest all their deeds.

—₁QH i.7

Before they were established, He knew their works . . .
for He knew the years of their existence and the number
and the explanation of their periods for all who exist in
the ages and the things that will come to pass, even that
which will come in their periods for all the years of
eternity.

—CD ii.7 f.

Thus far we find ourselves within the framework of
the Old Testament doctrine of creation. Psalm 139, for
example, points out how God knows each word before it
is on our tongue and that all the days of man were
written in his book before any of them existed (vss. 4,
16; cf. also Wisd. of Sol. 19:1). But the Qumran sect
goes further: that God knows man's deeds means not
only that he foresees them but that he has predestined
them. God's reign over the world is dependent on his
eternal counsel and predestination. Everything is fixed
beforehand by him from the beginning:

From the God of knowledge comes all that is and that is
to be, and before they came into being He prepared all
their thoughts. And when they came into being according to His predestination (*teʿûdāh*), according to His
glorious plan, they fulfill their work; without anything
being changed.

—₁QS iii.15 f.

. . . according to God's will
and predestination (*teʿûdāh*) concerning that which will
   come to pass:
and it comes to pass,

and it is not invalid,
and without that nothing has come to pass
neither shall it come to pass,
since the God of knowledge has prepared it,
and there is none beside Him.

—₁QH xii.9-11 [9]

Here the word $t^{e'}\hat{u}d\bar{a}h$ is of particular interest. It looks precisely the same as the word which otherwise means "testimony," but here it is a term for God's eternal decree or predestination. It is possible that at Qumran it was not connected with the verb $h\bar{e}'\hat{i}d$ (from the root 'WD), "to witness," "to assert," but with the root $Y'D$ "to appoint," "to agree on" (a time or place). As a matter of fact, the War Scroll uses the latter verb in a context which gives expression to the same deterministic point of view: there is an "appointed day" ($y\hat{o}m\ y\bar{a}'\hat{u}d$) for the great eschatological final battle (₁QM i.10).

In the Thanksgiving Psalms there is also the idea that "everything is engraved ($\hbar\bar{a}q\hat{u}q$) before God with the stylus of remembrance" (i.24) or that "God has recorded ($r\bar{a}\check{s}am$) the spirit of the righteous ones (xvi.10). Behind these expressions we may detect the idea of the heavenly book or tablet where everything is recorded—an idea which is also found in the pseudepigraphic literature, for example Jubilees 5:13 f. ("The judgment is decided and written on the holy tablets"), I Enoch 81:3 ("upon them are prefigured all the events of the world").[10]

[9] Cf. also: ₁QH iv.13.

[10] Nötscher, "Himmlische Bücher und Schicksalsglaube in Qumran," RQ 1 (1958/59), 405-411. On page 408 reference is made to unpublished texts which mention the heavenly tablets and the dependence of man's life on the course of the heavenly bodies.

This concept may go all the way back to the Babylonian idea of the tablets of destiny, with the help of which Marduk determined the fate of the world at creation and whose earthly symbols played an important role each year in the so-called determination of fate or fixing of destinies in the New Year festival.

It is a well-known fact that the Jewish apocalyptic literature also has a more or less deterministic view of the course of the world, since it presupposes that there exists a divine plan for the world which is established from the beginning and which goes irresistibly to its completion. The task which apocalyptic took upon itself was to reveal this world plan of God and in that way also to predict the end of this age and the breaking in of the coming age. But this idea has probably never been presented elsewhere within Judaism as consistently as here in Qumran.

GOD'S ORDERING OF THE UNIVERSE

The planned order of creation also manifests itself in the world of nature and can be observed in the wise and harmonious ordering of the universe. The cycles of the sun and moon, the succession of day and night, the stars, the winds and other powerful phenomena of nature all follow their unchanging and clearly demonstrable laws. Their movements and effects were established at the creation. God has "prepared" or "established" (*hēkîn*) their work (₁QH i.14, 19; ii.17; x.22; xi.34; xv.14, 19, 22; cf. the expression "was prepared," Greek: *hētoímasthai*, Matt. 20:23; Rev. 12:6).

In the first column of the Thanksgiving Psalms there is (although unfortunately somewhat damaged) a poetic description of the wonders of the universe where this idea of the purposefulness of all things is given especially clear expression. Each natural phenomenon has its fixed place in God's plan, its fixed aim which it inevitably fulfills. Everything moves in the course fixed by God— and so does man; this is the conclusion the author wants to draw from his reflections. This thought is so central in the theology of the Qumran community that the section should be cited *in extenso*.

It is Thou Who hast formed every spirit
and gave [rule and] law for all their works.
It is Thou Who didst stretch out the heavens to Thy
   glory
and [prepared] all its [hosts] according to Thy pleasure
and strong spirits according to their laws.
Before they became [holy] angels,
[Thou madest them] as everlasting spirits in their
   dominions,
the luminaries for their mysteries,
the stars for their courses,
[clouds] for their task,
meteors and lightnings for their service,
the resources of the deep for their aims,
[. . . . .] for their mysteries.
It is Thou Who hast created the earth through Thy
   power,
seas and deeps [. . .] their depths
hast Thou established through Thy wisdom,
and all that is in them hast Thou prepared according
   to Thy pleasure.

—₁QH i.8-15

These lines, like some similar phrases in the badly damaged column xiii, probably allude to the doctrine concerning elemental spirits, which is also known from the Book of Enoch: God has appointed spirits to rule over the elements and natural phenomena, and these spirits act in accordance with his will and the plan which he has established.

The order of nature and the regular course of the heavenly bodies receives special meaning for man, since they control the calendar and mark the holy seasons, i.e., the religious festivals.[11] This is the reason why the Qumran congregation attached such importance to questions concerning the calendar: the times for the festivals are decided by the order which God laid down in the universe at the creation. This is indicated, for example, in a somewhat damaged section in the War Scroll (1QM x.15), where the various natural phenomena and the distribution of the human race on earth are first mentioned and later as a direct continuation from this "the holy festivals, the course of the years and the (established) periods of eternity." One as well as the other is based on the divine order of creation and cannot be altered by man's actions.

[11] This idea is also found in the Book of the Wisdom of Jesus the Son of Sirach (Ecclesiasticus), as for example, Sir. 33.8. Cf. J. C. Rylaarsdam, *Revelation in Jewish Wisdom Literature* (1946), p. 33. There are also reflections on creation and predestination in chapter 39 of Sirach which have rather close affinities with Qumran: ". . . whatever He commands will be done in His time. . . . At His command whatever pleases Him is done, and none can limit His saving power. . . . No one can say, 'What is this?' 'Why is that?' for everything has been created for its use." (Sir. 39:16, 18, 21).

GOD'S ACTING IN HISTORY

The divine plan and predestination apply to an equally high degree, however, both to nature and mankind. This thought can probably most clearly and obviously be seen in the section of the War Scroll just mentioned, where it is said:

> . . . he who created the earth and the regulations for its divisions into wilderness and desert plain and all that grows therein with its fruit, [and who made] the circle of the sea and the gathering place of streams, who divided the depths and made animals and birds, the form of man and his gen[erations . . .], who caused the confusion of tongues and apportioned to the peoples habitations according to their families and let them take lands into their possession [. . .] holy festivals and the courses of the years. . . .
>
> —₁QM x.12-15

Not without reason has this section been compared with Paul's speech on the Areopagus in Athens, where it is said: "And he made from one every nation of men to live on all the face of the earth, having determined allotted periods and the boundaries of their habitation . . ." (Acts 17:26).[12]

That God acts in history is one of the well-known themes in the Old Testament. And bearing in mind the Qumran congregation's general attitude on the question of God as sovereign ruler of everything it is only natural that this particular side of the general thought concerning God's rule of the world occurs many times in the

[12] Cf. F. Mussner, "Einige Parallelen aus den Qumrântexten zur Areopagrede (Apg. 17, 22-31)," *BZ* 1 (1957), 125 ff.

Dead Sea Scrolls. The introductory part of the Damascus Document is a brief philosophy of history or,
more correctly, theology of history, an interpretation of
the whole of Israel's history in the light of the insight
into God's just rule of the world, the general principle
of which is expressed in the sentence: "When those who
deserted Him acted disloyally, He hid His face from
Israel and from its temple and gave them over to the
sword" (CD i.3-4). This to be sure is hardly more than
an example of the Deuteronomic view of history. A
faint trace of another concept is however seen, when
the author continues: "But when He considered the
covenant with the fathers, He left a remnant in Israel
and did not abandon them to destruction" (i.4-5). Here
it is not the moral or religious quality of the remnant
which is the focus of interest, but God's initiative in
saving his people from total destruction.

Again in the War Scroll there are some reflections concerning God's intervention in history on behalf of Israel
in its battles; and hence the conclusion is naturally drawn
that he will help his people also in the last eschatological war:

For Thine is the battle, and through the strength of Thy
hand their corpses were scattered about without burial.
And the Gittite, Goliath, the mighty hero, didst Thou
deliver into the hand of Thy servant, David . . . and
[Thou] hast humiliated the Philistines many times through
Thy Holy Name, and also through the hand of our kings
hast Thou delivered us many times . . . and Thou doest
with them (i.e., Belial's hosts) as with Pharaoh and his
charioteers at the Red Sea.

—₁QM xi. 1-3, 9 f.

We are here once again within the framework of the Old Testament's teaching about God. But against the background which has been sketched it is clear that even in this simple statement of God's acting in history there is an underlying idea of divine predestination of the course of the world and of history. The fact that God's action is emphasized more strongly than the role of the human instrument in the event is probably connected with this idea of predestination.

A similar deterministic view of history is also found in other contemporary documents, for example, II Esdras:

> Before the present years were reckoned,
> and before the imaginations of those who now sin were estranged,
> and before those who stored up treasures of faith were sealed—
> then I planned these things,
> and they were made through me and not through another,
> just as the end shall come through me and not through another.
>
> —II Esdras 6:5-6

GOD'S MYSTERIES

God's plan for the universe and for history is a secret, a mystery (*rāz*).[13] God has made the sun and the moon

---

[13] The word "*rāz*" is Persian in origin; it occurs several times as a loanword in Dan. 2:18 ff., and in Sir. 8:18. Concerning the concept "mystery" in the Dead Sea Scrolls, see E. Vogt, " 'Mysteria' in textibus Qumrān," *Biblica* 37 (1956), 247-257; R. E. Brown, "The Pre-Christian Semitic Concept of 'Mystery,' " *CBQ* 20 (1958), 436 ff.; *ibid.*, "The Semitic Background of the New Testament *Mysterion*," Part I. *Biblica* 39 (1958), 426 ff.; Part II, 40 (1959), 70 f.

"for their secrets" ($_1$QH i.11; cf. i.13). In the mysteries
of his insight has he appointed a time for the dominion
of evil ($_1$QS iv.18) and it is averred that "all God's
times ($q\bar{e}\d{s}$)[14] come according to His appointed order,
which He has fixed for them in the mysteries of His
wisdom" ($_1$QpHab. vii.14), and "God's mysteries are
wonderful" ($_1$QpHab. vii.8). In the eschatological final
battle some will fall "through God's mystery" ($_1$QM
xvii.17). A $r\bar{a}z$, therefore is, as Licht expresses it, a
"divine, unfathomable unalterable decision."[15] There is
a fragment of the Thanksgiving Psalm Scroll which apparently reads: God "preserved man (?) for the mysteries of His good pleasure (or His will) (= His secret
aims)" ($_1$QH fr. iii.7); another, that not even the angels
can grasp these mysteries (fr. i.2-3).

Moreover, there is also mention of "the mysteries of
sin" ($_1$QH v.36; The Book of Mysteries [$_1$Q 27] i.2; cf.
$_1$QM xiv.9),[16] which naturally can be an intimation that
the dominion of evil is ordained by a divine decree[17]
(cf. $_1$QS iii.23), but can also simply refer to the hidden
activity of the evil powers.

God's mysteries are, at least to some extent, laid down
in the holy writings, but in order that they might appear

---

[14] The word $q\bar{e}\d{s}$ literally means "end," but in the Dead Sea
Scrolls it has a special technical meaning of "appointed, exact
time"; cf. Wallenstein, "Some Lexical Material in the Judean
Scrolls," *VT* 4 (1954), 213 f,; and Wieder, "The Term QṢ in the
Dead Sea Scrolls and in Hebrew Liturgical Poetry," *JJS* 5 (1954),
22 ff.

[15] Licht, "The Doctrine . . . ," *op. cit.,* p. 8

[16] Cf. II Thess. 2:7.

[17] Licht seems to imply this in "The Doctrine . . . ," *op. cit.,*
p. 8.

clearly they must be interpreted; and for that purpose God has given the Teacher insight. "He made known to him all the secrets of the words of His servants the prophets" (₁QpHab. vii.4 f.; cf. ii.8 f.). The meditations concerning the divine plan of the world in the Thanksgiving Psalm scroll's first column ends with the words:

> These things I know through Thy understanding,
> for Thou hast opened my ears
> unto wonderful mysteries,
> although I am a vessel of clay, etc.
>
> —₁QH i.21

In the so-called Book of Mysteries (₁Q 27) the word *rāz* has a clearly eschatological implication: "They (the wicked) do not know the mysteries to come, and they do not heed those things that are past; and they do not understand what shall come upon them, and their souls (= their life) shall they not be able to save from the mystery to come" (i.3-4). One specific detail of those eschatological events which are foreseen in God's plan, i.e., judgment of the wicked, has here received primary attention and is designated by the word "mystery." This shows in any case, that the word has a tendency to take on an eschatological coloring.

The insight into God's mysteries, which sometimes also can be called "the truth" (cf. ₁QS ix.18 f.), is thus given to man, or perhaps rather to the elect, through divine revelation. For the sinners, the children of destruction, the truth remains hidden (₁QH v.25 f.; cf. ix.24: "Thou hast hidden the truth until its time"). It is thus a question of an esoteric teaching, which may not be imparted to the uninitiated. It has been hidden for a long time, but now it has thus been revealed to the elect.

But each one who has been initiated into the mysteries must strive to subordinate himself to God's plan and take his assigned place in it. As ₁QS i.14 expresses it, he shall not hasten or delay any of God's times. This might just as well allude to the epochs of world history as to the stated times established for festivals, since both are grounded in the divine plan for the world.

Allegro points out that the idea of the mystery of God, long hidden but now revealed, occurs in several passages in the New Testament.[18] Thus Paul speaks of ". . . the mystery which was kept secret for long ages but is now disclosed . . ." (Rom. 16:25 f.), or of ". . . a secret and hidden wisdom of God, which . . . none of the rulers of this age understood . . . ," but which ". . . God has revealed to us through the Spirit" (I Cor. 2:7 f., 10; cf. also Eph. 3:3-9). Even if there may be no direct influence here, in any case the line of thought and the ideological background are the same.

GOD'S RIGHTEOUSNESS

What the Qumran texts have to say about God in other respects agrees largely with the point of view of the Old Testament. Against those who oppose him God is the righteous and severe judge (₁QH v.4; vi.4; vii.12) before whose wrath no one can stand (ix.14 f.; xii.30 f.): "Thou art righteous, and all Thine elect are truth, and all error and wickedness dost Thou destroy forever" (₁QH xiv.15 f.; cf. CD vii.9 ff.).

[18] Allegro, *The Dead Sea Scrolls* (1956), pp. 130 ff.

But God's righteousness is not only condemning and punishing but also cleansing. Wrath is coupled with mercy and grace:

> Through Thy wrath all afflicting judgments come to pass,
> and in Thy goodness is abundant forgiveness.
>
> —₁QH xi.8 f.

The discipline of God's righteousness leads to the soul's salvation (₁QH ix.33), his righteousness and long-suffering are sometimes mentioned together (₁QH i.6; xvii.17). God's faithfulness, grace and compassion are strongly emphasized; he who turns to him in penitence receives forgiveness of sins:

> All their works shalt Thou judge
> in Thy truth (faithfulness) and Thy grace
> with a wealth of compassion and abundant forgiveness.
>
> —₁QH vi.8 f.

> I lean upon Thy grace
> and on Thine abundant compassion,
> for Thou atonest for iniquity
> and cleansest man from guilt through Thy righteousness.
>
> —₁QH iv.36 f.

(Cf. also ₁QH i.32; vii.27, 30, etc.). How this forgiveness is related to the idea of predestination will be discussed later.

The way in which the concept of righteousness is combined with both judgment and forgiveness is striking. Actually, for the Qumran congregation, God's righteousness is somehow at the center of God's nature. But the shades of meaning of the word are not quite the same as in the Old Testament. The aspect upon which attention is immediately focused is God's absolute righteousness in contradistinction to man's total depravity. God is righteous, and truth is his judgment (₁QS i.26). "Who is righteous before Thee when he is judged?" asks the psalmist (₁QH vii.28); "none is righteous in Thy judgment and none is innocent in trial before Thee" (₁QH ix.14 f.; cf. xii.19). It is characteristic of the Thanksgiving Psalms that God's righteousness is associated with his absolute sovereignty over the world as its Creator. "To Thee, to Thee alone belongs the righteousness (cf. xi.18), for Thou hast made all things" (xvi.9).

This is clearly a continuation of a line of thought which is also represented in the Old Testament. Thus, for example, Ecclesiastes says: "Surely there is not a righteous man on earth who does good . . ." (7:20), and it is an obvious fact that no man can argue his right against God (Isa. 45:9; Job 9:32). God who is the greatest in righteousness cannot fall under man's condemnation (Job 34:17).

But no matter how strongly God's righteousness is stressed at Qumran, it is nevertheless an exaggeration to say, as does Licht, that this righteousness is "God's unquestionable right to do as He pleases." [19] It is correct, that God "is just in whatever He does," but that does not mean that he may do something which is evil or even capricious. God is righteous in all his works (₁QH i.6) and there is no defense or answer to his chastisement

[19] Licht, "The Doctrine . . . ," *op. cit.*, p. 9.

for he is righteous and none compares to him (xii.31). But this is only one side of the matter, and it is particularly emphasized when there is a question of the contrast with man's lack of righteousness. God's righteousness is also a redeeming righteousness:

> If I totter,
> God's mercy is my salvation forever,
> and if I stumble in iniquity of the flesh,
> my vindication through God's righteousness shall stand
> eternally. . . .
> In His compassion has He brought me near,
> and in grace He causes my vindication to come,
> and in His faithful righteousness does He vindicate me,
> and in His abundant goodness does He atone for all of
> mine iniquities.
> And in His righteousness does He cleanse me from the
> impurity of man.
>
> —₁QS xi.12-15

In this passage God's righteousness is more or less identical with his grace and compassion, his saving goodness. Therefore the author of the hymn can say that man should "thank God for His righteousness" (₁QS xi.15). Therefore will he open his mouth with thanksgiving and recount God's righteousness (₁QS x.23), and therefore shall the priests at the ceremonies of entrance into the covenant "recount God's righteousness in His powerful deeds and proclaim all His merciful acts of grace toward Israel" (₁QS i.21). It is true that this aspect is stressed more strongly in the Manual of Discipline than in the Thanksgiving Psalms, but neither is it entirely absent in the later writings, where it is said once:

Thou atonest for iniquity
and cleansest man from guilt through Thy righteousness.

—1QH iv.37

In agreement with this, it belongs to the eschatological fulfillment that "God's righteousness will become manifest before all His works" (1QH xiv.16); that means not only that all evil and unrighteousness will be forever annihilated (xiv.15 f.), but it also means the final salvation of the elect. "As smoke vanishes and is no longer, so will wickedness vanish forever. And righteousness will be revealed as the sun" (Book of Mysteries, i.5 f.). This means that God's innermost nature, his righteousness, has become fulfilled.

2

Dualism

As a logical consequence of God's absolute sovereignty it must in a way follow that he is in the last analysis also the originator of evil, or as the Qumran literature says, that he has created the two spirits which determine and govern the course of the world and human life. God is at the head of a dualistic system, in that he alone has created the two fundamental powers of the universe. This dualistic outlook[1] is most clearly described in the theological section of the Manual of Discipline.[2] After it has first been established that "from the God of knowledge comes all that is and all that is to be" (₁QS iii.15), it continues:

> He created man to have dominion over the world and made for him two spirits, so that he may walk by them until the time of His visitation: they are the spirits of truth and of error.
>
> In the dwelling of light are the origins of the truth, and from a spring of darkness are the origins of error. In the hand of the Prince of Lights is dominion over all the children of righteousness; in the ways of light they walk.

[1] For a monograph on dualism in Qumran see: Huppenbauer, *Der Mensch zwischen zwei Welten* (1959).

[2] A study of this section is given by Licht, "An Analysis of the Treatise of the Two Spirits in DSD," *Scripta Hierosolymitana* 4 (1958), 88-100.

And in the hand of the angel of darkness is all dominion
over the children of error; and in the ways of darkness
they walk.

And through the angel of darkness come all the aberra-
tions of the children of righteousness, all their sin and
their iniquity and their guilt and the transgressions of their
deeds under his dominion until his appointed time (*qēṣ*),
and all their afflictions and the times of their distress stand
under the dominion of his enmity (*maśṭēmāh*). And all
the spirits of his "lot" (*gôrāl*) try to cause the children
of light to stumble, but the God of Israel and the angel
of His truth have helped all the children of light.

For He created the spirits of light and of darkness, and
upon them He founded every work and upon their ways
every service. One of the (spirits) God loves in all the
ages of eternity, and in all his deeds He has His pleasure
(*rāṣāh*) forever; the other, its counsel He abhors, and all
its ways He hates eternally.

—₁QS iii.17-iv.1

This section immediately gives the following information:

1) In the beginning, God has created two spirits, one
   good and one evil, and all the doings and dealings in
   the world are dependent upon them.

2) The good spirit is connected with light, truth and
   righteousness, and God loves him and his work; the
   evil spirit is connected with darkness, error (*ʿāwel*),
   sin and guilt, and God hates him and his works
   despite the fact that he created him. It is never said
   that the spirit of error had been created other than
   evil, or that he may have become evil through a fall.

3) Each of the two spirits has a "lot" (*gôrāl*), an area
   of activity or a band of followers.

4) Even the sins of the "righteous" are caused by the evil spirit.

5) God has measured out an appointed time for the activity of both spirits and this predestination belongs to the "mysteries" (*rāz*) of God.

6) The dualism is not physical-cosmological—as, e.g., between spirit and matter—but has a religious-ethical basis.

7) The dualism is not absolute and consistent: God created both spirits and fixed times for their dominion.

The passage just cited is followed by a section which describes the deeds and activity of the two spirits and which in many respects is reminiscent of the "catalogs of virtues and vices"[3] known from the epistles of the apostolic literature:

These are their (the good spirits') ways in the world: to illuminate the heart of man and to make smooth before him all the ways of righteousness (and) truth and to make his heart fear God's statutes; a spirit of humility and long-suffering of great compassion, eternal goodness, insight, understanding, mighty wisdom, which believes in all God's works and leans upon His abundant grace: a spirit of knowledge in every intention of action, zeal for righteous judgments, holy thought (intention) in a steadfast purpose, great devotion to all the children of truth, glorious purity, loathing all unclean idols and walking humbly (with self-restraint) in all things, concealing the truth of the mysteries of knowledge. These are the spirit's "counsels" (or rather: the fruits of his fellowship, Hebrew *sôd* in the

[3]S. Wibbing, *Die Tugend- und Lasterkataloge im Neuen Testament, und ihre Traditionsgeschichte unter besonderer Berücksichtigung der Qumran-Texte* (Beih. ZNW 25). (1959).

plural) for the children of truth in the world (cf. Gal. 5:22). . . .

But to the spirit of error belong: greediness, slackness in the service of righteousness, wickedness, falsehood, pride and haughtiness, treason and deceit, cruelty and great wickedness, a quickness to anger and much folly and unrestrained jealousy, shameful deeds in a spirit of fornication and filthy ways in the service of impurity, a blasphemous tongue, blind eyes, deaf ears, a stiff neck and hard of heart to walk the ways of darkness and evil cunning.

—₁QS iv.2-6, 9-11

After that it continues:

In these (two spirits) are the origins (or nature?)[4] of all men, and in their two divisions all the host of men have their inheritance in their generations, and in their two ways do they walk. And the performance of all their works happens in their divisions according to the inheritance of each, whether much or little, in all periods of eternity.

For God has placed the two spirits side by side until the last times and He has put eternal enmity between the two portions. An abomination to truth are the deeds of error and an abomination to error are all the deeds of truth. And envy of strife rests upon all their judgments, for they cannot walk together.

—₁QS iv.15-18

The sharp contrast between the two spirits is here brought to clear expression, and it becomes even more

[4] The Hebrew *tôlᵉdôt* which is usually translated "lineage, genealogy" (from the root *YLD*, "to bring forth, bear, beget") sometimes has the meaning "nature" in later Hebrew. It is perhaps possible that this is already the case here. (Cf. the review of Licht's "An Analysis . . . ," *op. cit.*, in *RQ* 1 [1958/59], 287.)

evident that man's good or evil behavior is dependent on his belonging to one or the other group or party (*miplāg*, as is modern Hebrew). Man's whole personality and his ethical conduct is therefore determined by which of the two camps or "lots" he belongs to.

"But," the text further states, "in the mysteries of His insight and in the wisdom of His glory God has appointed a time for the existence of error, and at the appointed time of visitation He will destroy it forever" (₁QS iv.18-19). Thus, the dualism is limited also by the fact that the dominion of the evil spirit is established up to a certain time which was predetermined by God.

"But," it says finally, "thus far the spirits of truth and error strive in a man's heart: man walks in wisdom or folly, and according to each one's share of his inheritance in truth is he righteous and so hates error, but according to his inheritance in the lot of error is man wicked therein and loathes truth. For side by side has God placed them (the two spirits) right up to the firmly decreed time and the new creation; and it is He who knows the performance of their works in all the periods of eternity. And He causes them to be inherited by the children of men, so that they may know good and evil, in that He casts lots for all the living in accordance with His (its) spirit in the world until the time of visitation" (₁QS iv.23-26).

From this section it appears that God has determined man's place in the "lots" or spheres of power of two spirits even from the beginning. Something similar also appears to be suggested in one of the Thanksgiving Psalms, where it says:

I know that in Thy hand is the forming of every spirit,
[his deeds] didst Thou determine before Thou didst
   create him;
and how should anyone be able to change Thy words?
Yea, Thou [didst form] the righteous,
and from the womb Thou didst prepare him for the
   appointed time of [Thy] good pleasure
in order that he be preserved in Thy covenant and
   walk in all . . .
unto everlasting salvation and endless peace without
   want;
and Thou didst raise his glory over the flesh.
But the wicked Thou didst create [for the time of] Thy
   [wrath],
and from the womb Thou didst set them apart for the
   day of slaughter,
for they have walked in a way which is not good,
and they have rejected Thy covenant . . .
and they have not had pleasure in all that which Thou
   hast commanded,
and they have chosen that which Thou hatest;
For [according to the mystery of Thine insight] hast
   Thou prepared them
to execute great judgments upon them before all Thy
   works,
and that they shall be a sign [and a wonder] forever,
that all may know Thy glory and Thy great power.
                                        —₁QH xv.13-20

Thus, on the one hand it is said here that God has predestined the righteous to "good pleasure," salvation and
glory and the wicked "to a day of slaughter" and
through his severe judgment on them to reveal his glory.
On the other hand, one gets the impression that the
righteous have indeed been predestined to a life according to God's will, whereas punishment befalls the wicked

because they themselves have done what is evil. It is very doubtful whether this should be taken to mean only that the general principle or norms for retribution are fixed beforehand. But if such is not the case, then there is a certain inconsistency on this point in the doctrines of the sect, or at least the expression of their doctrine is not quite clear.

Licht[5] is doubtless correct, when he says that preoccupation with the sharp contrast between the righteous and the unrighteous is genuinely Jewish; but this concept of predestination is decidedly new.

It should be pointed out that the dualistic point of view appears in very varied degrees in the different writings.[6] As we have seen, the clearest expression is in the Manual of Discipline; in which, moreover, it is said that the evil spirit is called Belial ($b^e liyya^c al$) (₁QS i.18, 23 f.: "The dominion of Belial").[7] This name was known prior to the finding of the Scrolls particularly from the Testaments of the Twelve Patriarchs, where it is the common name for the prince of the evil spirits. Aside from these occurrences, it appears only very occasionally in the late Jewish literature and once in the New Testament (II Cor. 6:15).

In the War Scroll the struggle of the children of light against the children of darkness is the actual leitmotiv and there again Belial is named as the ruler of the evil "lot." This is especially clear in the following section:

[5] Licht, "The Doctrine . . . ," *op. cit.*, p. 5.

[6] This also appears clearly in Huppenbauer's description (see note 1, above) which treats of each writing separately.

[7] Huppenbauer, "Belial in den Qumrantexten," *ThZ* 15 (1959), 81-89.

Into the lot of light didst Thou cause us to fall for Thy
truth, and the prince of light hast Thou appointed from
of old as our helper. And in [his hand are all righteous
works], and all spirits of truth are in his dominion. And
Thou hast made Belial for destruction, an angel of enmity
(*maśṭēmāh*), and in dark[ness is his dominion] and in his
counsel is it to practice wickedness and guilt. And all
spirits of his lot are angels of destruction; they walk in
statutes of darkness and to him is all their desire. But we
rejoice in the lot of Thy truth through Thy strength and
delight in Thy salvation and we rejoice in Thy might and
in Thy peace.

—₁QM xiii.9-12

It is interesting to note another section in column xiii
of the War Scroll, where priests and Levites praise and
bless God and curse Belial (lines 2-4). Here, then, it is
not a question of two spirits under God's supremacy but
of God and Belial.

In the Habakkuk Commentary the dualism does not
appear as clearly, but the opposition between truth and
falsehood is obvious (viii.9; x.9 f., 12; xi.1). In the Damascus Document Belial is mentioned once as instigator
of an evil plan (v.17-19). In the Thanksgiving Psalms
in addition to the quotation given above there are
allusions several times to the dualistic doctrine, and still
more often it may be surmised in the background,[8] but
it is not found as consistently formulated as in the Manual
of Discipline and the War Scroll, with the possible exception of a somewhat damaged passage in xiv.11: "for

[8] On the other hand, *bᵉliyyaʿal* does not seem to have been
personified in the Thanksgiving Psalms; see Huppenbauer, *Der
Mensch* . . . , *op. cit.*, p. 73, with a discussion of iii.28-29 see
below pp. 156 ff.

according to the command of the eternal spirits [. . .] good and wicked [. . .] their reward (or work)." In any event goodness and wickedness are here combined with a dependence on the two spirits.

It is clear that the dualism here, and especially in the Manual of Discipline has two aspects: a human (psychological) and a cosmic. The two spirits struggle with each other in the heart of man,[9] and when the "righteous" sin, then it is because the evil spirit made them stumble. But this is not only a struggle in the heart of man, it is also a world-wide battle between two principles, which finally will end in a terrible war between the children of light and of darkness.

In this connection Otzen [10] has called attention to an interesting fact. In the Testaments of the Twelve Patriarchs—which, as is known, also exhibits similarities to the Dead Sea Scrolls in some other respects—there is a similar doctrine of two spirits, but here only on the psychological plane.[11] Thus, for example, the Testament of Judah 20:1 has: "Know therefore, my children, that two spirits wait upon man—the spirit of truth and the spirit of deceit."

The dualism is no more absolute in the Testaments of the Twelve Patriarchs than at Qumran. Thus, the Testament of Asher 1:3 ff. reads: "Two ways hath God given to the children of men, and two wills, two places and

---

[9] O. J. F. Seitz, "Two Spirits in Man: An Essay in Biblical Exegesis," NTS 6 (1959/60), 82-95.

[10] B. Otzen, "Die neugefundenen hebräischen Sektenschriften . . .," StTh 7 (1953), 135 ff.

[11] Cf. P. A. Munch, "The Spirits in the Testaments of the Twelve Patriarchs," AcOr 13 (1935), 257-263.

two goals." Hence it is God who has set man the choice between the two possibilities.

In certain respects, the doctrine of the conflict of the two spirits in man is a special form of the usual Jewish doctrine of the two "impulses" (*yēṣer*): the good and the evil impulses. That a tendency to mythologize these concepts also exists within rabbinic Judaism is evident.[12] But for the Qumran sect the cosmic aspects are typical. Whether this is a later development, as Otzen maintains— in which case the Testaments of the Twelve Patriarchs and the Damascus Document which do not have these cosmic aspects would represent an earlier stage—may be left open. It is perhaps rather a question of two different solutions of one and the same problem, each of which achieves a compromise between a dualistic tendency of foreign origin and the biblical teaching.

It has recently been argued that the dualistic doctrine as set forth above is due to an overinterpretation of the passage in the Manual of Discipline.[18] In the opinion of such writers the word "spirit" should be taken in a psychological sense much as in the way it appears in the Testaments of the Twelve Patriarchs. The truth the Manual of Discipline sets out to explain is simply that "man was created by God with two 'spirits'—the Old

---

[12] W. Bousset and H. Gressmann, *Die Religion des Judentums im späthellenistischen Zeitalter* (3rd ed.; 1926), pp. 402 ff.; H. L. Strack and P. Billerbeck, *Kommentar zum Neuen Testament aus Talmud und Midrasch* (1928), IV, 466-468.

[18] Wernberg-Møller, "A Reconsideration of the Two Spirits in the Rule of the Community," *RQ* 3 (1961/62), 413-441; M. Treves, "The Two Spirits of the Rule of the Community," *ibid.*, pp. 449-452.

Testament term for 'mood' or 'disposition.' " [14] In this case the doctrine of the scroll would come closer to the rabbinic teaching of the good and evil *yêṣer* than was suggested above.

However, it can hardly be denied that the language of the Manual of Discipline is so concrete and "mythological" that it suggests somewhat more than a psychological theory. And even if "spirit" be taken as a psychological term, the fact remains that the passage refers also to the prince of light and the angel of darkness, which can hardly be disposed of as psychological entities. A dualistic conception is present even if a little more stress should be placed on the psychological aspect.

There can probably be no doubt that the dualism of the Dead Sea Scrolls is inconceivable without some form of Iranian influence. As early as in 1952, Kuhn [15] called attention to the obvious similarity between the dualistic section of the Manual of Discipline and a section from the Gâthas of the Zoroastrian Avesta, Yasna 30:3-5:

3. The two primal-spirits, the twins, were, as it has been handed down in tradition, the Better and the Evil in thought, word and deed. Between them the wise choose aright, but not so do the foolish.
4. When these two spirits came together, they created the first Life and Non-Life and ordained that finally the Worst would fall to the share of the followers of falsehood, but the Best Mind to the followers of right.
5. Of these two spirits the Spirit of Falsehood chose to do the worst, but the Most Holy Spirit, clad in the firm

[14] Wernberg-Møller, "A Reconsideration . . . ," *op. cit.*, p. 422.
[15] K. G. Kuhn, "Die Sektenschrift und die iranische Religion," *ZThK* 49 (1952), 296-316.

heavens, chose to do the right, and so, too, do they who with truthful deeds seek willingly to please Ahura Mazda.

Here then are two spirits, on which man's thoughts, words, and deeds depend; there is the opposition: truth-falsehood, and the concept of the eternal consequences of man's taking a stand with respect to the two conflicting spirit-powers.

Somewhat later Michaud [16] pointed out striking parallels between the section in question and Plutarch's description of the Persian religion in its Zervanite form. There again two spirits are found: Horomazes (Ohrmazd), born of purest light, and Areimanios (Ahriman), born of darkness as well as their struggle with each other until an "appointed time," when the evil spirit will be conquered. This observation should, perhaps, be supplemented with the information that Zervanism in fact also offers a parallel to a limited dualism and God's supremacy: according to this form of doctrine the two spirits have not existed from eternity but emanate from the highest god, Time or Zervan. In Zervanism there is also a clearly deterministic view. Bearing in mind that, to all appearances in that time it was a Zervanite movement which was predominant in any case in the religion of western Iran, then the probability of dependence in some form appears so much the greater. But there is no doubt that the Qumran dualism bears the stamp of compromise. The Old Testa-

[16] H. Michaud, "Un mythe zervanite dans un des manuscrits de Qumrân," *VT* 5 (1955), 137-147; cf. also: J. Duchesne-Guillemin, "Le Zervanisme et les manuscrits de la Mer Morte," *Indo-Iranian Journal* 1 (1957), 96-99.

ment doctrine of God was too strong to be pushed aside by a dualistic conception. The Dead Sea Scrolls stand here on the foundation of Deutero-Isaiah (Isa. 45:6 f.):

> I am Yahweh and there is no other,
> I form light and create darkness,
> I make weal and create woe.

It should be mentioned that this verse is often taken as a polemic against Iranian dualism. In any case, it is in good agreement with the monistic tradition of the Old Testament.

It is usually accepted as obvious that dualistic tendencies in late-Judaism in general are due to Iranian influence. This is probably correct, but one should not forget that the presuppositions for this tendency existed in the Israelite image of God which combined good and "evil," light and darkness, precisely in the manner of the Isaiah passage just cited. But nowhere is the Iranian stamp so apparent as at Qumran.

3

Angels and Demons

That with emphasis on God's transcendence he becomes increasingly more elevated has, as is well known, in late Judaism led to the development of the belief in a series of intermediaries, who stand between God and the world and, so to say, mediate his actions to the world. First and foremost among these intermediary beings are the hypostases (Wisdom, the Skekinah, the Word [*mêmrā'*, *dibbûr*, etc.]) and angels, of which Judaism knows a number each with his particular individuality.

Strangely enough concepts of hypostases are lacking in Qumran. Granted there is often mention of God's wisdom, but it is never personified or hypostatized. One does not say: "The Word said so and so," but: "God said." Of course there is avoidance of naming the divine name, Yahweh, as has been seen, but it is not replaced by such words as The Name, The Word or The Shekinah. Thus, the Qumran congregation knows itself in spite of God's sublime distance to stand in a nearer and more immediate fellowship with God than is the case with rabbinic Judaism; and therefore stands nearer to older Jewish mysticism as found in the so-called *hêkālôt* and *ma'aśē* literature.[1]

[1] Compare pp. 229 and 251 f. below.

This observation is also of importance for the understanding of the doctrine of angels. For here the angels seem to be—as in the Old Testament—God's heavenly court rather than actual intermediary beings.[2] They have not been created to bridge the gulf between the divine, or heavenly, and the earthly, but they have simply been taken over from the Bible and the thought world of contemporary Judaism and been understood as God's messengers and servants.

The Prince of Light (or Lights) has already been mentioned as identical with one of the two spirits (₁QS iii.20; also CD v.18: Moses and Aaron arose through the Prince of Lights, while Belial raised Jannes and his brother).[3] Whether "His (God's) angel of truth," which is mentioned in ₁QS iii.24 is identical with the Prince of Light or not is not clear. Otzen supposes two different figures, since a particular Angel of Truth also occurs in the Testaments of the Twelve Patriarchs.[4] This is, however, by no means necessary; why should "the angel of His truth" and "a spirit of truth" not be able to stand for the same figure?

Among individual angelic figures is Michael, who appears several times in the War Scroll as the helper of the children of light (ix.15 f.; xvii.6 f.). It has been sug-

[2] K. Schubert, "Der gegenwärtige Stand der Erforschung der in Palästina neu gefundenen hebräischen Handschriften, 25. Der Sektenkanon von En Feshcha und die Anfänge der jüdischen Gnosis," *TLZ* 78 (1953), col. 502.

[3] Jannes and Jambres (or Mambres) are two opponents of Moses who are also mentioned in the Talmud and Targums. The legend is connected with the story of the Egyptian magicians in Exod. 7:11 f. and is behind the allusion in II Tim. 3:8.

[4] Otzen, *op. cit.*, p. 144.

gested that he should also be identified with the good spirit, since the Prince of Light and Michael in the War Scroll (xiii.10; xvii.6-8) both are given the task of helper of the children of light.[5] However, such an identification would not appear to be actually necessary. The good spirit gives the impression of being more a figure in his own right. In addition to Michael, there is also mention of Sariel, Raphael and Gabriel (ix. 15 f.). The last two of these also belong to the traditional archangels in other Jewish literature, while Sariel only occurs in one passage in the Greek version of I Enoch, chapter 20, where the Ethiopic text has instead Saraqâêl.

In a couple of passages (₁QSb, The Blessings, iv.25 and ₁QH vi.13) there is also mention of angels of the presence, i.e., angels of a special higher rank who stand before the face (presence) of God; this term is also known from the rest of Judaism. The so-called Angelic Liturgy names a large number of angels and classes of angels as participants in adoration and worship.[6]

Otherwise in the texts published thus far there is mostly mention of angels in general. They are called "sons of heaven" (₁QS iv.22; xi.8; ₁QH iii.22); in the last passage just mentioned the expressions "the host of the holy ones" is used parallel to that expression (also ₁QH x.34 f.; simply "holy ones": CD xx.8., ₁QSb iii.26).[7]

[5] Compare the discussion in *MLS*, chap. 24, pp. 277-289.

[6] See: Strugnell, "The Angelic Liturgy . . . ," *VT Suppl.* 7 (1960), 330 ff.; and Benoit, *et al.*, "Editing the Manuscript Fragments . . . ," *BA* 19 (1956), 81 on Angels of the Presence in a fragment from Cave 3.

[7] Cf. Nötscher, "Heiligkeit in den Qumranschriften," *RQ* 2 (1959/60), 321 ff.

As designations for angels one should also understand such expressions as "the host of heaven" and "heroes of heaven" (₁QH iii.35), and, further, "hosts of eternity" (*s^eba̅' 'ad* ₁QH xi.13), "the communion of the holy ones" (₁QH iii.22), "valiant heroes" (₁QH viii.11; x.34 f.; cf. Ps. 103:20). So, too, when God is called "Prince of gods (*sar 'ēlîm*, ₁QH x.8), the King of the glorious ones (cf. Slavonic Enoch 22:9) and Lord of every spirit," it only means that he stands above all angels.[3] *'Elîm* most probably then is to be taken as "divine beings" or something similar.

A particularly characteristic concept is encountered in the War Scroll, where it is said several times that the angels fight on the side of the children of light together with the human armies. Thus it says, for example, in xii.1-9: "A multitude of holy ones are in heaven and hosts of angels in Thy holy dwelling . . . in order to muster the army of thine elect according to their thousands and ten thousands together with Thy holy ones [. . .] thine angels . . . the congregation of Thy holy ones is among us as an eternal help. . . . For the Lord is holy, and the king of glory is with us, a people of holy ones is our strength and hosts of angels are among our leaders." The thought is reminiscent of Jesus' words in Matthew 26:53, that he could have asked the Father to send more than twelve legions of angels to his help; this then is something that belongs to the messianic time.

The presence of these angels puts demands on the children of light: no one shall be impure, it says in the War Scroll vii.6, "for holy angels are together with their

---

[3] Schubert, "Der gegenwärtige Stand . . . ," *op. cit.*, col. 502.

armies," and in a fragment of the Damascus Document it is said that fools, madmen, simpletons and imbeciles, the blind, the maimed, the lame and the deaf may not enter into the community, "for holy angels are in their midst" (4QD[b]).[9] In the Rule of the Congregation (The Two Column Fragment, 1QSa), it is enjoined that no one who is impure or has any bodily defect may "take his place in the congregation of the men of renown, for holy angels are in their congregation" (ii.3-9). Fitzmyer has associated this thought with the enigmatic explanation in I Corinthians 11:10 that "a woman ought to have a veil on her head, because of the angels." [10]

What the presence of these angels means may be seen from a couple of other passages. In the concluding hymn of the Manual of Discipline it is said:

> He has given them an inheritance in the lot of the holy ones,
> and with the sons of heaven has He associated their company
> to be a council of unity and a foundation for a holy building,
> to be an eternal plantation for all coming time.
>
> —1QS xi.7 f.

It is thus an immediate fellowship with the heavenly world that is granted to the elect. In the Thanksgiving Psalms the same thought is expressed as follows:

> The perverted spirit didst Thou cleanse from much transgression,

[9] J. A. Fitzmyer, "A Feature of Qumrân Angelology and the Angels of I Cor. XI.10," *NTS* 4 (1957/58), 58. See also: Milik, *Ten Years of Discovery* . . . (1959), p. 114.

[10] Fitzmyer, *op. cit.*, pp. 48 ff.

that he may take his place in the host of the holy ones
and enter into community with the congregation of the
    sons of heaven,
and Thou hast cast for man an eternal lot with spirits of
    knowledge.

—₁QH iii.21 f.

This idea of a fellowship with the angels apparently
played a central role and deserves special attention. It is
probably connected with the conviction of living in the
last times, when God with his heavenly hosts intervenes
in the fight. Perhaps also, as Gaster maintains, a half-
mystical experience of the nearness of the divine world
contributed to the foundation of this concept.[11] Important in this connection is a section in one of the
Thanksgiving Psalms which has often been incorrectly
translated:

Thou hast caused [. . . .] to come in into Thy [. . . .][12]
to all men of Thy counsel
and in the lot of association with the angels of the
    Presence,
and there is no mediator.

—₁QH vi.12 f.

The word *mēlîṣ*, which was translated by many investigators as "scoffer," here obviously has the same meaning
as in Job 33:23, i.e., "interpreter, intercessor, mediator."[13] Thus, the point is that the elect have direct

[11] T. H. Gaster, *The Dead Sea Scriptures* (1956), pp. 6 f.

[12] Or, perhaps rather as Licht reconstructs the passage: Thou
hast caused Thy [glo]ry to come to (all the men of Thy counsel).

[13] My former translation in *Handskrifterna från Qumran IV-V.*
("Symbolae Biblicae Upsalienses, 15.") (1956), *loc. cit.*, should be
corrected in accordance with this observation.

fellowship with the angels and the heavenly world without needing anyone as a mediator.

Finally, a special problem is associated with the expression "the holy spirit" (or "spirit of holiness"—sometimes also simply "God's spirit"). The holy spirit appears several times as an intermediary of salvation, forgiveness or knowledge. "A man's conduct ('way') will not be right except through the spirit, which God formed for him" (₁QH iv.31). "Thou didst uphold me with Thy strength, Thou didst cause Thy holy spirit to fall upon me (or: sprinkled me with the holy spirit)" (₁QH vii.6; cf. xvii.26 where the context is, however, obscure). Through the holy spirit man is cleansed from all deeds of wickedness, and God sprinkles him with the spirit of truth as with water of purification (₁QS iv.21; cf. iii.7: Through the holy spirit, *rûah qedôšāh* he is cleansed from all sins). "Through truth hast Thou supported me and through Thy holy spirit hast Thou delighted me" (₁QH ix.32).

> I have insight, I know Thee, my God,
> through the spirit which Thou hast given me,
> and what is sure have I heard in Thy wondrous
> council.
> Through Thy holy spirit hast Thou opened to mine
> inmost parts
> the knowledge of the mystery of Thine insight.
> —₁QH xii.11-13

What then is this "holy spirit," "spirit of truth," "the spirit which God has given," etc.? The answer is not so easy to give, for all statements which concern the spirit are remarkably vague and indistinct; and this is connected especially with the fact that the word *rûaḥ* itself is ambiguous and particularly in the Dead Sea Scrolls is used with several different meanings.[14] Disregarding the meaning "wind" which occurs in a couple of cases, and also, at this point, the use of the word "spirit" for angels (₁QH viii.12; xi.13) and demons, it can first be established that *rûaḥ* often designates man's personality, that part of man which is understood as the bearer of his non-bodily characteristics. This can then also often be rendered with "disposition," "character" or similar expressions. Thus it is said, for example, that God has cleansed "man's perverted spirit" (₁QH iii.21) or that he has made man's spirit strong in affliction (₁QH i.32; cf. ix.12). The author of the Thanksgiving Psalms says that he "became a zealous spirit" (ii.15) or that he was endowed with a spirit of knowledge (xiv.25) which simply means that he had received knowledge.

The two spirits as manifestations of the two opposing principles in God's plan of the world have already been noted. Now it appears, however, that the concept "spirit of truth," i.e., the good spirit and various other "spirits" as expressions for God's "turn of mind" often, so to speak, overlap. Thus it is said, for example, in ₁QH xvi.8-11:

> Thou hast graced me with a spirit of Thy compassion . . .
> Thou hast recorded the spirit of the righteous one . . .
> I entreat Thee (lit.: appease Thy face) with the spirit, which Thou hast given me.

In ₁QS iv.21 and ₁QH ix.32, and to a certain extent also in ₁QS ix.3 truth or the spirit of truth and the holy spirit are juxtaposed in such a way that they must be understood as practically identical.

Thus, *rûaḥ* also stands for various manifestations of God's gracious disposition which, so to speak, finds a comprehensive expression in "the spirit of truth," the good spirit in the dualistic system.

"The holy spirit" (*rûaḥ qôdeš*) must also be understood as a manifestation of God's grace.[15] The expression is taken from the Old Testament (Ps. 51:11; Isa. 63:10), where God's spirit often occurs as an intermediary of divine activity, as the divine power which is active in Israel, particularly in its political and spiritual leaders (judges, kings, prophets), sometimes simply hypostatized and taken as a more or less independent being. In the Dead Sea Scrolls, "the holy spirit" is especially connected with cleansing and forgiveness or with the granting of knowledge and insight. In the former case the spirit is compared through the use of the verbs *hēnîp* (₁QH vii.6 f., xvii.26) and *nāzāh* (₁QS iv.21) with the water of purification which "is sprinkled" on one who has become impure. As Nötscher[16] quite correctly observes, the spirit is "a power granted by God which becomes active in man for salvation."

Thus the holy spirit is not as an hypostasis or a "person in the Godhead" but simply a manifestation of God's

---

[15] Nötscher, "Heiligkeit . . . ," *op. cit.*, pp. 333 f.; J. Coppens, "Le don de l'esprit d'après les textes de Qumrân et le quatrième évangile," in *L'Évangile de Jean (Recherches Bibliques III)* (1958), pp. 209-223.

[16] Nötscher. "Heiligkeit . . . ." *op. cit.*, p. 339.

saving activity. The tendencies to hypostatization of the
spirit which actually appear in the Old Testament have
thus not been followed up by the Qumran community.
Neither does such hypostatization appear to have been
so pronounced in the rest of Judaism. It is mainly in
the Wisdom of Solomon that the spirit as well as wisdom
receives a more independent function (1:5, 7; 9:17).
Further, there are a series of expressions in the Testaments of the Twelve Patriarchs which are strongly
reminiscent of the Dead Sea Scrolls' "spirit of truth,"
"spirit of fornication," "spirit of falsehood," "spirit of
enmity," etc. It should be noted that here as in Qumran there is always mention of a "spirit of something,"
never of the spirit in general or as an independent entity.[17] This is entirely in agreement with the meaning
of the word *rûaḥ* developed above.

It should be pointed out that in Qumran there is also
no reference to the spirit as the driving force in
prophecy.

Concerning demons or evil spirits there are two different ideas represented in Judaism. On the one hand,
in the pseudepigraphic literature demons are associated
with the fallen angels and are understood as seducers
to and instigators of evil deeds. On the other hand, in
the rabbinic literature they are understood primarily as
beings which cause sickness and, as such, are morally
neutral. In Qumran, the aspect first mentioned is
dominant.

This, of course, is closely connected with the general

[17] Cf. R. Eppel, *Le piétisme juif dans les Testaments des douze
Patriarches* (1930), p. 124.

view which is represented by the doctrine of the two spirits. The spirit of error, Belial, is as has been seen, the root of all evil in the world of men. From him come all evil thoughts and deeds. In a Thanksgiving Psalm fragment he is called Satan ($_1$QH fr. iv.6), in the War Scroll xiii.11 and the Damascus Document xvi.5 he is called the angel of enmity (*mal'āk maśṭēmāh*), and also elsewhere he is related to *maśṭēmāh*, enmity. This carries over easily into the idea of the use of Mastema as a name for the prince of the evil spirits as, for example, in the Book of Jubilees, where it is he who tempts Abraham (17:15-18), wants to kill Moses (48:2, 9), hardens the hearts of the Egyptians (48:17) and kills the first-born in Egypt (49:2).

However, the Dead Sea Scrolls' mention of Belial is more reminiscent of the Testaments of the Twelve Patriarchs. In both, Belial is God's adversary ($_1$QS ii.5; CD v.18; T. Simeon 5:3), a tempter and seducer ($_1$QS iii.20 f.–"angel of darkness"–CD iv.15; T. Joseph 7:4), prince of the evil spirits ($_1$QS iii.23 f.; CD xii.2; T. Judah 25:3; T. Issachar 7:7). Whether it is he who is meant by Azazel in a fragment from Cave 4 is uncertain –this is the identification found in later Judaism.

Belial has subordinate to him a great multitude of evil angels or spirits. Thus the Thanksgiving Psalms (iii.18) speak of "spirits of vipers" (or possibly: "spirits of nothingness"); the text has *rûḥê 'ep'êh*,[18] behind which the gates of eternity finally will be closed–but it is possible that this also refers to men of an evil disposition. A psalm fragment ($_1$QH fr. v.4, 6) mentions "spirits of

[18] For further discussion of this expression, see p. 192, below.

wickedness" (*rûḥôt riš'āh*) and "spirits of error" (*rûḥôt 'awlāh*), but the context is so broken that it is impossible to draw any sure conclusions as to their function. On the other hand, the War Scroll speaks plainly of "angels of the dominion" of Belial (i.15) and of "spirits of his lot" (xiii.11 f.; the same phrase is found in ₁QS iii.24), while "spirits of error" in ₁QM xv.14 once again are in a broken context; in any case these refer to enemies of God.

An interesting passage in the so-called Book of Mysteries tells of how "the offspring (*môlādîm* or possibly: *môlīdîm* 'begetters') of wickedness" shall be closed in, whereupon guilt will yield to righteousness (i.5). This seems to signify that the evil spirits are the cause of error ("*môlādîm* of error"), and when they no longer exist then neither will there be any error or sin.[19]

Huppenbauer [20] finds in this passage an allusion to the imprisonment of the fallen angels—a motif which occurs in I Enoch—but it does not appear to be quite certain that such an allusion actually exists. On the other hand, it actually says once in the Damascus Document ii.18 that the watchers of heaven fell when they walked in the hardness of their hearts; but here the context shows that the passage refers to the well-known sons of God from Genesis 6:1 ff. It is thus a question of the use of the same biblical stories which underlie the ideas in the Book of Enoch concerning the fallen angels, and the expression "watchers of heaven" actually occurs in

---

[19] Huppenbauer, *Der Mensch zwischen zwei Welten, op. cit.*, pp. 89 ff.

[20] *Ibid.*, p. 92.

I Enoch 91:15. In the Thanksgiving Psalms nothing is said about the origin of the evil spirits. The Manual of Discipline, as has been seen, has its familiar doctrine of the two primal spirits.

Finally, in some passages "angels of destruction" (*mal'akê hébel*) are mentioned. In ₁QS iv.12 and CD ii.6 they carry out punishment of the evil men. The War Scroll (xiii.12) names them together with the spirits of Belial's lot. In the first two examples, these beings seem to stand in God's service to execute his punishment on the evil. But it should be noted, that it also can be said that the disobedient shall "be visited by the hand of Belial" (CD viii.2). I Enoch is also acquainted with these "angels of punishment" (56:1, etc.).

It is of interest to note how the evil spirits in the Dead Sea Scrolls rarely become quite concrete demon figures. The emphasis is on their activity as tempters and seducers, and hence it becomes quite difficult to distinguish them from such concepts as evil states of mind or temptations. They are servants of the evil spirit, to induce those who are in his dominion to do what is evil. Thus the evil spirits take on a demythologized, "spiritualized" character, which makes them evil principles rather than actual demons.

4

Man

Between the two struggling worlds stands man. The view of man in the Dead Sea Scrolls [1] is marked by this fact. But it is also, and perhaps to a greater extent determined by the Old Testament view of man. It is perhaps not entirely consistent, and in any case certain peculiar features are emphasized more in some writings than in others. In its essentials it is however a particular development of the Israelite view of man, and it is not without importance for the understanding of the New Testament concept of man and his place in God's world.

NOTHINGNESS

In contrast with God's omnipotence the writings from the Dead Sea emphasize man's weakness and insignificance, and this is especially so in the Thanksgiving Psalms. Man is by nature an insignificant, weak and perishable being, and it is stressed again and again how he is molded of clay, formed of dust or kneaded with water. In itself the awareness of man's insignificance and nothingness is, of course, a general religious phenomenon, and many of the thoughts in the Qumran writings can in this regard be traced back to the Old Testament.

[1] J. P. Hyatt, "The View of Man in the Qumran 'Hodayot,'" *NTS* 2 (1955/56), 276-284.

But these ideas are presented here with such emphasis
that they almost become the leading motif in the Qumran concept of man. In any case they are repeated so
often in the psalms that there is an overwhelming impression of man's nothingness and depravity. This
probably has its explanation at least partially in a radical,
personal experience on the part of the author of the
Thanksgiving Psalms. One must carefully avoid regarding these personal and subjective outpourings as dogmatic
statements designed to be universally applicable.

This is best demonstrated by a few examples:

> What then is a man? He is earth,
> [of dust] is he formed,
> and to dust he will return.
>
> —₁QH x.3-4

Even with regard to the wording itself this is clearly
based on the Old Testament. The question is derived
from Psalm 8:4; the play on the word *'ādām* (man)—
'ᵃdāmāh (earth) occurs in Genesis 2:7 and the clause
concerning the return to dust comes from Genesis 3:19.

The same applies to the phrase "I am dust and ashes"
which occurs a couple of lines further down in the same
psalm (₁QH x.5)—and is found in Genesis 18:27.

> But I am a vessel of clay; what am I?
> kneaded with water; for what can I be counted?
>
> ₁QH iii.23-24

The expression "kneaded with water" (*migbal māyim* or
something similar)[2] occurs in two or three additional

[2] J. C. Greenfield, "The Root *'GBL'* in Mishnaic Hebrew and
in the Hymnic Literature from Qumran," *RQ* 2 (1959/60), 155-
162.

places (i.21; xiii.14 f. and probably xii.25 f.); there is, in addition, the phrase "kneaded of dust" ($_1$QS xi.21). The idea apparently is that man was molded as an earthen vessel is molded by a potter, and is based in all probability on the Yahwistic creation story: "Then the Lord God formed (molded) man of dust from the ground" (Gen. 2:7). Despite the fact that the expression, "kneaded with . . . ," is not itself biblical (the word, however, is found in rabbinic literature) this does not seem to assume any different concept of man's creation:

> I am a vessel of clay,
> kneaded with water,
> a foundation of shame,
> and a spring of impurity,
> a furnace of iniquity,
> and a building of sin,
> an erring spirit,
> perverse and without understanding.
>
> —$_1$QH i.21-23

This is similarly stated in $_1$QH xii.24-26:

> But I, from dust am I taken,
> [from clay] am I formed
> unto a flood of impurity
> and in shameful nakedness,
> to a compound of dust,
> knead[ed with water],
> and to a dwelling place of darkness.
> And a return to dust
> is the destiny of the earthen vessel;
> at the time [which is ordained,
> it returns] to the dust,
> from which it is taken.

Thus the author of the Thanksgiving Psalms asks again and again: What am I, I who am born of woman, I who am taken from the dust (xiii.14 f., xii.31), that I shall count for something before God or be an object of his grace? It is a feeling of complete unworthiness that dominates the psalmist's reaction before that which has befallen him from God; and it is this feeling that takes its expression in the rather sharpened formulations here cited.

It should be noted that in the three sections cited just above there is the use of sexual expressions such as *'erwāh*, shame (lit.: nakedness, pudenda) and *niddāh*, impurity (lit.: menstrual blood). They have lost their original literal meanings, but they give an impression of the deepest abhorrence of the impurity of human nature.[3] Possibly Ezekiel 36:17 (*ṭum'at niddāh*, the uncleanness of a woman in her impurity) has contributed to the shaping of these ideas.[4]

In this connection the word "flesh" (*bāśār*) is also used now and again. But this word is ambiguous and since it can have some significance for our understanding of the New Testament *sárx*—concept, it deserves a closer investigation.[5] Sometimes the word is used in a completely

[3] Licht, "The Doctrine . . . ," *op. cit.*, p. 10.
[4] Cf. O. Betz, "Die Proselytentaufe der Qumransekte und die Taufe im Neuen Testament," *RQ* 1 (1958/59), 221.
[5] On this see: K. G. Kuhn, "New Light on Temptation, Sin and Flesh in the New Testament," in *SNT*, pp. 94-113 (a translation with some revisions of the article in *ZThK* 49 [1952], 200-222); W. D. Davies, "Paul and the Dead Sea Scrolls: Flesh and Spirit," in *SNT*, pp. 157-182; Huppenbauer, "*BŚR* 'Fleisch' in den Texten von Qumran (Höhle 1)," *ThZ* 13 (1957), 298-300. Compare also Flusser, "The Dualism of 'Flesh and Spirit' in the Dead Sea Scrolls and the New Testament," *Tarbiz* 27 (1957/58), 158-165;

neutral sense of "body" or the like. The expression,
"afflicted in his flesh" (₁QSa ii.5), simply means bodily
sickness or affliction. It can be synonymous with a person, a being, as when it says: "My flesh melts like wax"
(₁QH viii.32 f.), and it can be used collectively of man
in general, as when it stands parallel to "born of woman"
(₁QH xviii.23). But often the idea bears with it an echo
of human weakness and mortality, and "flesh" is then
more or less synonymous with such concepts as dust,
vessel of clay, etc. Thus the author of the Thanksgiving
Psalms asks:

> What is flesh (= a mortal being) compared with these
> things?
> And what is a vessel of clay, that it should perform
> great wonders?
>
> —₁QH iv.29

> And what is flesh, that it should have insight?
> That which is [formed] of dust, how should it be able
> to guide its steps?
>
> —₁QH xv.21 [6]

So far, as Huppenbauer points out, no change of the
content of the concept can be established which is in
opposition to the Old Testament idea. But there are
some passages which, to use the same author's expression,
"give rise to questions." [7] In the War Scroll iv.3 and
xii.12 the opponents of the children of light are desig-

E. Schweizer, "Röm. 1,3 f. und der Gegensatz von Fleisch und
Geist vor und bei Paulus," *EvTh* 15 (1955), 563-571; R. E.
Murphy, "*BŚR* in the Qumrân Literature and *SARKS* in the
Epistle to the Romans," *Sacra Pagina* (1959), II, pp. 60-76.

[6] Cf. also ₁QH xv.12, 17.

[7] Huppenbauer, "*BŚR* 'Fleisch' . . . ," *op. cit.*, p. 298.

nated as "flesh of evil" or "of guilt," but it probably
only means the same as guilt-laden men. In the Thanksgiving Psalms xvii.25 the author calls himself a "spirit of
flesh" ("a *rûaḥ bāśār* is thy servant")[8]—but this could be
taken to mean "a creature with a fleshly, i.e., human,
weak character"—and according to xiii.13 such a "spirit of
flesh" has received insight; here too it appears to be a
question of the weakness and insufficiency of man *qua*
man. In ₁QS iii.9, where the cleansing of the flesh is mentioned, and in iv.20, where it is said that God removes
"every spirit of evil from the inward parts[9] of his (man's)
flesh" through cleansing in the holy spirit, it seems to
be presupposed that the flesh in itself is impure and
sinful. Thus, as Kuhn has expressed it, the flesh represents "die Sphäre des Widergöttlichen," the sphere of
ungodly power, i.e., of everything which opposes God.
Similarly ₁QS xi.12 reads:

And if I stumble in iniquity of the flesh,
my vindication through the righteousness of God,
will stand eternally.

Here flesh is clearly set in relationship to sin and guilt.
It is perhaps only a matter of definition as to whether
the flesh is to be called "the sphere of ungodly power"
or not. This much must be granted: the flesh stands in
relationship to God as that which is mortal and imperfect
stands in relationship to the Eternal and the Perfect One.

[8] Huppenbauer, *Der Mensch zwischen zwei Welten, op. cit.,*
p. 70.

[9] The word *TKM* is hitherto unknown, but there can now be
no doubt as to its meaning. See: Yadin, "A Note on DSD IV 20,"
JBL 74 (1955), 40 f.

Huppenbauer admits that the flesh "certainly has a part in sin." But he cannot find any instance of its being, so to speak, the driving force and ultimate cause of sin. On the other hand, he says, flesh designates man "to the extent that he does not stand under the gift of the divine spirit." [10] This is about the same as that which Licht expresses as follows: ". . . 'flesh' means humanity without the ennobling gift of divine grace." [11] In short: if flesh does not characterize man as inimical to God then in any case it characterizes man without God.

What has been said can possibly be understood as a statement of a dualism between flesh and spirit in the Dead Sea Scrolls. This is, however, only partially correct. As Flusser quite correctly has pointed out, there is a dualism between flesh and spirit not as an opposition between two forces in man but as the opposition between man as flesh and the divine spirit which is the means for man's salvation. [12] In certain respects this agrees with the Old Testament view of man: man is a whole and as such he is of flesh and is weak, incomplete, impure, sinful; but the impurity is more strongly emphasized here than ever in the Old Testament.

SIN

From what has already been said it appears that sin is inseparably associated with the conditions of human life. [13]   Man's sinfulness is connected with his general

[10] Huppenbauer, "*BSR*, 'Fleisch' . . . ," *op. cit.,* p. 300.
[11] Licht, "The Doctrine . . . ," *op. cit.,* p. 11.
[12] Flusser, "The Dualism . . . ," *op. cit.,* pp. 158 f.
[13] See the sections on *Sin* in Licht, "The Doctrine . . . ," *op. cit.,* pp. 11 f.

wretchedness. Sin cleaves to all that is human. God is righteous, but "to the children of men belong the service of iniquity and works of deceit" (₁QH i.27).

> What is a vessel of clay, that it should perform great wonders?
> He (man) is in sin from the womb
> and unto old age in guilt of faithlessness.
>
> —₁QH iv.29-30

> [. . . to confess] my former sins,
> to pray and make supplication for [the evil] of my deeds
> and the perversity of my heart.
> For in impurity (*niddāh*) have I wallowed. . . .
>
> —₁QH xvii.18-19

Man is therefore altogether evil. But this sinfulness is apparently not traced back to the fall of the first man, neither is original sin expressly mentioned. The Manual of Discipline has, as is known, its theory of the two spirits; the Thanksgiving Psalms seem to presuppose a similar teaching. Licht raises the question as to whether the expression *peša' ri'šôn*, "the first (former, earlier) sin" in ₁QH ix.13, and xvii.18 (the plural form) could designate some kind of original sin, but he admits that the thought "does not entirely crystallize." Rather, for the author of the Thanksgiving Psalms, man's sinfulness is a corollary of God's absolute righteousness:

> And I know that a man does not have righteousness
> nor a son of man blamelessness of conduct (lit.: walking, way).
> To God, the Most High, belong all works of righteousness,

and the way of man is not established
except through the spirit which God has fashioned for
   him
to make blameless the conduct of the children of men.

—₁QH iv.30-32

If there is thus no explicit reference to original sin, there are on the other hand a couple of examples of the feeling of solidarity in responsibility and confession of sin with past generations. ₁QH iv.34 reads: "For I remember my guilt together with the faithlessness of my forefathers." And in the confession of sin in ₁QS i.25 f. (with a parallel in CD xx.28 f.) "those who enter into the covenant" confess: "We have done evil, we have been guilty of transgression, we have sinned, we have been wicked, we and our fathers before us. . . ."

It is also conceivable that the word *yêṣer*, "forming" or "inclination," [14] in some places in the Thanksgiving Psalms (v.6; vii.13, 16; ix.16; xv.13; xviii.11) and in CD ii.16 possibly could allude to a sinful inclination or evil nature in man. But it is rather a question of human weakness in general; the same word is used to characterize man as a "vessel" of clay. If there were not the rabbinic teaching concerning the good and evil *yêṣer* the idea of impulses or inclinations in man would probably not suggest itself immediately. It is probably not a question of original sin but of a certain "predisposition" to sin, which clearly follows from man's total dissimilarity to God.

This sinfulness of man is in no way just a theory or

[14] Concerning this word, see: R. E. Murphy, "*Yêṣer* in the Qumran Literature," *Biblica* 39 (1958), 334-344.

teaching that is of purely theoretical interest. The author of the Thanksgiving Psalms has in any case experienced his sin as a frightening reality. He speaks of it with constantly new expressions, pursues it in all its nuances, exhausts the whole rich vocabulary which the Bible has put at his disposal.[15] In images which are often drawn from the Bible but often are also original and expressive, he paints his feeling of sin and his despair:

> For me is opened a spring
> of bitter sorrow [. . . . .]
> trouble was not hidden from mine eyes,
> for I came to know the inclinations of man
> and mankind's return [to dust
> . . . . . .] to sin and sorrow over guilt.
> And they entered into my heart
> and penetrated my bones [. . . . .]
> and to mutter murmurs of grief
> and sighs with a harp of lamentation
> for all grievous sorrow
> and bitter complaint until evil cease. . . .
>
> —₁QH xi.19-22

> As for me, trembling and terror have gripped me,
> and all my bones become broken,
> and my heart melts like wax before a fire,
> and my knees become fluid as water
> which rushes over a precipice.
> For I remember my guilt
> together with the faithlessness of my fathers.
>
> —₁QH iv.33-34 [16]

[15] Molin, "Die Hymnen von Chirbet Qumran," in *Vorderasiatische Studien. Festschrift für Prof. Dr. Viktor Christian . . .*, ed. K. Schubert, *et al.* (1956), p. 78.

[16] Note the allusions one after another to Ps. 22:14, Ezek. 7:17 and Mic. 1:4.

It is a question whether this repeated emphasis on man's sinfulness does not ultimately have a psychological basis, caused by a profound religious experience, a conversion which made all former things appear to be corrupt and worthless.

HOPE, ELECTION, CONVERSION

The experience of sin is not the last word in the Thanksgiving Psalms. For the poet emphasizes equally strongly as sinfulness the fact that "there is hope for him, whom Thou hast formed of dust, for an eternal fellowship. And the perverse spirit Thou hast cleansed from much transgression" ($_1$QH iii.20 f.). Man's sinfulness and wretchedness is not the whole truth about him. Not a single psalm deals exclusively with nothingness, sin and guilt, but as a complement there is always a reference to God's grace and compassion:

(Man) is in sin from the womb
and unto old age in guilt of faithlessness.
And I know that a man does not have righteousness
nor a son of man blamelessness of conduct.
To God, the Most High, belong all works of righteousness,
and the way of man is not established
except through the spirit which God has fashioned for him,
to make blameless the conduct of the children of men,
that they may know all His works
in the might of His power and the abundance of His compassion
upon all the sons of His good pleasure.

—$_1$QH iv.29-33

"I know," it is said in ₁QH vi.6 f., "that there is hope for those who turn from transgression and abandon sin [. . . . .] and walk in the way of Thy heart without evil." And in ₁QS iii.6-12:

> For by the spirit of God's true counsel are all the ways (= conduct) of man atoned for, all his iniquities, so that he may see the light of life. And by a holy spirit toward union with His truth is he cleansed from all his iniquities. And by an upright and humble spirit is his sin atoned for. And by his soul's humiliation under all God's ordinances (i.e., by his humbly subordinating himself to all God's statutes) is his flesh cleansed, so that he may be sprinkled with the water of purification and be sanctified with the water of purity. Then can he guide his steps, so that he walks blameless in all God's way . . . and does not turn aside to the right or to the left and does not transgress a single one of His words.

This certainly implies that the hope is based on the work of God's spirit; but at the same time it becomes apparent that salvation presupposes a conversion and a new willingness to fulfill God's law. ₁QS v.1-3 presents this demand for a conversion even more clearly: "This is the regulation for the men of the community, who are willing to turn away from all evil and hold fast to all that which He (God) has commanded according to His pleasure. . . ."[17] And in ₁QH xiv.24 it says: "Thou forgivest those who turn away from transgression but avengest (lit.: visitest) the iniquity of the wicked."

Is it thus in the power of man to turn away from evil and do the will of God? Allegro is of the following opinion: "Man must prepare himself by self-discipline,

[17] E. Nielsen, *Håndskriftundene i Juda ørken* (1956), p. 143.

but the action of cleansing is entirely dependent on the will of God. Man has no claim to justification merely on the grounds of his good works; it is an act of divine grace. . . ."[18] Allegro supports this statement with two quotations from the Manual of Discipline; ₁QS iii.8 f. just cited which speaks of humble obedience to God's command, and a section from the concluding hymn: "As for me, my justification (*mišpāṭ*)[19] belongs to God, and in His hand is the perfection of my way, etc." (xi.2 f.).

Molin says something similar in his study of the religion of the Thanksgiving Psalms: "But the worthless, sinful man, surrounded by God's predestination has, however, freedom for decision. He can feel the impact of the call of God, Who calls, elects and cleanses him and installs him in God's service. God's Holy Spirit grasps and sanctifies him. With this the anxiety of judgment which had formerly filled him also vanishes. He can take comfort in God's grace and help."[20]

But none of the passages from the Thanksgiving Psalms which Molin uses as evidence state unambiguously that man can of himself bring about his salvation. In ₁QH v.6, for example, it says: "Thou didst not abandon me to the evil design of my inclination, and Thou didst rescue my life from the grave." Here it is God who is the one who acts: he has not given the psalmist up to his evil inclination but has saved him. And in vii.29-31 it is said:

[18] Allegro, *The Dead Sea Scrolls* (1956), p. 126.
[19] Allegro translates *mišpāṭ* as "justification"; the rest of the quotation as it is given is far from correct.
[20] Molin, "Die Hymnen von Chirbet Qumran, (₁QT)," *op. cit.*, pp. 77 f.

All the children of Thy truth Thou leadest into forgiveness . . .
Thou cleansest them from their transgressions . . .
to place them before Thy presence (face) forever and
  ever.

Here the expression "the children of Thy truth" would
even indicate that only those who are elected from the
beginning and predestined become objects of God's
salvation.

This predestination idea is still more explicitly expressed in xv.13-18:

I know that in Thy hand is the "forming" (purpose)
  of every spirit;
[his deeds] didst Thou determine before Thou didst
  create him;
and how should anyone be able to change Thy words?
Yea, Thou [didst form] the righteous,
and from the womb Thou didst prepare him for the
  appointed time of [Thy] good pleasure
in order that he be preserved in Thy covenant. . . .
But the wicked Thou didst create [for the time of] Thy
  [wrath],
and from the womb Thou didst set them apart for the
  day of slaughter.

This seems to imply a double predestination: the righteous man is created from the beginning for righteousness, the wicked for sin, and both redound to God's
glory (xv.20).

Strangely enough the next line begins with a "for,"
which seems to lay the responsibility on the wicked:
"For they have walked in a way which is not good. . . ."
There is good evidence, however, that Licht is right

when he maintains that predestination is the view which is typical of the Thanksgiving Psalms.[21] "The author of the Thanksgiving Scroll," he says, "has been granted the gifts of righteousness by divine mercy." One may also say that God *willed* it thus or that it is God's *good pleasure;* and *both* concepts are expressed by the same Hebrew word (*rāṣôn*),[22] e.g., xiv.13: "I know that through Thy good pleasure [. . .] Thy holy spirit"; xvi.4, 12: "I know that through Thy good pleasure hast Thou increased in man [. . .] truth"; ". . . to cleanse me by Thy holy spirit and let me come near in Thy good pleasure according to Thine abundant grace." God's grace and good pleasure are not granted to everyone but only to those who have been predestined to belong to the "lot" of the righteous; or, in other words, to the elect:

I know that Thou hast chosen them from among all
  (others),
and they shall serve Thee to eternity.

—1QH xv.23 f.

And I understood, that he whom Thou hast chosen,
his ways hast Thou (also) [prepared][23]
and through insight Thou preventest him
from sinning against Thee.

—1QH xvii.21 f.

[21] Licht, "The Doctrine . . . , Part 2," *op. cit.*, pp. 89 f.; cf. the detailed discussion in Nötscher, "Schicksalsglaube in Qumrân . . . , Parts 1 and 2," *op. cit.*

[22] Concerning the word *rāṣôn* see Vogt, " 'Peace among Men of God's Good Pleasure' Lk. 2:14" in *SNT*, pp. 114-117 (a translation with some revisions of " 'Pax hominibus bonae voluntatis' Lc. 2,14," *Biblica* 34 [1953]. 427 ff.).

[23] Cf. Rom. 8:30.

It appears as if the question of predestination cannot receive an unambiguous answer. Nevertheless, it seems that the deterministic-predestinarian statements predominate. Therein the Manual of Discipline and the War Scroll (col. xiii) are more objective and establish the fact that there are two spirits and two "lots," to which mankind belongs in accordance with God's decision, while the author of the Thanksgiving Psalms sees the matter more from the subjective side: he knows that he belongs to the elect, that God has placed him in the "lot" of the righteous and appointed him for salvation, and therefore he thanks God. He knows that he himself has not contributed to his salvation; he has experienced the whole course of events as directed by God, and thus he praises God because he is not among the wicked (vii.34). And on this basis he thinks that he sees a meaning even in the attack of his enemies: they, too, are dependent on God in their actions "in order that God may be glorified (or: show Himself glorious) through judgment of the wicked" (ii.23 f.).

Under these conditions it may seem strange that such a word as *mitnaddēb*, "voluntary," "willing," plays an important role in the Dead Sea Scrolls and it can even be said that "volunteer" is a designation for the member of the community (₁QS v.8, 10, etc.).[24] One voluntarily, with a free will, offers himself to perform the statutes of God (₁QS i.7), one is "a volunteer for His truth" and brings knowledge, power and wealth with him into

---

[24] See: Nielsen, *Håndskriftfundene, op. cit.*, p. 135. For further discussion of this point, see Nötscher, "Schicksalsglaube . . . ," *op. cit.*, pp. 218 f.

the community (i.11-12), he offers himself willingly (volunteers) to turn away from all evil and to hold fast to all that God has commanded (v.1). In the Micah Commentary it is said (line 16): "That alludes to the Teacher of Righteousness, who interprets the law for his congregation and for all those who are willing to join God's elect [who do the law] in the council of the community and who are saved from the day [of judgment?]." Thus, one has voluntarily become one of the elect, and he is to make an effort to become one of the elect.

According to Licht, however, a word found in ₁QS ix.24 which is from the same root has a slightly different meaning. When one goes out into the desert to prepare the way for the Lord, he shall in everything do God's will and fulfill all his commands, "then everything that is done shall be done gladly in willingness; apart from God's will (or: good pleasure *rāṣôn*) nothing is acceptable." Licht interprets this as follows: a member of the community shall voluntarily and humbly subordinate himself to God's predestination,[25] but it could just as well allude to willingness to obedience. However, the translation is far from certain in this line. The last clause can also mean: "Beyond the will of God one shall desire nothing."

Naturally these statements which presuppose man's cooperation are from a strictly logical point of view irreconcilable with the teaching of predestination. But they are not impossible because of this. Within the frame of a living religious experience these two ideas may coexist. A study of comparative religion reveals

[25] Licht, "The Doctrine . . . ," *op. cit.*, p. 94, note 101.

several parallels to this. In the Koran Mohammed teaches both strict predestination and man's possibility of free decision; and it has become the task of later Islamic dogmatics to find a formula to unite all these different statements. And in Paul, both the adherents and opponents of the teaching of predestination have found or would like to find support for their view. It is possible that a formula might be found which expressed the relationship between predestination and human decision in Qumran. But since the texts themselves give no definite answer to this question and furthermore, since parts of them are damaged in decisive places, it would not seem wise to try to make a final judgment, particularly as it is probable that the Qumran community itself was not aware of the contradiction, or in any case did not try to express its belief in a form which was free of contradiction. One can entirely agree when Davies says concerning perfection: "The attainment of 'perfection' . . . is clearly a matter of works and yet it is a gift of God ($_1$QS xi.2)." [26]

It should be pointed out that the deterministic attitude is by no means unique for the Dead Sea Scrolls. On the contrary it is very widespread in the Hellenistic world at this time. In Gnosticism and related movements revelation and election are central concepts. Knowledge, gnosis, can be imparted to man through God's revealing Himself to him, and the reception of this revelation makes him elect, having the *mystērion* at his disposal, the

[26] Davies, " 'Knowledge' in the Dead Sea Scrolls and Matthew 11:25-30," in *Christian Origins and Judaism* (1962), p. 121 (originally published in *HTR* 46 [1953], 115).

secret, the mystery that remains hidden from the masses.[27]

On the other hand, it must be remembered that the general atmosphere in the Qumran writings is in good agreement with late Judaism in general. That man is "a small, wretched, weak and mortal creature,"[28] is also taught very clearly in the apocryphal and pseudepigraphic books. And it is well known that Judaism at this time was characterized by a trembling reverence for God and a strong submission to whatever fate he ordains.[29] However, it is striking that this deep reverence and submission is coupled with joy and confidence in the consciousness of being elect and saved and participating in God's wonderful knowledge.

THE WAY OF SALVATION

Bardtke[30] has directed attention to the fact that one of the Thanksgiving Psalms, xi.3-14, contains a description of the way of salvation which could almost have been part of a catechism. It seems appropriate to orient this presentation of the doctrine about salvation around this psalm, and especially its latter half, which is cited here *in extenso:*

[27] A. J. Festugière, "Cadre de la mystique hellénistique," in *Aux Sources de la Tradition Chrétienne. Mélanges offerts à M. Maurice Goguel.* (1950), pp. 74-85.

[28] L. Couard, *Die religiösen und sittlichen Anschauungen der alttestamentlichen Apokryphen und Pseudepigraphen.* (1907), p. 102.

[29] Bousset and Gressmann, *Die Religion des Judentums, op. cit.,* pp. 373 ff.

[30] H. Bardtke, "Considérations sur les cantiques de Qumrân," *RB* 63 (1956), 228 ff.

. . . and Thy compassion is for all the children of Thy
good pleasure.
For Thou hast given them knowledge through (or: in)
the counsel of Thy truth,
and through (or: in) Thy wondrous mysteries hast
Thou given them insight.
And for the sake of Thy glory hast Thou cleansed man
from transgression,
that he may consecrate himself to Thee from all filthy
abominations and from the guilt of faithlessness
to unite himself [with] the children of Thy truth
and (to be) in the lot of the people, Thy holy ones,
to raise from the dust the worms of the dead
unto [a holy? or: everlasting] fellowship
and from a perverse spirit unto [Thine] insight,
and to stand in position before Thee
with the hosts of eternity and spirits [of knowledge?],
to be renewed with everything which has come into
being
and with those who have knowledge, in the community
of jubilation.

—₁QH xi.9-14

Bardtke finds here six components or stages, but it
seems more correct to speak of three pairs of concepts:

1) Knowledge of God's truth and insight into his
   mysteries.
2) Cleansing from sin, and consecration to God, being
   set apart from impurity and faithlessness.
3) Unification with the children of the truth—i.e.,
   joining the community—and participation in the
   "lot" of the holy ones.

The content of the third point is then developed further
in the following lines where it is said of the saved man,
that he

a) is as one who is dead and who is lifted up out of the dust,

b) is freed from a perverse spirit (= mind),

c) takes his place before God,

d) has fellowship with the angels and

e) belongs to the community of jubilation.

These stages will now be studied somewhat more closely, beginning with "knowledge."

KNOWLEDGE

The psalm just cited mentions knowledge and insight [31] as the first stage on the way of salvation. A couple of times in the Thanksgiving Psalms it is explicitly said that man comes close to God only in relationship to his knowledge or insight (xii.23; xiv.18 f.). And every one who wishes to enter into the community will be tested with regard to "his insight and his deeds according to the law" ($_1$QS v.21). The concluding hymn in the Manual of Discipline also states clearly that "from a spring of His knowledge He has opened up His light, and my eyes have perceived His wonders and the light of my heart a mystery to come" ($_1$QS xi.3). And there is hardly any phrase that recurs so often in the Thanksgiving Psalms as the expression "I know": "I know Thee" (xii.11); "I know that man does not have

[31] On "knowledge" in the Dead Sea Scrolls, see: Davies, " 'Knowledge' . . . ," *op. cit.*, pp. 119-144; Reicke, "Traces of Gnosticism in the Dead Sea Scrolls?" *NTS* 1 (1954), 137-141; Nötscher, *Zur theologischen Terminologie der Qumran-Texte* (1956), pp. 15 ff.; Ringgren, "Gnosis i Qumrantexterna," *SEÅ* 24 (1959), 41-53; J. de Caevel, "La connaissance réligieuse dans les hymnes d'action de grâces de Qumran," *EphThLov* 38 (1962), 435-460.

righteousness" (iv.30); "I know that man can not direct his own steps" (xv.12); "I know that there is hope" (iii.20; cf. ₁QS x.16 f.); "I know that of Thy good pleasure I have a part in the holy spirit" (₁QH xiv.13); etc. Time after time the psalmist praises his God for having given him insight:

> I thank Thee, O Lord
> that Thou hast given me insight into [32] Thy truth
> and given me knowledge of Thy wonderful mysteries.
> —₁QH vii.26-27

There is thus no doubt that knowledge is an extremely central concept in Qumran.

It should first be noted that there is no fixed terminology, no *one* particular word for this saving knowledge, but a whole series of different expressions. The entire arsenal of synonyms for "wisdom" and "insight" from the biblical wisdom literature are used: first the verb *yādāʿ* "to know," with its derivatives *daʿat* and *dēʿāh*, "knowledge," then *śēkel*, "insight," *bînāh*, "understanding" and less often *ḥokmāh*, "wisdom," *ʿormāh*, "prudence," and similar terms.

Another linguistic or rather stylistic observation concerns the expression "I know." It is certainly dependent on biblical prototypes such as Job 19:25: "I know that my Redeemer lives," or Psalm 20:6: "I know that Yahweh will help His anointed," Psalm 41:11: "By this I know that Thou art pleased with me" (cf. also Ps. 39:4, 135:5). It was evidently a fixed formula in the cult

---

[32] For the translation of these expressions see the suggestion of Mansoor, "Some Linguistic Aspects of the Qumran Texts," *JSS* 3 (1958), 41.

language to express assurance. This original function had probably been forgotten when the Qumran psalms were written, but the formula was retained as a biblical expression—it is a well-known fact that the language of the Qumran writings is permeated with biblical expressions.

The objects of knowledge are manifold.[33] The phrase, "I know Thee," (i.e., God) was cited above. God is thus one of the foremost objects of knowledge. But this cannot be said without further qualification. To know God is a fundamental concept, for example, in the Book of Ezekiel, or in Jeremiah 31:33 f.: (In the days of the new covenant) ". . . no longer shall each man teach his neighbor . . . , saying 'Know the Lord,' for they shall all know me, from the least of them to the greatest, says the Lord. . . ." The Thanksgiving Psalms say, for example: "I know Thy truth" ($_1$QH ix.9 f.) or: "I know that truth is in Thy mouth" (xi.7), i.e., God's truth or his true nature is an object of knowledge. To this knowledge concerning God belongs also recognition that he is righteous and always abides by his word ($_1$QH xiii.18 f.) and that he is the judge of all mankind ($_1$QS x.16 f.).

But this knowledge is also insight into God's work, the wonder of the creation and the divine plan for the universe. The detailed description of God's world-plan in $_1$QH i is followed by the words:

These things I know through Thy understanding
for Thou hast opened mine ear to wonderful mysteries.
—$_1$QH i.21

[33] Licht, "The Doctrine . . . ," *op. cit.*, p. 98.

That "the forming of every spirit is in God's hand" and that he has predestined their deeds are also objects of knowledge (₁QH xv.13); in other words, knowledge applies to dualism and predestination. The insignificance of man and his sinful nature is another important point: "I know that man does not have righteousness" (₁QH iv.30); "I know through Thine understanding, that it is beyond the power of the flesh [to do good?] . . . and that a man cannot guide his steps aright" (₁QH xv.12).

But it is also knowledge concerning salvation and forgiveness, concerning hope of eternal fellowship for him whom God has formed of dust (₁QH iii.20 f.); certainty that through God's good pleasure he will receive the holy spirit and be brought near in order to understand God (₁QH xiv.12 f.). Further, it is the right understanding of God's command (cf. perhaps ₁QH vi.4: "Thou hast opened mine ear for the chastisement of righteous judgments"; this occurs several times in the Damascus Document and in ₁QS i.12 where purifying one's knowledge through God's ordinances is mentioned) and understanding of the prophetic word and its application in the final age which is present (₁QpHab. ii.9 f.; vii.4-5: God has allowed the Teacher of Righteousness to know all the secrets of the words of his servants, the prophets; xi.1). In other words, Licht is right when he says that knowledge refers to practically all of the teachings of the community.[34] But doubtless the emphasis lies on the divine plan for the world and on the place of man therein, his insignificance and his possibility for salvation; thus, in short, God's plan of salvation.

[34] *Ibid.*

This knowledge is, however, entirely a gift of God to the elect, a result of divine revelation: [35]

I have insight, I know Thee, my God,
through the spirit, which Thou hast given me,
and what is sure have I heard in Thy wondrous council.
Through Thy holy spirit hast Thou opened to mine
    innermost parts
the knowledge of the mystery of Thine insight.

—₁QH xii.11-13

For Thou givest him insight into wondrous things such
    as these,
and the counsel of Thy truth hast Thou made known
    to him.

—₁QH x.4

God is the "source of knowledge" (₁QS x.12), in him one beholds wisdom, prudence, righteousness and power, and he gives all these to those whom He has chosen (₁QS xi.6 f.). He opens the hearts of his servants unto knowledge (₁QS xi.15 f.) and it is he who imparts all knowledge, and there is no other who can grasp or know his counsel, his mysteries and his wonders (xi.17-19).

Finally, it should be noted that this knowledge may not be imparted to just anybody. It is reserved for those who are worthy, the initiated:

With the counsel of understanding I conceal knowledge,
and with prudent knowledge I fence in wisdom
with a firm boundary in order to preserve faithful-
    ness. . . .

—₁QS x.24 f.

It can be added that knowledge sometimes is equated

[35] *Ibid.*, pp. 98 f.

with enlightenment. Thus, it is said, for example, in
$_1$QH iv.5: "Thou hast illumined my face concerning
Thy covenant," and in iv.27 f.: "Through me hast Thou
illumined the faces of the many . . . , for Thou hast made
known to me the mysteries of Thy wonders." One
could possibly think that to "illumine someone's face"
would be synonymous with making someone glad, but
the paraphrase of the Aaronic benediction in $_1$QS ii.2-4
clearly puts the expression in connection with insight:
"May He illumine thy face with insight of life."

It is, apparently, then, by its very concentration on
man's situation and the way of salvation that knowledge
becomes a way of salvation. This is the way which God
himself has opened through his word and above all
through the authoritative interpretation of the word
which was given by the Teacher of Righteousness. It is
through this that man has received the possibility of
finding his place in God's plan and fulfilling his purpose.

An unavoidable question now remains: How is this
"knowledge" related to the gnosis of Gnosticism? [36] The
question has been much debated and no consensus has
been reached. To a large extent, however, it seems to
be a question of definitions of terms. Festugière has
defined gnosis as a) knowledge of God, above all as
Savior, b) knowledge of oneself, one's origin and destiny,
and c) knowledge of the way to salvation and the return
to the divine origin. The two first points are applicable
also in Qumran but only half of the third point since
Qumran teaches salvation but not the deification which

[36] See the discussion of this problem in Ringgren, "Gnosis . . . ,"
op. cit.

is found in Gnosticism. But through this the Qumran community's teaching is still not established as gnostic. If Gnosticism is taken to mean any form of religion that considers esoteric knowledge as the road to salvation, then one may also perhaps call the religion of the Dead Sea Scrolls Gnosticism.[37] But there is much beside this in the Gnosticism of the first Christian centuries that is missing in Qumran: the dualism is of a different sort, the aeon speculations are missing, etc. But one may still venture to say that Qumran and Gnosticism have so much in common that they must be considered as two branches of the same tree. Perhaps one may speak of a preparation for Gnosticism, a pre- or proto-Gnosticism.

FORGIVENESS AND PURIFICATION

The second stage of the way of salvation was cleansing from sin: forgiveness, sanctification. Here the Thanksgiving Psalms are our most productive source. The author of these hymns has painfully experienced the depravity of his heart and his sinfulness. But by having come to know the riches of God's compassion he has been saved from despair. Thus, for example, after first having spoken of his sin and guilt, he confesses:

And when I remember the strength of Thy hand
and Thine abundant compassion,
I arise and stand,
and my spirit holds its ground before adversity.
For I lean upon Thy grace
and on Thine abundant compassion,
for Thou atonest for iniquity

[37] Licht, "The Doctrine . . . ," *op. cit.*, p. 97.

and cleansest man from guilt through Thy righteousness.

—₁QH iv.35-37

Or in the words of the concluding hymn in the Manual
of Discipline:

In His compassion has He brought me near,
and in His grace He causes my vindication to come,
and in His faithful righteousness does He vindicate me,
and in His abundant goodness does He atone for all mine
    iniquities.
In His righteousness does He cleanse me
from the impurity of man and the sin of the children
    of men.

—₁QS xi.13-15

This certainty concerning purification and forgiveness
is the poet's only way out of despair, his only hope. "I
know there is hope through Thy compassion," is a
phrase which is met four times in the Thanksgiving
Psalms (iii.20; vi.6; ix.14; fr. i.8).

The feeling of regained hope, of being delivered from
despair and of being freed from sin is dominant in the
Thanksgiving Psalms. The wonderful experience of the
transition from despair to certainty of divine grace is
described several times (iii.19 ff.; iv.33 ff.—just cited
above—ix.4-13; xi.15 ff.). It is easy to understand that
the psalmist often exaggerates his original hopelessness
and worthlessness in order to permit the greatness of
what has befallen him to stand out that much more
clearly.

The author of the Thanksgiving Psalms also knows
that his sins are forgiven and atoned for, and that he is

cleansed from his guilt. All these terms, which are well
known from the Old Testament, are used apparently
without differentiation. Thus, for example, "to atone for,
expiate" (*kipper*)[38] is parallel with "to cleanse" (*ṭihar*)
in ₁QS xi.14 (cited above). "Forgiveness (*sᵉlîḥôt*) is
parallel to "cleansing" (pi'el of *ṭāhar*) in ₁QH vii.30; cf.
also xi.30 f.:

> Cleanse me through Thy righteousness,
> as I hope in Thy goodness
> and wait upon Thy grace and Thy forgiveness.
> Thou hast opened (= removed?) my torment(?),
> and in my sorrow hast Thou comforted me,
> for I leaned upon Thy compassion.

Here a series of well-known terms are added: *ḥesed*
"grace," *ṭûb* "goodness," *raḥᵃmîm* "compassion." As
regards the last of these words, the combinations *rôb
raḥᵃmîm* "abundance of compassion" and *hᵃmôn raḥᵃmîm*
"heap (or abundance) of compassion" are particularly
frequent.[39]

How these terms are used interchangeably also may
be seen from an example from the Manual of Discipline:

> For by the spirit of God's true counsel are all the ways
> (conduct) of a man atoned for (*yᵉkupperû*), all his in-
> iquities, so that he may see the light of life. And by a
> holy spirit toward union with His truth will he be cleansed
> from all his iniquities. And by an upright and humble

---

[38] Concerning this term, see S. Lyonnet, "De notione expiationis,"
VD 37 (1959), 349 ff., cf. Chamberlain, "Toward a Qumran
Soteriology," *NT* 3 (1959), 311 f.

[39] *rôb raḥᵃmîm:* ₁QH iv.32; vii.27; xiii.16 f.; xviii.14; ₁QS iv.3;
hᵃmôn raḥᵃmîm: ₁QH iv.35 f.; vi.9; vii.30, 35; ix.7 f., 34; x.20 f.;
xv.15 f.

spirit is his sin atoned for. And by his soul's humiliation
under all God's ordinances is his flesh cleansed. . . .

—₁QS iii.6-8

In this passage another question comes to the fore to
which Licht has given some attention:[40] Does forgiveness apply to all men and can man do anything to win
it? The section of the Manual of Discipline quoted
seems to imply that man's right disposition ("spirit") is
in some way a prerequisite for forgiveness. In one
Thanksgiving Psalm it says: "Thou forgivest those who
turn away from transgression and avengest (lit.: visitest)
the iniquity of the wicked" (xiv.24). Licht believes that
this implies that only the elect receive forgiveness, while
the wicked are simply not allowed to repent. The expression šabê pešaʻ "those who turn away from (repent
of) transgression"[41]—an appellation which, in fact,
comes from Isaiah 59:20—would then mean "those
who are allowed to repent" and almost become a title
for the members of the sect (₁QH ii.9; vi.6; ₁QS x.20;
CD ii.5). It is doubtful, however, whether the concept
of predestination may be carried so far. The tendency
is there, but the passages cited seem more probably to
imply that the consequences referred to have not been
drawn. Forgiveness is a gift of God, it is true, but at the
same time, it is inseparably connected with repenting
of sin and a proper frame of mind.

However, another observation is more important.
Since sin is often taken as defilement or impurity, de-

[40] Licht, "The Doctrine . . . ," *op. cit.*, p. 96.
[41] Cf. H. Braun, " 'Umkehr' in spätjüdisch-häretischer und in
frühchristlicher Sicht," *ZThK* 50 (1953), 243-258.

liverance from sin is described correspondingly as *cleansing*.[42] Concerning the concept "pure" in the Manual of Discipline, Huppenbauer says: "While man's purity is brought about through atonement (*kippûrîm*, cf. $_1$QS iii.4; xi.14), nevertheless—and this is decisive here—this is not through the flesh of offerings and animal sacrifices (ix.4). To the extent to which man himself contributes anything to the atonement, he can do it by turning away from evil behavior (v.13), by meekness and submission before God's command (iii.7-8). But then (iii.8 f.) cleansing follows from 'sprinkling with the water of purification' and from 'sanctification with running water' (iii.4, 9; v.13). In the last analysis it is, however, God Himself who reconciles (xi.14) and purifies."[43]

The situation is roughly the same in the Thanksgiving Psalms except that lustrations or cleansing with water are not mentioned. The psalmist repeatedly gives thanks to God for having cleansed him from grave guilt (i.32; iii.21; iv.37; xi.10, 30; xvii.11). This cleansing is often described with expressions which are taken from the language of ritual—as has been noted above, this was also true of sin as impurity. The conferring of the spirit is especially described in terms of this kind: God has poured out (or sprinkled, *hēnîp*) the holy spirit "in order to atone for guilt" ($_1$QH fr. ii.13). An example has already been given of how the cleansing of man is connected with "a holy spirit" ($_1$QS iii.7). In $_1$QS iv.21 it

---

[42] Forms of both *ṭahēr* and *zākāh* occur.

[43] Huppenbauer, "ṬHR und ṬHRH in der Sektenregel von Qumran," *ThZ* 13 (1957), 350-351.

is expressly said that "God cleanses (man) by the holy spirit from all works of wickedness and sprinkles him with a spirit of truth like water of purification (for cleansing from) all abominations of falsehood."

The relationship between ritual and moral purity is clarified in the upper half of the third column of the Manual of Discipline: one cannot be had without the other. He who does not abandon sin but walks in the hardness of his heart will not be cleansed through atonement or be made pure through water. He who wishes to do penance will be sprinkled with water of purification and God will lead him in the right way.

Finally it should be noted that this cleansing (salvation) is twice described as passing from death to life:

I praise Thee, O Lord,
for Thou hast delivered my soul from the grave,
and from the abyss of the kingdom of death hast Thou
    led me up
unto an eternal height.

—₁QH iii.19 f.

I thank Thee, O Lord,
for Thou hast bound my life in the bundle of the living.
—₁QH ii.20

The question is whether the psalmist is dependent here on the Old Testament vocabulary and phraseology—for every act of deliverance is there presented as deliverance from the power of death—or whether he actually has a theory concerning the dominion of sin as a kingdom of death and salvation as life. The instances of occurrences of this terminology are too few to permit a definite

answer to this question. The passages that speak of
death and the realm of death ($\check{s}^{e'}\hat{o}l$) are either built on
Old Testament expressions or are to be understood in a
general figurative sense. Instances of "life" and "to live"
are perhaps somewhat more clear: "to see the light of
life" ($_1$QS iii.7), to be illumined with "insight of life"
and twice even "eternal life" ($\d{h}ayy\hat{e}$ $ne\d{s}a\d{h}$ CD iii.20;
$_1$QS iv.7). A particular type of imagery is found in the
rather puzzling psalm in column viii of the Thanksgiving
Psalms. The psalmist thanks God for having placed him
at a spring in the desert which waters a holy plantation
of "trees of life." These trees will "put forth a branch
for an eternal plantation" and this branch will become
food for all the beasts of the forest and shelter for all
birds. After that a hedge around the fruit of the plantation is mentioned, with evident allusion to the garden of
Eden. There is a clear reference to the fact that man
cannot reach the fountain of life. But the word of the
psalmist is a fountain of living water and he says that by
his hand God has "opened their source." When he
moves his hand, the trees grow abundantly, when he
withdraws it, there will be a wasteland. It appears as
though the plantation were the community and the
psalmist the Teacher of Righteousness. Thus he has
opened the way for man to the life-giving trees and the
fountain of life in Paradise.[44] But here, too, the author
seems to be dependent on Old Testament imagery. No
clear theory or teaching concerning spiritual death and
spiritual life can be discerned.

[44] Cf. below, pp. 187 ff., and see: Ringgren, "The Branch and
the Plantation in the *Hodayot*," *Bibl. Res.* 6 (1961), 3-9.

FELLOWSHIP WITH THE HOLY ONES

In the psalm which was used as a starting point ($_1$QH xi.3-14) the result of salvation was defined as joining with the children of truth and fellowship with the holy ones. The first expression apparently alludes to association with the sect, whereas the latter is ambiguous. Several times in the Manual of Discipline the members of the order are referred to as "the holy ones": he who enters into the order is united with "the holy congregation" (*ʿadat qôdeš*, v.20), the fully initiated members are called *anšê ḥaq-qôdeš*, "men of holiness," i.e., "holy men" (viii.17, 20, 23; ix.8), and they are "a holy house for Aaron" (ix.6). But it is also expressly said that the members "stand in one and the same lot as the angels of the presence" ($_1$QH vi.13), and it is apparently thought that the elect as the result of their entrance into the community become in some way citizens of the kingdom of heaven:

> Thou didst cleanse the perverse spirit . . .
> that he may take his place in the host of the holy ones
> and enter into fellowship with the congregation of the
> sons of heaven.
> > —$_1$QH iii.21-22

> . . . who came together for Thy covenant . . .
> and arrange themselves before Thee in the fellowship of
> the holy ones.
> > —$_1$QH iv.24-25

> To them whom God elects He gives this as an eternal
> possession
> and gives them a share in the lot of the holy ones,

and to the sons of heaven does He join their circle
(*sôd*).

—₁QS xi.7-8

It has already been seen that these passages presuppose
a fellowship with the heavenly world which is allotted
to those who are saved. The angels and those who are
saved constitute one great community. But its visible
manifestation on earth is, of course, the Qumran community itself.

This fellowship is often called a covenant (*bᵉrît*). To
"enter into the covenant" means the same thing as to
become a member of the order (for example, ₁QS i.18,
20; ii.10; v.8, 20). God has chosen those who are blameless for an eternal covenant (₁QS iv.22), and he who
walks blamelessly in all of God's ways becomes well
pleasing to God "and this becomes for him a covenant
of eternal fellowship" (₁QS iii.11 f.). What this means
becomes clear if we turn to the Damascus Document.
As is known this speaks explicitly of the establishment
of a new covenant in the place of that which Israel's sin
had made invalid (CD xx.12; vi.19). This is clearly based
on Jeremiah's prophecy of the new covenant (Jer.
31:31), and it is clear that the community within which
the Damascus Document came into existence is taken
to be this new covenant. In the Thanksgiving Psalms
it was learned that sin excludes man from the covenant
(iv.35; xv.18) but that God gives strength to the elect to
be steadfast in the covenant (₁QH ii.22; xvi.7; xviii.9) or
also that he strengthens them *through* the covenant
(ii.28).

Everything granted to man in the covenant is a gift

of God's grace. The Thanksgiving Psalms' "I thank Thee, O Lord" can, in fact, be said to be man's thankful acknowledgment of this fact, and the Thanksgiving Psalms as a whole are only one great elaboration of this theme. It is therefore understandable that there is no systematic enumeration of the gifts of grace. A short but comprehensive list is found in ₁QS iv.2-6, which stresses the ethical and is reminiscent, as has been noted (p. 70) of the so-called catalogs of virtues. A series of important concepts occur in ₁QH vii.6-20, from which some selections follow:

I thank Thee, O Lord,
that Thou hast sustained me with Thy strength
and caused Thy holy spirit to fall upon me. . . .
And that Thou hast strengthened me in the face of
  battles with wickedness. . . .
And Thou hast made me as a strong tower,
as a high wall. . . .
And Thou hast established me in Thy covenant
and my tongue in Thy teaching. . . .
And Thou hast made my heart secure
in Thy teaching and Thy truth
to direct my steps in the paths of righteousness,
that I might walk before Thee . . .
and Thou hast made me a father for the children of
  grace.

In this section there is particular emphasis on the way in which God upholds and guides the pious, a feature familiar in these writings (₁QH ii.7 f., 28; ix.32; xviii.13; ₁QM xiv.7).

Seen from another point of view, this support is described as help in battle against enemies and adversaries.

False teachers and lying prophets, who are at the service of Belial, deny the new revelations and persecute their bearer and seek to persuade him to apostasy and unbelief:

They did not listen to Thy voice
and they did not harken to Thy word.
They said of the vision of knowledge: it is not true,
and of the way of Thy heart: it is not (anything). . . .
But those who are according to Thy mind
shall stand before Thee forever,
and they who walk in the way of Thy heart
shall stand fast eternally.
And I, since I cleave to Thee,
I will be steadfast and rise up
against those who despise me,
and my hand shall be against all those who despise me.
—₁QH iv.17-18, 21-22 [45]

Against all opposition the psalmist can rely on God's help, which places him on a firm foundation and which guides his path:

They made a mockery and disgrace of me
in all the mouths of those who seek deceit.
But Thou, my God,
hast rescued the afflicted and needy soul
out of the hand of him who was stronger than he.
And Thou didst deliver my soul out of the hand of the mighty,
before their reviling Thou didst not cause me to be terrified
into giving up Thy service
because of terror before the greediness of the wicked.
—₁QH ii.34-36

Regardless of who the "I" of these lines is, the feeling

[45] Cf. also ₁QH v.12-19.

of security against all attacks because of God's help is unmistakable. He who with the help of God prevails in battle will finally reach his glorious destiny: to form with the angels before God's throne a community which praises and magnifies him forever and which rejoices in his presence:

> Thou shalt bring their justice to victory
> and truth to success.
>
> —₁QH iv.25

> But my foot stands on level ground,
> in the congregations shall I praise Thy name.
>
> —₁QH ii.29 f.

> And he gives strength to tottering knees
> and mighty power to sore shoulders,
> courage to those distressed in spirit
> and endurance to those whose hearts are timid. . . .
> And Thou raised up with Thy power those who have
>   fallen,
> but the great in height dost Thou hew down. . . .
> But we are Thy holy people,
> in works of Thy truth we will praise Thy name,
> And in Thy mighty acts will we exalt it.
>
> —₁QM xiv.6-7, 10-11, 12-13 [46]

The jubilation is not only something that belongs to the consummation—even now the pious are members of the "community of jubilation":

> My heart rejoices in Thy covenant
> and in Thy truth is my soul satisfied.
>
> —₁QH x.30-31

[46] The translation given here is somewhat free.

Thou didst give [47] man an eternal lot
with the spirits of knowledge
to praise Thy name in unanimous jubilation
and to tell forth Thy wonders before all Thy works.

—₁QH iii.22-23

Thou hast given me understanding through Thy won-
derous works
and put thanksgiving in my mouth
and jubilation on my tongue . . .

—₁QH xi.4 [48]

Hence despite everything the key note in the piety
of the Qumran congregation is jubilation, and songs of
praise are both a holy duty for him who is saved and
a wonderful gift of God. It is at the same time both
thanksgiving for his own salvation and a proclamation
before the world. It has at least one of its concrete expressions in the cultic praise of God at definite times,
which will be more closely examined in connection with
the cult of the community.

ETHICAL IDEAS

The ethical demands most often receive a very general formulation, for example, "to love all that which God
has chosen and to hate what He has rejected" (₁QS i.3 f.;
₁QH xiv.10; xvii.24; cf. Ps. 139:21)—apparently a fixed
formula, cf. the description of the opposite attitude and
behavior in ₁QH xv.18 f.—"to walk in the way of
(God's) heart" (₁QH iv.24; xv.18; cf. vi.6; vii.14; I En.
91:4, etc.) or simply to live (walk) according to God's

[47] Literally: didst let fall to.
[48] Cf. also ₁QH xi.23 ff.; x.20 f.

will or his command. These are, of course, the fundamental virtues of all Judaism, and are also placed first in the Manual of Discipline (i.7): "to bring all who are willing to do God's statutes (= to fulfill God's command), into a covenant of grace to be united in the council of God, to walk blamelessly before Him in accordance with all that which is revealed in their ordained times." Similarly it is said in the Manual of Discipline ix.13, that one should "do God's will in accordance with all which is revealed in each time." [49]

The ethical demands are stated in equally general terms in the section of the Thanksgiving Psalms where to some extent there is explicit mention of them:

I know through Thy great goodness,
and by an oath have I enjoined my soul
not to sin against Thee
and not to do anything which is evil in Thy sight.
—₁QH xiv.17-18

. . . to despise all the ways of error,
and I love Thee willingly and with all my heart.
—₁QH xiv.26, par. xv.10 [50]

Behind these general demands lies the fundamental ethically based dualism. On the one hand there is truth (*'emet*), righteousness (*ṣᵉdāqāh*), perfection (*tom*), uprightness (*yoŝer*), communal faithfulness (*ḥesed*), love (*'aheᵃbāh*), etc.; and opposite to them stand error (*'āwel*),

---

[49] Precisely what is referred to by the expression "revealed in each time (era, epoch)" is not clear. Either it is a quite general expression, much the same as "every time something is revealed," or behind it may lie a theory that each particular time has its revelation and its understanding of the law (see below, p. 134).

[50] Cf. ₁QH xiv.14 f.; xv.24; xvii.22 f.

wickedness (reša'), falsehood (šeqer), vanity (šaw), etc. Thus, for example, the Habakkuk Commentary speaks of "men of truth, who live according to the law (tôrāh) and serve the truth" (vii.10 f.) and of the false preacher (maṭṭîp hak-kāzāb) who establishes a congregation in falsehood (šeqer) in order that many will weary themselves in the service of vanity (šāw) (x.9-11).

On the basis of the passages cited it is nevertheless possible more closely to define the ethical demands: one should "do the will of God in accordance with all that has been revealed"; "the men of truth . . . live according to the Law." Further, it is said at the beginning of the Manual of Discipline: "One shall do what is good and right before Him as He commanded through Moses and through all His servants, the prophets" (i.2-3). Hence it refers primarily to carrying out the law of Moses, the Torah, and in the Manual of Discipline it is even decreed that "each man who transgresses a word of the Law of Moses shall be banished from the fellowship of the congregation" (viii.22).

Here two points should be noted. First, the passages noted above seem to indicate that the ethical demands revealed depend on the period in which one lives. It is possible that this implies that each period has its own understanding of the Law and that in the present time God has revealed through the Teacher of Righteousness the right and true understanding of his commandments. The Qumran congregation lives in the final age and its ethic is therefore eschatologically motivated.[51]

[51] Cf. E. Beijer, *Kristologi och etik i Jesu bergspredikan* (1960), pp. 136 ff.

Second, it is known that piety based on the Law is characteristic of late Judaism in general. Despite this, the ethics of the Qumran congregation are not fully in accordance with that of Pharisaic rabbinic Judaism.[52] Otzen has attempted to describe this distinction in greater detail.[53] He calls the ethics of Pharisaic Rabbinism a legal ethic while Qumran and the Testaments of the Twelve Patriarchs represent an ethic with its center in piety and the relationship to the neighbor. This does not mean that the Law is not central for the latter groups. On the contrary, such concepts as "truth," "right," and "righteousness" have both at Qumran and in the Testaments of the Twelve Patriarchs a very clear connection with the Law and the words can sometimes almost be synonymous with "Law." Hence one can speak of "doing the truth" or "transgressing the truth," etc.

As is well known the fundamental virtue in the Testaments of the Twelve Patriarchs is *haplótēs*, "single-mindedness" or perhaps rather "wholeheartedness," "unity of thought and deed in the moral man," (Eppel)[54] or "sincerity and straightforwardness in one's actions"; its opposite is hypocrisy. In the same way, says Otzen,

---

[52] There are also certain differences between the various writings. The Damascus Document seems to be more "legalistic" or perhaps, rather, more casuistic than the other writings, but that can partly be due to its particular character and aim. For a discussion of some halakhic questions, see: Rabin, *Qumran Studies, op. cit.*, pp. 82 ff.

[53] Otzen, "Die neugefundenen . . . ," *op. cit.*, pp. 126 ff.

[54] R. Eppel, *Le piétisme juif dans les Testaments des douze Patriarches, op. cit*, pp. 148 f.; cf. C. Edlund, *Das Auge der Einfalt. Eine Untersuchung zu Matt. 6, 22-23 und Luk. 11, 34-35* (1952).

the parallel concepts to this wholeheartedness *tom* "blamelessness, perfection" and *yoŝer* "uprightness, honesty, integrity" are central in the Dead Sea Scrolls.

One thing must, however, be stressed here. Ethical actions are not a human achievement but a gift of God. "Man does not have perfection of behavior" ($_1$QH iv.31). "My right is with God and from His hand comes perfection of behavior and uprightness of heart" ($_1$QS xi.2). Moral behavior is hence a work of God's grace. At the same time that the author of the Thanksgiving Psalms confesses that he loves God willingly and with all his heart (xiv.26) and with his whole soul (xv.10) and says that he does not wish to stray from that which God has commanded or abandon any of his statutes (xv.11-12) he explains that it is not within the power of his flesh to do this or to direct his steps rightly (xv.12-13). Everything comes from God who has chosen man and made him willing to obey his commandments.

The goal is the establishing of a pure community, one which will be found suitable to have fellowship with God and the angels. This is described partly in a negative way as the separation from evil people. Those who enter the covenant are expected not only to "turn to the law of Moses with all their hearts" but also to "separate themselves from all the men of error who walk in the way of wickedness" ($_1$QS v.7 ff.). So they are "separated from the congregation of the men of error" and "become a community in the Law" ($_1$QS v.1 f.). Separated from the men of error the community withdraws into the wilderness to prepare the way for God ($_1$QS ix.19 ff.).

In this way the congregation is to become a pure and holy community, which through their obedience to the Law becomes a holy temple and atones for the sins of the people, thus preparing the way for the fulfillment of the promises and God's final victory. Behind this we sense the conviction that the community represents the true Israel which was chosen by God to be his holy people. The community aims at the realization of the ideal of the chosen people,[55] as is also learned from a prayer in a liturgical fragment, ₁Q 34 bis., where it says: "Thou hast chosen for Thee, at the time of Thy good pleasure, a people, for Thou hast remembered Thy covenant, and Thou hast established them, separating them from all the peoples for a holy possession, and Thou hast renewed Thy covenant . . ." (ii.5 f.).

Love of one's neighbor is expressed in the Manual of Discipline with the phrase taken from Micah 6:8 *'aḥᵃbat ḥesed*, which may be translated as "steadfast love" and which Otzen is inclined to translate as "love of neighbor." It occurs in ₁QS ii.24 and v.25 together with "truth" and "meekness."[56] In viii.2 it is expanded as in Micah 6:8 with the phrase *haṣnēaʿ leket* which is difficult to translate (RSV, "to walk humbly," or perhaps rather "to walk with great care" or "with self-restraint") and it is clarified with the addition *'iš ʿim rēʿēhû* "with one another." It should be noted that this love of the neighbor applies, however, only to members of the community: one should "love all the children of light and

---

[55] See Gärtner, "Bakgrunden till Qumranförsamlingens krig," *RoB* 19 (1960), 35-72, especially 46 ff.

[56] The expression *'aḥᵃbat ḥesed* also occurs in ₁QS v.4 and x.26.

hate all the children of darkness" (₁QS i.10), a phrase
which is very close to what according to Jesus' Sermon
on the Mount was the accepted teaching: "You shall love
your neighbor and hate your enemy" (Matt. 5:43).[57]

This two-edged ethic also occurs in a section of the
concluding hymn of the Manual of Discipline:

> I will not return evil to anyone,
> but with good will I pursue a man,
> for with God is the judgment of all the living;
> and He repays man for his actions.
> I will not be envious against a spirit of wickedness. . . .
> Nevertheless my wrath will I not turn back from men of
> error,
> and I will not be content until He establishes judgment.
> I will not keep wrath against those who repent of
> transgression
> but I will not have compassion on any who stray from
> the way,
> I will not pity those who are smitten, until their way be
> perfect.
>
> —₁QS x.17-21

The first principle advanced, not to repay anyone with
evil, is justified by a reference to the fact that all judgment and all vengeance is God's. The same justification
is found in the Testament of Gad 6-7 and in Romans 12:
19.[58] In the following lines the differing attitude con-

[57] Cf. E. F. Sutcliffe, "Hatred at Qumran," RQ 2 (1959/60),
345-355. Sutcliffe correctly calls attention to the fact that hatred
of those outside the community is limited to the time appointed
by God for his vengeance (note particularly ₁QS i.10 f.: "to hate
all the children of darkness each according to his guilt, with the
vengeance of God").

[58] See Stendahl, "Hate, Non-Retaliation, and Love," HTR 55
(1962), 343-355.

cerning members and outsiders becomes evident. Obviously the sanction is a religious one: if sinners repent of their evil ways and join the community then the situation changes at once. They thereby show that they belong to the elect and share in the fight against the children of darkness, or perhaps rather against the evil principle.

The lines which follow in the hymnic portion cited above also are occupied with ethical questions, and in it there is formulated as Otzen expresses it, an ideal of perfection, to which he finds close parallels in the Testaments of the Twelve Patriarchs. The concluding hymn continues:

> Baseness (*b*ᶜ*liyyaʿal*) will I not keep in my heart,
> nor from my mouth shall be heard folly,
> nor shall sinful deceit, treachery and lies
> be found on my lips,
> but the fruit of holiness shall be on my tongue,
> and abominations shall not be there.
>
> —₁QS x.21-23

To this total negation of all sinful ways the Testament of Issachar offers a good parallel: "Guile arose not in my heart, a lie passed not through my lips" (7:4), and while this parallel has a less general character than the Qumran passage, the resemblance is, however, striking.

Otzen points out further that the ideal of chastity and the practice of fasting do not play an equally significant role in Qumran as in the Testaments of the Twelve Patriarchs although, however, certain expressions in warnings against fornication are common to both (₁QS i.6; CD

ii.16; ₁QS iv.10; cf. T. Issach. 7:2, 3:4; T. Reuben 3:3).[59]
Strangely enough the Manual of Discipline seems to
assume a community without women while the so-called
Rule of the Congregation (Two Column Fragment)
speaks of women and children (₁QSa i.4) and gives instructions concerning the age one should have reached
before having sexual intercourse (i.8 f.). The Damascus
Document also assumes a community of families with
women and legislates concerning the case in which "they
take wives according to the Law and beget children"
(CD vii.6 with par. xix.3). At the cemetery at Qumran
female skeletons have also been found. The only solution seems to be that there were different groups within
the community which had different attitudes toward this
question. The same would also be true of the Essenes
as described by Josephus.

On the other hand, fasting which in the Testaments
is very important as a penance and as a means of pre-
serving chastity, is hardly mentioned at all in Qumran.
The Habakkuk Commentary mentions in passing a fast
day (xi.8), the Damascus Document *perhaps* contains a
prohibition against fasting on the Sabbath (xi.4) and in
one place the Manual of Discipline gives directions for
deprivation of one-fourth of the food ration as a punishment (vi.25). In any case, asceticism is not a means of
disciplining the body in its capacity as sinful flesh.[60]

The question of the ideal of poverty merits particular
attention, especially since it has already been the object

[59] Otzen, "Die neugefundenen . . . ," *op. cit.*, pp. 133 f.
[60] S. Szyszman, "Ascèse et Pauvreté dans la Doctrine Karaïte,"
ZRGG 11 (1959), 373-380.

of considerable discussion. Words like *'ebyôn* "poor" and *'ānî* "oppressed" and similar terms occur fairly often in the Qumran texts as designations for the pious—a fact which has led some scholars to think of the Ebionites, the Jewish-Christians—although most have not gone so far as Teicher who simply sees the Qumran community as a congregation of Jewish-Christians.[61] The decisive question is, however, the following: is the poverty to which reference is made here to be understood literally or figuratively, that is: is it a question of actual voluntary poverty as in Christian monasticism or is it a question of being poor in spirit?

It must first be recalled that both terms are of course dependent on linguistic usage of the Old Testament. The Psalms of the canonical Psalter often speak of the poor and the oppressed, although here too investigation has not been successful in arriving at a generally acceptable interpretation of these terms. Thus it is very probable that the use of these words at Qumran simply is intended to present the community as the fulfillment of the prophecy which was seen in the words of the Psalms.

An interesting investigation of the poverty motif in Qumran has been made by Kandler.[62] He observes that

[61] J. L. Teicher, "The Dead Sea Scrolls—Documents of the Jewish-Christian Sect of Ebionites," *JJS* 2 (1950/51), 67-99; "The Damascus Fragments and the Origin of the Jewish Christian Sect," *ibid.*, 115-143; "The Teaching of the Pre-Pauline Church in the Dead Sea Scrolls," *ibid.*, 3 (1952), 111-118, 139-150; 4 (1953) 1-13, 49-58, 93-103, 139-153.

[62] H.-J. Kandler, "Die Bedeutung der Armut im Schrifttum von Chirbet Qumran," *Judaica* 13 (1957), 193-209; cf. also: S. Légasse, "Les pauvres en esprit et les 'Volontaires' de Qumran," *NTS* 8 (1961/62), 336-344.

it is true that the poor (*'ebyônîm*) appear as a definite
entity but that one may not go so far as to understand
this word as a name of the sect. Thus the identification
with the Ebionites becomes even less probable. None of
the passages considered lends any support to the assumption that *'ebyônîm* stands for the poor in a literal social
sense; it probably refers to being poor in spirit. This
is doubtless correct with regard to the quotations from
the Thanksgiving Psalms (ii.32; iii.25; v.15 f., 18, 22; fr.
iii, iv); whereas the passages in the Habakkuk Commentary (xii.3, 6, 10) which speak of persecution and
plundering of the poor and a few passages in the War
Scroll (xi.9, 13, xiii.14; and in addition $_4$QpPs. 37 ii.10)
in themselves do not give any conclusive answer to the
question. As Schubert notes, it is however quite close
to a technical meaning as a self-description of the community.[63] The context in the War Scroll indicates rather
a figurative usage, since the poor are equated with those
who bow down in the dust (xi.13).

Kandler points to the expression *'aniyyê rûaḥ* in $_1$QM
xiv.7, which he translates "those who are voluntarily
poor," i.e., those who are willing to accept poverty and
are poor by choice, and he later compares this with "the
poor in spirit" (*ptōchoì tō pneúmati*) of the Gospel
according to Matthew (5:3) which would hence also
mean "those who are willing to be poor." The context
shows, however, that *'aniyyê rûaḥ* goes together with
"the weak," "tottering" and "timid" and it should therefore perhaps be translated "oppressed in spirit" or some-

[63] K. Schubert, *The Dead Sea Community*, trans. J. W. Doberstein (1959), p. 88.

thing like that. The similarity to the New Testament expression remains, however, but its traditional meaning appears to stand firm.

Concerning the attitude toward wealth and property Kandler refers especially to the Habakkuk Commentary xii.10 where *hôn 'ebyônîm* "the wealth of the poor" is mentioned. The fact that the sect possessed its own *hôn*, shows that *hôn*—i.e., property, wealth—has by no means a simply negative evaluation. On the other hand community of goods was practiced and this offers certain parallels to early Christianity. But in any case according to Kandler, it was demanded that those who entered into the community should be prepared to give up private property. Poverty is thus not to be taken to have solely a spiritualized meaning. The immediate proximity of the end time has necessitated abstaining from everything that fetters man to that which is earthly.[64]

Thus it says in the concluding hymn of the Manual of Discipline:

I shall not be envious toward a spirit of wickedness, and my soul has no desire for wealth of violence.

—₁QS x.19

It appears from the context that it possibly refers to a question of property of outsiders which should not offer any temptation to those who have already entered the community and left their wealth to the common administration. But it is apparent that the community was well aware of the dangers of wealth and knew that they

[64] Cf. H. Braun, *Spätjüdisch-häretischer und frühchristlicher Radikalismus, I* (1957).

possessed something more valuable: "I know that no riches can compare with Thy truth" (₁QH xv.22 f.).

REWARD AND PUNISHMENT

The good receive their reward, the evil their punishment, but both are in God's hand. He who "has made both the righteous and the wicked" and who "forgives those who turn from transgression but avenges (lit.: visits) the iniquity of the wicked" (₁QH xiv.24), it is also he who allots reward and punishment according to his pleasure. But the principle remains: righteousness brings reward with it and sin is inseparably united with punishment.

> Only through Thy goodness is a man made righteous
> and through Thy great compassion [is he saved?]
> In Thy splendor Thou glorifiest him
> and [. . . him with] abundant delight
> together with eternal peace and long life.
> —₁QH xiii.17-18

> . . . to spare him in Thy mighty compassion
> and to relieve all the distress of his soul
> unto eternal salvation and endless peace without want;
> and Thou didst raise over (or: from) the flesh his glory.
> —₁QH xv.15-17

Concerning punishment it is said:

> But the wicked Thou didst create for [the time of] Thy [wrath],
> and from the womb Thou didst set them apart for the day of slaughter,
> for they have walked in a way which is not good.
> —₁QH xv.17-18

And if he is wicked,
he shall become a sign in eternity
and a symbol for all generations. . . .

—₁QH xiii.16

Of what then do reward and punishment consist? The
texts quoted only give a series of very general and indefinite expressions: delight (in abundance: *rôb ʿᵃdānîm*),
eternal peace (*šᵉlôm ʿôlām*), eternal salvation (*yᵉšûʿat
ʿôlām*),[65] long life. Of these only the last can be unambiguously defined. The expression "Thou dost raise
his glory *mibbāśār*" is ambiguous, since *mibbāśār* may
be translated either "from the flesh" or "more than (all
other) flesh." As far as evil is concerned the expressions
in the quoted passages are even more indefinite. There
are, however, a series of other passages which speak of
total annihilation:

Thou shalt judge them in Thy power
according to their idols and their many transgressions . . . ,
and Thou shalt exterminate in judgment all men of
deceit,
and seers of error shall nevermore be found.

—₁QH iv.18-20

Then shall God's sword speedily come at the appointed
time of judgment,
and all the children of His truth shall awaken
to put an end to [the children] of wickedness,
and there shall no longer be any children of guilt.

—₁QH vi.29 f.

[65] To these expressions, the following must be added: *ḥayyê
neṣaḥ*, "eternal life" (CD iii.20); concerning the same term in
₁QS iv.7, see below.

The description in column iv of the Manual of Discipline is somewhat more clear. There it is said concerning the good:

> And the reward (*p*e*quddāh*, lit.: visitation) of all who walk therein consists of healing and abundance of peace (bliss, happiness, *šālôm*) in length of days and bearing fruit with all eternal blessings and eternal joy in an everlasting life and a crown of glory with splendid raiment in eternal light.
>
> —₁QS iv.6-8

This seems to imply both long life on earth with all conceivable happiness and eternal life in the heavenly glory. The latter is then probably thought of as communion with the angels, and this as a continuation of the fellowship experienced already here and now. But it must be admitted that almost every word can be taken in several different ways. It is especially unclear as to what lies behind the different words for eternity ('*ôlām*, '*ad*, *nesah*). They could connote a long period of time (thus something like: lasting peace, abiding salvation, perpetual blessing, etc.). But they could equally well refer to what we call "eternity." [66]

Considering the Manual of Discipline's general view as to the course of the world it seems possible, however, that it actually is a question of an *eternal* blessedness.[67] It is of particular interest that the reward of the righteous comprises exactly the same things that Adam, according to the pseudepigraphic literature, lost in the Fall

[66] Coppens, "La Secte de Qumrân et son attente eschatologique," *Nouvelle Clio* 5 (1953), 5-9.

[67] *Ibid.*, pp. 7 f.

(cf. particularly: The Life of Adam and Eve). Thus it concerns a restoration of the conditions of Paradise (cf. ₁QH viii, above p. 126).[68]

Similar expressions are used of the evil:

> And the reward of all those who walk therein consists of many plagues through all angels of destruction for an eternal perdition through the wrath of the God of vengeance, eternal torture and everlasting disgrace together with destroying shame in the fire of darkness. And all their times in their generations will be in sorrowful mourning and bitter woe in dark depths. . . .
>
> —₁QS iv.12-14

This seems to offer an exact contrast to the eternal bliss of the good. But characteristically enough, the author adds some significant words: "until they are destroyed so that there is no remnant or survivor among them." Thus, misfortune and sorrow in this life and final annihilation in fire in the other world. It should be mentioned that the description of the wicked priest's plagues in the Habakkuk Commentary (ix.1 ff., 9 ff.) show many parallels to the section just quoted and that the commentary ends with the words: "On the day of judgment God will exterminate from the earth all those who serve idols, together with the sinners" (₁QpHab. xiii. 2-4).

According to a report an unpublished fragment from Cave 4 contains a description of the torments of the evil and the blessedness of the righteous.[69]

It is clear that this picture of the fate of the individual

[68] This was pointed out by Otzen, "Some Text-problems in ₁QS," *StTh* 11 (1957), p. 96 f.

[69] See: *MLS*, p. 347.

is very closely connected with the general eschatology, a subject to be dealt with below.

At this stage, however, two other questions of a more special nature present themselves: Did the Qumran sect believe in the resurrection of the dead, and, Did they teach the immortality of the soul?

The first question was apparently not present in their minds. There is nowhere any statement which can be taken as a substantiation of a belief in the resurrection of the dead. There could possibly be an allusion in $_1$QH vi.34 where in speaking of the great final battle it is said that "they who lie in the dust will raise a flagstaff and the worms of the dead will lift up an ensign." Here in fact it seems as though the dead will arise to take part in the battle. Unfortunately the text is so damaged that the context is not fully clear. But it is possible that the dead here, as probably in $_1$QH xi.12 (see above p. 113), refer to weak insignificant men.[70] In itself an unconcerned attitude toward the question of the resurrection of the dead would be understandable. The members of the Qumran sect were convinced that they lived in the last time and that the end was immediately at hand; thus they would enter directly into the eternal glory. The earlier generations, those who had already died, are apparently given little attention. On the other hand, it must be remembered that the resurrection of the dead is taught in the Book of Daniel and this book seems to have been known at Qumran. Therefore it may perhaps

[70] Cf. Schubert, *The Dead Sea Community, op. cit.,* p. 11, who cites $_1$QH xi.12 in support of a resurrection of at least the righteous dead.

be assumed that the idea at least was not foreign to the people of Qumran. But it should furthermore be recalled that Judaism by no means was consistent and of a unanimous opinion on this point and that great variations evidently were possible—as is well known, the Sadducees completely denied resurrection.

The second question is even more difficult to answer. The immortality of the soul was taught in late-Judaism particularly in the apocryphal Book of the Wisdom of Solomon, probably under at least indirect Greek influence. Dubarle believes he has found in the Dead Sea Scrolls a source of some of the thoughts which are maintained in the Book of Wisdom; [71] it would then be relevant to ask: What is the view concerning the immortality of the soul? Delcor has made an investigation of the question [72] and has arrived at a surprisingly positive result. He points out that in 1QH iii.19 f. there is mention of the fellowship of the pious with the angels, which seems to assume a resurrection body, since man who is created of dust otherwise could not be destined for fellowship with the angels. We have above (see p. 85) interpreted this passage in a different way. Another passage, 1QH iv.18-21 which speaks of judgment of the evil and the eternal continuation of the good, is, to be sure, somewhat unclear but still it leaves the possibility of resurrection and immortality open. Delcor further cites 1QS iv.7-8, where eternal joy, eternal life

---

[71] A.-M. Dubarle, "Une Source du livre de la Sagesse?" *RSPhTh* 37 (1953), 425-442.

[72] M. Delcor, "L'immortalité de l'âme dans le livre de la Sagesse et dans les documents de Qumrân," *NRTh* 77 (1955), 614-630.

and eternal light are mentioned; this he considers to presuppose a resurrection. But in the first place resurrection and the immortality of the soul are not the same thing; and in the second place, as has already been noted, there is in the Dead Sea Scrolls no mention of any dualism between body and soul. We are thus still within the realm of Old Testament thought: man is an indivisible unity, and if there were a question of immortality it would have to refer to man as a whole. Such a view would of course be compatible with belief in resurrection from the dead, even if this question never comes to the fore in the texts.[73]

Laurin arrives at a completely different result in a later investigation.[74] First he points out that $_1$QH iii. 19-23 is altogether concerned with the salvation of the individual here on earth as a deliverance from death; fellowship with the angels he interprets in the same way as we have above. He devotes the rest of his investigation to an analysis of $_1$QH vi.7-35 which he correctly assigns to this world and not to a heavenly consummation. He considers that the use made in the Thanksgiving Psalms of words like "eternal" and "everlasting" should be taken in a "figurative" sense and finally comes to the conclusion that the Thanksgiving Psalms conceive neither of the immortality of body or soul. It is rather

[73] van der Ploeg, "L'immortalité de l'homme d'après les textes de la Mer Morte," *VT* 2 (1952), 171-175; cf. van der Ploeg, "The Belief in Immortality in the Writings of Qumran," *Bib. Orient.* 18 (1961), 118-124.

[74] R. B. Laurin, "The Question of Immortality in the Qumran Hodayot," *JSS* 3 (1958), 344-355.

a matter of a kingdom of God on earth with a new Jerusalem, but not of resurrection or immortality.

If this be correct then all possibility of identification of the Qumran sect with the Essenes would be excluded, since Josephus reports that the Essenes believe in the immortality of the soul and teach that "the soul once delivered from the bonds of the flesh . . . will with joy fly up on high" (*Jewish War*, II, 8, 11). But as will be seen, there is much else that indicates that the Qumran community either was identical with the Essenes or was very close to them. Has Josephus then to some extent manipulated his report of the teaching of the Essenes in order to make it more understandable and perhaps more appreciated by Greek readers? Or is it not rather the case that a radical either/or in this matter is unrealistic? It appears most probable that Qumran embraced the hope of a new earth and a new Jerusalem, where eternal bliss would be the portion of the people of God, and at the same time experienced a union with God "here and now" which can be described as participation in the eternal world. This comes very near to the teaching of the Gospel of John concerning eternal life as something which the believer possesses already here but which at the same time belongs to another world in its consummation. But in the final analysis if the identification with the Essenes be correct, then the idea of the immortality of the soul still must be ascribed to Josephus' Hellenizing tendency.

5

Eschatology

It has been observed that according to the Qumran texts the course of the world is fixed by God and follows his plan. It has also been seen that it can be described as a battle between two powers or spirits, the good and the evil. But God's plan also includes an end to this conflict.[1] God has placed the two spirits side by side "until the appointed time and the new creation" (*'ad qēṣ neḥerāṣāh wa'ʻaśôt ḥᵃdāšāh;* ₁QS iv.25); or "until the last time" (*'ad qēṣ 'aḥᵃrôn;* ₁QS iv.16; the same term is found in ₁QpHab. vii.7). The expression "the end of days" also occurs (*'aḥᵃrît hay-yāmîm*) as a designation for the time when God will carry his plan for the world to its conclusion and lead the good to victory (₁QpHab. ii.5 f.; ix.6). This last term is well known from the Old Testament.

On the other hand, one term which is specific for the Dead Sea circle is *pᵉquddāh*, an ambiguous word, in itself neutral, but which can take on both positive and nega-

[1] Delcor, "L'eschatologie des documents de Khirbet Qumran," *RScRel* 26 (1952), 363-386; Daniélou, "Eschatologie sadocide et eschatologie chrétienne" in *Les Manuscrits de la Mer Morte* (Colloque de Strasbourg, 1955) (1957), pp. 111-125; O. A. Piper, "The 'Book of Mysteries' (Qumran I 27) A Study in Eschatology," *JR* 38 (1958), 95-106.

tive connotations so as to be translated "visitation" in either the sense of reward or punishment.[2] God has made for man two spirits "so that he may walk in them until the time of His visitation" ($_1$QS iii.18), it is said, and we have seen how the word connotes the act through which God rewards or punishes man according to his deeds ($_1$QS iv.6, 11). At the time of this visitation God will once and for all exterminate the evil ($_1$QS iv. 18). The expression seems to have been well known within Judaism; its Greek equivalent occurs in Wisdom 3:7 concerning the time when the righteous will receive their final vindication; and in Luke 19:44 concerning the time of God's "visitation" of Jerusalem. The Damascus Document also mentions a "visitation" which is to take place before the end time, since it distinguishes between "the first visitation," when the faithful were saved but the evil given over to the sword, and a final judgment when "the poor" who remained faithful will be saved and the evil destroyed (CD vii.9—viii.3; xix. 9-13). The first visitation is probably the destruction of Jerusalem in 587 B.C.

"Visitation" implies judgment, and this brings about the end of the present mixture of good and evil in the world. The evil will be destroyed: "On the day of judgment God will exterminate from the earth all those who serve idols, together with the sinners" ($_1$QpHab. xiii.2-4). On the other hand, for the good it is a time of salvation. Directly after the words concerning the extermination of the evil at the time of visitation the Manual of Discipline continues: "And then shall the

[2] Daniélou. "Eschatologie . . . ." *op. cit.*, pp. 115 f.

truth go forward in the world forever (or: to victory, *lānesaḥ*), for it has wallowed in the ways of wickedness in the dominion of error until the determined time of judgment which has been fixed. And then will God in His truth purify all the deeds of a man—and He will sprinkle him with a spirit of truth . . ." (₁QS iv.19-21). Strangely enough this does not seem to be a description of eternal blessedness but simply a description of deliverance such as is also encountered in a series of other passages. The explanation is probably that the community considered the end time to be at hand, so that deliverance is experienced already here and now in this world. The community itself is the beginning of the eschatological age.

This also makes understandable the role that the "elect" play in the events of the end time. According to ₁QS viii.6 f. the council of the community are "those who are chosen of God's good pleasure to provide atonement for the earth and to avenge the wicked." [3] And this is brought out clearly in the Habakkuk Commentary's interpretation of Habakkuk 1:12 f.: "This means that God will not destroy His people through the Gentiles, but into the hand of His elect God will give the judgment of all the Gentiles, and through their chastisement will the wicked among His people be punished; since they (the elect) kept His commandments when they were in distress" (v.3-6). In other words, the loyalty and obedience of the elect will be rewarded with the mission of carrying out God's judgment.

[3] Chamberlain, "Toward a Qumran Soteriology," *op. cit.*, pp. 311 f.

The Thanksgiving Psalms allude several times to God's judgment, but in most cases the texts are so damaged that a clear idea of how the course of events was conceived of can not be determined. Of the passages which Coppens [4] cites as referring to the end time and God's judgment (iii.1-18; iii.19-36; xvii.1-8; fr. 5-9, 11-13 and the two fragments $_1$Q35) in his interesting article on the piety of the psalmists of Qumran, it is actually only possible to read and interpret the two first mentioned; in the others only individual isolated words and phrases can be made out. To these passages, however, vi.29 ff. should be added, to which attention will be turned presently.

Thanksgiving Psalm iii.1-18 belongs to a very special context and should be dealt with in connection with the messianic concepts. On the other hand, iii.19-36 has played such a role in discussions concerning concepts of the destruction of the world in Qumran that it should be quoted in full or at least from line 25. After giving thanks for salvation and deliverance, the author refers to his human weakness, where he stands "in the region of wickedness"; then he continues:

And the soul of the poor man was in dread amidst great dismay,
and furious [5] destruction followed my steps
when all the traps of the pit were opened

[4] Coppens, "La Piété des Psalmistes à Qumrân," in *La Secte de Qumrân et les Origines du Christianisme. (Recherches Bibliques IV.)* (1959), pp. 149-161; see especially p. 157, n.1.

[5] The Hebrew, *madhēbāh*, is a word of unknown meaning which occurs in the Old Testament only in Isa. 14:4. The translation in the RSV, "insolent fury," reads *marhēbah*, now found also in the great Isaiah Scroll at Qumran ($_1$QIsa^a).

and all the snares of wickedness were stretched out
and the nets of the wretched upon the water,
when all the arrows of the pit flew and could not be
    diverted
and were shot without hope.
When the plummet falls according to (? Hebr. 'al)
    judgment
and the lot of wrath upon those who are forsaken
and the outpouring of indignation upon hypocrites
and the time of their blaze over all perdition (beliyya'al)
and the cords of death encompass without escape;
and torrents of perdition (of Belial) go over all the high
    banks
like a fire which devours all their shores [6]
and consumes all green and dry trees along their canals,
and advances with blazing flames,
until there are none who drink of them;
it devours the foundations of clay
and the expanse of dry land,
the foundations of mountains (yield) to burning,
and the roots of flint become torrents of pitch;
and it devours to the great deep,
and torrents of perdition (of Belial) burst into the abyss,
and the recesses of the deep clamor
with the noise of (waves) which stir up mire,
and the earth shrieks because of the destruction
which comes to pass (or: will come to pass) in the
    world,
and all its recesses cry out
and all who are on it lose their senses,
and they are dissolved in the great disaster;
for God thunders in the noise of His strength,
and His holy dwelling echoes with His glorious truth,

[6] This word is probably from the Persian, šināb; see: J. P. de
Menasce, "Un mot iranien dans les Hymnes," RQ 1 (1958/59).
133-134.

and hosts of heaven let their voice be heard,
the eternal foundations melt and tremble,
and the war of the heroes of heaven advances over the
  world
and turns not back
until the firmly decreed eternal devastation (has begun);
and there is nothing like it.

There is no doubt that the last lines of this psalm describe the final decision, God's intervention and the final
battle through which the evil are annihilated. But the
question is: where does this description begin? Where
is the transition from the description of the dangers and
the sufferings which the psalmist has to endure to the
description of the events of the final time? The obscure
sentence construction with a rather inconsistent alter-
nation of infinitives and imperfect finite verbs makes it
almost impossible to answer this question. Ever since
this psalm was first published it has been assumed that
at least the description of the stream of fire which anni-
hilates the foundations of the earth belongs to the
eschatological context, and that this indicates that under
the influence of Iranian ideas the Qumran congregation
expected the destruction of the world by fire (cf. also
II Pet. 3:10).

Now in the first place, it is clear that two of the
phrases that occur in the text are derived from Psalm
18:4 ("cords of death encompass" and "torrents of perdition [beliyya'al]"), that the idea of a devouring fire
is by no means foreign to the prophets of the Old Testament (e.g., Amos 1:4 and 7:4 where even "the great
deep" occurs); and also that a number of other ex-

pressions in the psalm are likewise dependent on Old
Testament passages (e.g., "green and dry trees," Ezek.
17:24). Still more important is the fact that torrents of
fire are not an instrument of God's punishment but *of
perdition* or, as the Hebrew expression shows, simply
Belial's torrents. Hence it seems more correct to take
the torrents of fire as an image of error's last gathering
of strength before the decisive battle. That this is connected with the suffering of the psalmist can signify
that he regards himself as living in the last days and in
his experiences sees a foreboding of the final battle. Then
it is only at the end of the psalm, in the words concerning man's despair and God's intervention, that there
is an allusion to the final judgment. In the suffering of
the last days there is a counterpart to what is otherwise
known in Judaism as the messianic birth pangs. It should,
however, be mentioned that the Habakkuk Commentary
knows of a judgment in fire: in x.4 f. it is said that God
will judge "the house of judgment" in fire of brimstone
—probably on the pattern of Sodom and Gomorrah (cf.
also Ezek. 38:22, Ps. 11:6)—and in x.12 f. it is said
that they who deride and revile the elect of God will
be subject to "judgments of fire." But this is obviously
something other than that which is referred to in the
Thanksgiving Psalm cited.

In this connection another Thanksgiving Psalm should
also be mentioned. In vi.17-19 it is said, apparently
alluding to the last days:

> . . . the source of light becomes an eternal spring,
> which does not run dry;

in the sparks from it will all the children [of error]
  burn,
[and it becomes] a fire, which consumes
all men of guilt even unto annihilation.

The mixture of images is strange: a spring (or: source)
and fire appear to us to be incompatible concepts, but if
it is recalled that the reference is to a source of *light*,
the whole thing becomes somewhat more understandable. The train of thought is quite reminiscent of Isaiah
10:17: "The light of Israel will become the fire, and his
Holy One a flame; and it will burn and devour his
thorns. . . ." It is God's light or, bearing in mind the
passage above, possibly rather the congregation of his
elect, which will destroy the children of darkness.

As has been noted, Thanksgiving Psalm vi.29-35 speaks
of the last great battle against the powers of error:

Then shall God's sword speedily come at the appointed
  time of judgment,
and all the children of His truth shall awaken
to put an end to [the children] of wickedness,
and there shall no longer be any children of guilt.
And the hero will stretch his bow
and undo the distress [7] [. . . . . .]
to a spacious place without end
and (open) the gates of eternity
to bring forth the weapons of war,
and they shall be strong
from one end (of the earth) even to the other,
[. . .] and there will be no deliverance
for the sinful inclination.
To annihilation shall they trample them down,
so that no re[mnant will be left

[7] The translation of this word is uncertain.

. . . .] hope in a great number of [. . .]
and there is no escape for all the heroes of war.
For to God the Most High belongs [the power and
strength,
. . . .],
and they who lie in the dust will raise a flagstaff
and the worms of the dead will lift up an ensign
|. . .] to exterminate [. . . .] in the wars of the pre-
sumptuous,
and the blow of the lashing whip shall not come into the
fortress.

That the reference here is to the eschatological final
battle is completely clear. God will intervene—it is probably also he who is meant in the words concerning
the hero who bends his bow—and all evil will be annihilated. One thing remains unclear: when it says that "the
children of His truth shall awaken" and that "they who
lie in the dust" shall arm themselves for battle, does this
mean that the dead will arise and participate in the
battle? This is not necessarily so. "To awaken" can be
used of any transition at all from inactivity to activity,
and "they who lie in the dust" can be a figurative expression for the members of the sect in their capacity of
being weak and oppressed people.

The belief in a coming final battle holds good in any
case, and the entire War Scroll deals with this battle.
The children of light, it says, will attack the children of
darkness, and the hosts of heaven will fight on their side.
The dominion of the Kittim shall disappear, wickedness
will be exterminated without a remnant and none of the
children of darkness shall escape (₁QM i.1, 6). But "that
is the time of salvation for the people of God and an

appointed epoch of dominion for all men of His lot, but
eternal annihilation for all the lot of Belial" (i.5). The
day when this will happen has been appointed (*yā'ûd*,
i.10) from of old, it is in other words included in God's
plan of the world. Three times shall the children of
light defeat the wicked, and three times shall Belial's
host drive back the children of light, but in the seventh
round (the original text uses the term for "lot") God
shall give his own the final victory (i.13-15).

Then a thirty-five year period of war service is spoken
of, which is divided into six years when "the whole
congregation together" "shall organize for battle," and
twenty-nine years, which are taken up with "the war
of the divisions" i.e., isolated war operations against different enemy peoples, carried out by only a part of the
whole force. Every seventh year will be a sabbatical
year when no war service will be performed. If the five
sabbatical years are added to the thirty-five service years
there is a total of forty years, a number that also occurs
in the Commentary on Psalm 37 where it says that the
wicked will be destroyed at the end of forty years.

It is not quite clear whether the six years are meant
as mobilization and arming years or whether they form
a part of the war itself. Yadin [8] assumes the latter and
finds that it is these six years when the whole force fights
together that are referred to in the beginning of column
i where there is mention of fighting against Edomites,
Moabites, Ammonites and Philistines (i.e., Israel's closest
enemies), the Kittim in Assyria and Egypt together with

[8] Yadin, *The Scroll of the War* . . . (1962), pp. 19 ff.; see also
MLS, pp. 348 ff.

"those who violate the Covenant," i.e., the enemies of the sect among their own people. He refers the seven phases to this first stage of the war.

The twenty-nine remaining years are carefully apportioned to different enemy nations according to the list of nations in Genesis 10; nine years against different Semitic nations, ten years against the sons of Ham and ten years against the descendants of Japheth.

Yadin points out that this division of the war has a certain counterpart in the rabbinic discussion concerning the final battle. In Genesis 15:18-21 there is a list of ten nations who will be conquered by Abraham's descendants. As a matter of fact, Israel succeeded in conquering only seven of these, and for this reason the rabbis concluded that the remaining three would be overthrown in the days of the Messiah. It appears that the first six years of the war of which the War Scroll speaks are devoted to precisely these seven nations, while the remaining twenty-nine years belong to the category of messianic war.

The rest of the War Scroll is devoted to a detailed description of the equipment and formation of the army. There is information as to how the trumpets should look and what is to be written upon them: watchwords and mottoes concerning God's might, etc. Similarly the standards, shields and arrows are to be furnished with mottoes and battle cries. Further there are regulations concerning the ages of the warriors and their physical perfection, concerning battle signals and the disposition of the army, etc. The priests play an important role and often appear in front of the line of battle with exhortations—to some extent based on Deuteronomy 20:2-4, Numbers 10:9, *et al.*—and prayers. A hymn of victory is also given; it provides a typical picture of the mood that dominates the book:

> Arise, O hero; take Thy captives, Thou man of glory,
> and take Thy booty, Thou who doest valiantly.
> Place Thy hand on the neck of Thine enemies
> and Thy foot upon the high places of the slain.
> Crush the nations, Thine enemies,
> and with Thy sword devour the guilt-laden.[9]
> Fill Thy land with glory and Thine inheritance with
>   blessing:
> abundance of cattle in Thy fields,
> silver and gold and precious stones in Thy palaces.
> Zion, rejoice greatly,
> and shine forth in shouts of joy, O Jerusalem,
> and be joyful, all ye cities of Judah.
> Open thy gates forever,
> that the wealth of all nations be brought to thee,
> and their kings shall serve thee,
> and all thine oppressors shall fall down before thee
> and lick the dust of thy feet.
>
> —₁QM xii.10-14

To a large extent this hymn is built upon Old Testament quotations,[10] and it gives an excellent picture of how Israel felt herself to be the chosen people and how the Qumran congregation felt itself to be the true Israel.

[9] Literally: guilty flesh.

[10] Among other quotations, the following occur in this passage: Judg. 5:12, Gen. 49:8, Deut. 33:29, Num. 24:8, Deut. 32:42, Ps. 48:11, Isa. 60:11, 10, 14; 49:23. Cf. the discussion of Old Testament quotations in the War Scroll by Carmignac, "Les citations de l'Ancien Testament dans 'La Guerre des fils de lumière contre les fils de ténèbres,'" *RB* 63 (1956), 234-260, 375-390.

The War Scroll has been called a "ritual for holy war at the end of days" (Molin), and this designation is certainly correct; it purposes to give instructions for the battle which will give the people of God the final victory over all enemies.

The eschatological concepts at Qumran are partly built on Old Testament and Jewish ideas which are already known, and partly on entirely new ones. The war against Gog from Magog is already mentioned in Ezekiel 38-39—"judgments upon Gog and all his congregation" is mentioned in ₁QM xi.16—and the holy war in the War Scroll is conceived of as a continuation of the holy war in ancient Israel. But these thoughts have been further shaped here in an original way. The difficult period of distress which precedes judgment corresponds to the messianic birth pangs, well known in apocalyptic literature (Jub. 20:11-15, II Esd. 5-6, cf. Matt. 24:8, Mark 13:8). The concept of a world conflagration is Iranian, but as has been noted the passages cited from Qumran hardly presuppose more than the Old Testament prophecies concerning a punishment by fire.

Whether a renewal of the world after the catastrophe was also conceived of is not clearly stated. Gaster finds the idea in ₁QH xi.13 f.: "to be renewed with everything that is and with those who have knowledge in the community of jubilation," but it is, unfortunately, far from clear what this renewal means; in any case it seems to refer to something which applies to the individual and not to the world as a whole. Perhaps ₁QH xiii.11 f. is somewhat more clear:

For Thou didst allow them to see that which no [flesh
has seen before],
to create new things,
to dissolve that which has been from times immemorial
and to [restore] that which has been from eternity.

Although the reconstructions in this section hardly yield
a sure text, this much is certain: that the reference to a
creation of something new alludes to Isaiah 43:19 and
48:6. Hence, in itself the passage could just as well refer
to God's power to carry out great and mighty works
the like of which have never before been seen. But this
does not exclude the possibility that here there may
actually be allusion to a destruction of the existing creation and the creation of a new world. Something similar
seems also to be implied in $_1$QS iv.25 where it says that
God has placed the two spirits side by side "until the
appointed time and the new creation" (*^{a}ṣ̂ôt ḥ^{a}dāšāh*).[11]
In other words, the dualistic order will remain until the
time which God has appointed for its destruction; then
God makes something new in its place.

Fragments from Caves 1, 4 and 5 seem to contain
descriptions of a new Jerusalem, and it has been assumed
that there were also directions concerning the way in
which God would be worshiped in the new temple.[12]
"The Blessings" ($_1$QSb) from Cave 1 also clearly mention priests who serve in an earthly temple.[13] Apparently

---

[11] E. Sjöberg, "Wiedergeburt und Neuschöpfung im palästinischen Judentum," *StTh* 4 (1950), 44-85; and Sjöberg, "Neuschöpfung in den Toten-Meer-Rollen," *StTh* 9 (1955), 135 ff.

[12] Perhaps the Angelic Liturgy mentioned above (p. 23) belongs
here.

[13] Cf. Laurin, "The Question of Immortality . . . ," *op. cit.*, pp.
352 f.

these ideas go back to the promise of new heavens and a new earth in Isaiah 65:17 and 66:22. Under these circumstances it is difficult to establish any clear traces of influence from Iranian ideas of the restoration of the world to its pristine good condition (*fraškart*). Such an influence would otherwise be natural in view of the similarities in the dualistic system in Qumran and Iran. Once again it seems that the Old Testament material, however, has played the strongest part and has determined the shaping of the ideas.

We have pointed out that the Qumran sect apparently considered itself to be living in the last days and that it awaited the final judgment as immediately imminent. Surely this is behind the Habakkuk Commentary's mention of "the last generation" (ii.7) and "the last epoch" (vii.2). But the Habakkuk Commentary also points out something else: this expectation has not been realized and it is necessary to seek an explanation for this. Thus the commentator explains that "the last time shall lengthen (or: shall be delayed) and will exceed everything that the prophets have said, since the mysteries of God are wonderful" (vii.7 f.). Therefore the children of truth should not slacken in their service "when the last time is delayed for them" (vii.10-12). Hence, what the congregation now experiences of difficulties and persecutions are not the end, but certainly are a preparation for it. "The end of days" (ix.6) shall surely come, and then shall the judgment fall upon all those who have resisted the truth ($_1$QpHab. vii.16; x.3-5, 12 f.; xii.5; xiii.3 f.).

THE MESSIAH

Messianic expectations [14] present a particular problem where eschatological concepts are concerned. Hence we must devote special attention to this question and in so doing be very careful not to read our own concepts into the Qumran texts, but interpret them from their own presuppositions. It is not necessary that there be "messianic" ideas each time the word "anointed" (*māšîaḥ*) occurs, nor is it certain that "Messiah" was always understood to mean exactly or even approximately the same thing that we with our Christian presuppositions put into the word.[15]

If the passages in which the word *māšîaḥ* occurs are examined, some may immediately be left out of the discussion since they clearly do not speak of a Messiah in a more precise meaning of the term. These are:

CD ii.12: (among them He raised up such as call upon His Name . . .) and He made them know—through the hand of His anointed (ones; i.e., those anointed by Him)

---

[14] See: A. S. van der Woude, *Die messianischen Vorstellungen der Gemeinde von Qumran* (1957); for further discussion see also: Schubert, "Die Messiaslehre in den Texten von Chirbet Qumran," *BZ* 1 (1957), 177-197; Brown, "The Messianism of Qumran," *CBQ* 19 (1957), 53-82; E. L. Ehrlich, "Ein Beitrag zur Messiaslehre der Qumransekte," *ZAW* 68 (1956), 234-343; J. Liver, "The Doctrine of the Two Messiahs in Sectarian Literature in the Time of the Second Commonwealth," *HTR* 52 (1959), 149-185; H. W. Kuhn, "Die beiden Messias in den Qumrantexten und die Messiasvorstellung in der rabbinischen Literatur," *ZAW* 70 (1958), 200-208; K. G. Kuhn, "The Two Messiahs of Aaron and Israel," in *SNT*, pp. 54-64 (revision of "Die beiden Messias Aarons und Israels," *NTS* 1 [1954/55], 168-180).

[15] Note Smith's warning about caution: M. Smith, "What Is Implied by the Variety of Messianic Figures?" *JBL* 78 (1959), 66-72.

with the Holy Spirit, and (through) His seers of truth—
their exact names.[16]

The plural form and the context show that here prophets
or men with some similar function are referred to. The
expression "anointed" is to be taken as an image of their
being endowed with the divine power of the Spirit:

> CD vi.1: . . . they have preached apostasy from God's
> commandments, which He has given through Moses and
> His holy anointed ones ($m^e\check{s}\hat{\imath}\underline{h}\hat{e}$ $qod\check{s}\hat{o}$), and they have
> prophesied falsehood.

Here again the reference is to the prophets.

A similar combination of Moses and the prophets,
although without the term "anointed" occurs in ₁QS
viii.15-16.

> ₁QM xi.7-8: And through Thine anointed ones, who see
> "testimonies" ($t^{e\cdot}\hat{u}d\hat{o}t$) (i.e., the things predestined), hast
> Thou made known to us [the epochs] for the wars of
> Thy hands.[17]

Here, too, it is a question of prophets. It should be
noted that "anointed ones" and "prophets" are found in
parallelism in Psalm 105:15.

But there are also passages which contain *truly messianic references:*

> CD xix.10-11: (The oppressed of the flock shall be de-
> livered in the time of visitation.) But those who shrink
> back shall be given over to the sword, when there shall
> come the anointed one (or ones?) of Aaron and Israel.

[16] For the reading and translation of this passage, see: Yadin,
"Three Notes on the Dead Sea Scrolls," *IEJ* 6 (1956), pp. 158 f.

[17] To this should be added the fragment, ₁Q 30, which mentions
a "holy messiah" ($me\check{s}\hat{\imath}a\underline{h}$ $\underline{h}aq$-$q\hat{o}de\check{s}$). Cf. CD vi.1, above, and
P. Winter, "The Holy Messiah," *ZNW* 50 (1959), 275.

Here it is obviously a question of something which will happen in connection with the last time and its visitation (*p*e*quddāh*). But the Hebrew text leaves some uncertainty as to whether one or two people are referred to:

> CD xx.1: . . . from the day when the unique teacher (or: the teacher of the community?)[18] was taken away, until an anointed one arises from Aaron and Israel.

> CD xii.23: (According to these rules shall one live) in the epoch of wickedness until there shall arise the anointed one (ones) of Aaron and Israel.

> CD xiv.19 is unfortunately damaged; but there appears to be mention of an "anointed one of Aaron and Israel."

Ever since the Damascus Document became known, the problem has been whether these passages refer to one or two messianic figures. The Hebrew text has the singular but the construction is such that it is entirely conceivable that the author could have meant two anointed ones, one priestly and one royal. This would be in agreement with what is taught in the Testaments of the Twelve Patriarchs (see below). A decision on this issue became possible when the Manual of Discipline was published. There it is said:

> 1QS ix.10-11: They shall be judged according to the first statutes by which the members of the community had begun to have themselves disciplined, until there shall come a prophet and the anointed ones of Aaron and Israel.

[18] The translation variants depend upon whether one reads *yāḥîd*, "only, unique" or whether it is emended to *yaḥad*, "oneness, community"; the former is the reading transmitted in the text; the latter would fit in well with the idea that *yaḥad* is the self-description of the community.

Here there is clear reference to three eschatological figures of which two are called "anointed ones." The anointed one of Aaron must be a priest, apparently a high priest; while the anointed one of Israel is the king:

4Q Patriarchal Blessings i.3-4: . . . until there shall come the anointed one of righteousness, the branch of David.

This must refer to the king, the anointed one of Israel.

The Two Column Fragment, 1QSa ii.11-12, 14, 20: These are (rules for) the meeting . . . when God causes the anointed one to be begotten [19] among them: [the priest] shall come at the head of (i.e., the foremost in) the whole congregation of Israel, (then) all the leaders of the sons of Aaron, the priests . . . and then the anointed one of Israel shall seat himself, and before him shall the commanders of Israel's thousands seat themselves. . . . And when they gather for the common table and to drink wine . . . no one may stretch out his hand to the first of the bread and the wine before the priest, for he shall bless the first of the bread and of the wine and first stretch out his hand to the bread. And then shall the anointed one of Israel stretch out his hand to the bread, and the whole congregation shall bless. . . .

[19] The reading of this phrase is much debated: with some emendation Gaster (*The Dead Sea Scriptures* [1956], p. 279) reads *yiwwāʿed* "(if the messiah) is present (among them)"; others read *yôlîk* "he causes (the messiah) to walk (with them)" (Milik); according to Smith: *yiwwāled*, (if a defect or a blemish) be begotten (= arise) (the Anointed Priest shall come with them [to judge about it] . . .): Smith, " 'God's Begetting the Messiah' in 1QSa," *NTS* 5 (1958/59), 218-224; see the discussion in *MLS*, pp. 300 ff. and Yadin, "A Crucial Passage in the Dead Sea Scrolls. 1QSa ii.11-17," *JBL* 78 (1959), 238-241. The reading *YWLYD* seems, however, to stand and the only probable vocalization for these consonants is *yôlîd*, "he caused to be born, begotten." See also Cross, *The Ancient Library of Qumran* (2nd ed., 1961), p. 87, note 67.

This apparently treats of a kind of "court ceremonial" for the last days, and it appears obvious that a priest, consequently the high priest, the anointed one of Aaron, will have the highest rank, and that the king, the anointed one of Israel, only comes in the second place.

In summary: When God one day renews the covenant with his people, two anointed ones shall arise, one high priest and one king; and of these the high priest has the higher rank. Whether one here understands the word "messiah" in the sense familiar to Christians, is of little consequence. The messianism at Qumran is apparently of a different kind, but for the Qumran congregation only this type of "messianism" was known.

As we have already suggested, this expectation of two anointed ones is not entirely unique; it is also found in the Testaments of the Twelve Patriarchs, and the most important passages will be cited for comparison:

T. Simeon 7:1 f.: (from Levi and Judah the salvation of God shall arise). For the Lord shall raise up from Levi as it were a high priest, and from Judah as it were a king . . .

T. Judah 21:1-3: . . . love Levi. . . . For to me the Lord gave the kingdom, and to him the priesthood, and He set the kingdom beneath the priesthood. To me He gave the things upon the earth; to him the things in the heavens.

In the Testament of Judah 24 the teaching concerning the two messiahs is introduced by an interpretation of Numbers 24:17, the oracle of Balaam concerning a star which shall come forth out of Jacob and the scepter which shall rise out of Israel. The star is the priestly Messiah and the scepter the royal Messiah. (As is well known, this oracle also plays an important role in the Damascus Document, although the application is somewhat different.) In the Testament of Levi 18:3 the messianic high priest is also represented as "the star." [20] Another Old Testament passage which could have been the basis of the idea of two anointed ones is Zechariah 4:14 which mentions two "sons of oil," i.e., "anointed ones" of which one is Zerubbabel and the other the high priest, Joshua. It is known that Zerubbabel had been hailed as Messiah by certain circles (Hag. 2:20-23), and everything points toward a revision of certain sections of Zechariah in order to make way for the high priest Joshua in his place (Zech. 6:9-14), after the messianic hopes centered on Zerubbabel had failed. Perhaps here may be a pointer toward the historical conditions required by the idea of the two anointed ones.[21]

There are also other facts that indicate that the teaching about two messiahs fits in quite well with the post-exilic expectations for the future. As early as in Ezekiel rights of "the prince" have been limited, to the priests' advantage (34:23; 37:25; 44; 45). Similarly the high position of the priests is emphasized in Sirach 45:6-24. But it is not until the Testaments of the Twelve Patriarchs and in Qumran that the teaching is systematically developed.

[20] Concerning the two anointed ones in the Testaments of the the Twelve Patriarchs, see among others, Schubert, "Zwei Messiasse aus dem Regelbuch von Chirbet Qumran," *Judaica* 11 (1955), 216-235; and Schubert, "Testament Juda 24 im Lichte der Texte von Chirbet Qumran," *WZKM* 53 (1957), 227-236.

[21] Cf. Schubert, "Der alttestamentliche Hintergrund der Vorstellung von den beiden Messiassen im Schrifttum von Chirbet Qumran," *Judaica* 12 (1956), 24-28.

When the Hasmonaeans as priests also assumed the royal title, many protested (Josephus, *Antiquities* XIII, 11.1; XIV, 3.2) and in the Psalms of Solomon 17:4-6 an echo of this protest can still be heard.

That the first place is given to the priests may be connected with the fact that the sect had built on traditions which had been fostered in priestly circles.

The three eschatological figures found in the Manual of Discipline, i.e., the prophet and the two anointed ones will now be discussed somewhat more closely.

The Prophet [22]

The expectation of a prophet who would come in the last days is based on Deuteronomy 18:18 ("I will raise up for them a prophet like you from among their brethren; and I will put my words in his mouth . . ."). In its original context this saying most probably alludes to any prophet whom Yahweh causes to arise; the use of the quotation at Qumran for the eschatological prophet is well in keeping with Jewish scriptural interpretation. In the post-exilic period the activity of the prophets diminished; instead of prophetic revelation the *tôrāh*, Law, was more emphasized; and the place of the prophets was taken by the scribes, *sop^erîm*. The Talmud even states that after Haggai, Zechariah and Malachi, the last prophets, had died, the Holy Spirit had ceased to be active in Israel (b. Soṭah 48b). But the Law is from heaven (b. Sanh. 99a). In the Syriac Apocalypse of Baruch

---

[22] J. Giblet, "Prophétisme et attente d'un Messie prophète dans l'ancien Judaïsme," in *L'Attente du Messie* (*Coppens Festschrift*) (1954), pp. 85-130.

(85:3-4) it says that no longer are there any prophets: "We have nothing now save the Mighty One and His Law."

According to the rabbinic teaching, everything is already found in the Law; the prophets have not added anything as to its substance. From this it finally followed that the learned became more important than the prophets and superseded them. "After the destruction of the temple prophecy was taken from the prophets and given to the wise" (b. Ber. 34b). But the hope remains that in the age to come in accordance with Joel 2:28 f. *all* shall prophesy (b. Baba Metzia 59b).

Despite this, however, popular circles cherished the hope that a prophet would come and decide difficult halakhic questions. Thus, for example, it was narrated in I Maccabees 4:45-46 that the altar of burnt offering which had been profaned was torn down and the stones laid aside "until there should come a prophet to tell what to do with them." And according to I Maccabees 14:41 Simeon is made leader and high priest "until a trustworthy prophet should arise." Thus a prophet is awaited who would be able to say the decisive word in troublesome questions, a prophet like Moses; and his appearance is in some way connected with the messianic age.

In the apocalyptic literature this expectation is concentrated on an Elijah *redivivus* (who would return) according to Malachi 4:5 f. (Hebrew Bible 3:23 f.; cf. Sir. 48:10 f., I En. 89:52, 90:31). Jeremias [23] thinks that in certain respects Elijah is a messianic figure but many

---

[23] J. Jeremias, "Hēl(e)ías," in *Theol. Wörterb. z. N.T.*, II, pp. 930-943.

scholars contest this view. On the other hand it is known from the New Testament that the people often regarded Jesus or John the Baptist as the prophet or Elijah (John 1:21, Matt. 11:9-14, 16:14)—but in any case here neither Elijah nor the prophet is identical with the Messiah.

The witness of the Qumran writings concerning the expectation of a prophet also belongs in this stream of popular ideas. To a certain extent the Teacher of Righteousness is also to be regarded as such a prophet since, according to $_1$QpHab. ii.5 ff., vii.3-5 he is the one who brings the decisive interpretation of the Holy Scriptures. But $_1$QS ix.11 clearly speaks of a prophet who belongs to the future, and employs the usual term *nābi'* for him. It appears from the context in this passage that he will settle questions which are not clearly elucidated in the Law.

A particularly troublesome passage is CD vii.18-21:

> The Star (in Num. 24:17) is the searcher of the Law (*dôrēš hat-tôrāh*) who came (comes, will come)[24] to Damascus, as it is written: "A star shall come forth out of Jacob, and a scepter shall rise out of Israel"; the Scepter is the prince of all the congregation, and when he arises, he shall strike all the sons of Seth.

Giblet sees in this searcher of the Torah the prophet who appears as the forerunner of the royal Messiah; Schubert interprets him as the priestly messiah.[25] "The Prince of the Congregation" is probably in any case the royal messiah. The Florilegium from Cave 4 also speaks of a

---

[24] The text has a participle which can mean either "comes," "came," or "will come."

[25] Schubert, "Die Messiaslehre . . . ," *op. cit.*, p. 182.

searcher of the Law, who will appear together with the Branch of David—these are probably the two anointed ones. In the Damascus Document, on the other hand, the "searcher of the Law" seems to have already come (cf. CD vi.7). Possibly three different persons are referred to here and the "searcher of the Law" is rather a title than the name of a particular individual.

The Messiah of Aaron.[26]

In addition to the passages just cited which directly employ this term for the high priest of the last days, two sections have just been mentioned which probably refer to the same figure: CD vii.18-21 which interprets the Star in Numbers 24:17 as a "searcher of the Law" and the so-called Florilegium from Cave 4 where to an abbreviated reference to II Samuel 7:11-14 (Nathan's prophecy concerning the Davidic kingship) is added the explanation: "This is the Branch of David, who will appear together with the searcher of the Law, who will arise in Zion at the end of days." From this it seems clear that the two messianic figures will appear simultaneously. In the so-called Two Column Fragment (The Rule of the Congregation), as has been pointed out above, there is mention of a priest who in the new age has a higher rank than "the Anointed One." It is very probable that here, too, it is a question of the priestly messiah.

[26] Schubert, "Die Messiaslehre . . . ," op. cit., pp. 181 ff.; J. Gnilka, "Die Erwartung des messianischen Hohenpriesters in den Schriften von Qumran und im Neuen Testament," RQ 2 (1959/60), 395-426; cf. also G. Friedrich, "Beobachtungen zur messianischen Hohenpriestererwartung in den Synoptikern," ZThK 53 (1956), 265-311.

In the so-called Blessings ($_1$QSb) ii.1 ff. a blessing of the high priest is given and it appears probable that it deals with the priestly messiah. Unfortunately only the beginning of some lines of column ii are preserved, but some allusions are nevertheless clear. There is repetition several times of the blessing, "may He be gracious to thee" (cf. Num. 6:25 and $_1$QS ii.3), in line 24 "holy spirit and grace" are mentioned, and further on "an eternal covenant" and "a judgment of righteousness." In iii.1-3 priestly sacrifice is mentioned, but in the following lines some messianic features appear: iii.5 "eternal peace and kingship . . ." (cf. Isa. 9:6 f.), iii.7 "may he fight at the head of Thy thousands," iii.18 f. "bring many nations under Thy dominion . . . riches of the world . . . ." Then a blessing of the priests, "Zadok's sons" follows, iii.22 ff., iv.1 ff. to iv.22 where again it seems to refer to the high priest:

He has chosen thee to stand at the head of the holy ones and to bless Thy people . . . through thee the men of God's council and not through princes. . . . And thou art as an angel of the Presence in the holy dwelling to the glory of the God of hosts . . . and thou shalt be a faithful (?) servant in the temple of the Kingdom and one who shares (or: casts) the lot with the angels of the Presence and the council of the community . . . for ever and for eternal ages. For [all] His judgments [are truth]. And may He make thee something holy among this people and a [great] light (or: luminary, *mā'ôr*) which [illuminates] the world with knowledge and enlightens the face of many [. . . .] diadems (or: consecrated?) for the Holy of Holies, for thou shalt be holy unto Him and glorify His name and His holiness.

—$_1$QSb iv.22-28

The first editors thought that this referred to priests in general but in that case it would also apply in a very high degree to the high priest: he will serve in the Holy of Holies in the temple of the New Jerusalem and have fellowship with the angels and be a light for the world.

Brownlee [27] has associated this passage with a puzzling section of the Manual of Discipline, where the letters *'ālep, mēm* and *nûn* (which together make up the word "amen") are introduced into the text in a mysterious way:

> . . . bless Him at the times which (the) L(ord)—[*'ālep* is probably an abbreviation for *'ᵃdônāy* here]—has ordained: at the beginning of the dominion of light and its course and at its in-gathering to its ordained dwelling . . . when they are renewed; *m* is large for the Holy of Holies and the sign *n* is for the opening of His eternal grace. . . .
>
> —₁QS x.1-4

The section deals with the various times for prayer and has by reason of its obscurity invited a great number of more or less ingenious interpretations.[28] Brownlee thinks that *h-m gādôl* in ₁QSb is an abbreviation for *ham-mā'ôr hag-gādôl*, the great light, which in Genesis 1:16 is the sun; and he points out that ₁QH fr. ii.11 f. seems to speak of a light (*mā'ôr*) which God has revealed and which will have the effect of banishing darkness forever —though the context is so broken that it is not possible

---

[27] Brownlee, "Messianic Motifs of Qumran and the New Testament," *NTS* 3 (1956/57), pp. 198 ff.

[28] Among other interpretations, see: Dupont-Sommer, "La sainteté du signe 'noun' dans le Manuel de Discipline," *Bulletin de l'Académie royale de Belgique, Classe des Lettres* (1952), pp. 184-193; and R. Goossens, "L'énigme du signe *nun* dans le Manuel de Discipline," *Nouvelle Clio* 6 (1954), 5-39.

to decide whether here it really refers to a person. But
if "the large M" really is the same as "the great light"
in the Blessings, it would also be a messianic title and
"the sign n" might mean *nēzer* "crown, diadem" a word
which also occurs in the Blessings.

Brownlee draws attention to the fact that something
similar occurs in the Jewish messianic prayer *Yoşer*,
which probably was of Essene origin. The reason for
its occurrence precisely here in the Manual of Discipline
would be that at this point there is reference to hours of
prayer and festivals, i.e., precisely the occasions when
the priest officiates in the temple. Since the Essenes did
not have access to the temple, it must refer to an eschatological ministry. Thus this also refers to a figure of
the same kind as the new priest in the Testament of Levi
18:2 ff., who is designated as "Star" and who is expected
to open the gates of Paradise (cf. the opening of His
grace, ₁QS x.4). These last words are reminiscent of
₁QH vii.20-21 where the author expresses something
similar concerning himself—but still it could hardly mean
that he considers himself to be the priestly messiah. An
archiereús christós, an "anointed high priest" is also
promised in the Testament of Reuben 6:8.

Finally, it should also be considered whether the chief
priest in the War Scroll who plays an important role
as leader in the War (ii.1; xv.4; xvi.13; xviii.5; xix.11)
might not also be the priestly messiah. It should be
noted that he does not directly take part in the battle;
he is too holy for this.

Nothing of that which has been learned about the
priestly messiah is in any way sensational. He is simply

the high priest of the last days, and he exercises all the priestly functions of such a figure. But as priest he has precedence over the king, his "co-messiah."

The Messiah of Israel [29]

Aside from the passages cited above there is little said concerning a messiah of Israel. However, it is probably he who is referred to with the title "prince of the congregation" ($n^c\acute{s}\hat{\imath}$ $h\bar{a}$-'$\bar{e}d\bar{a}h$) in ₁QSb v.20 ff. (the term also occurs in CD vii.20; ₁QM v.1). The text is worth quoting:

> (in order that he may . . . .) his [. . .] and renew for Him a covenant of unity to restore the kingdom of His people forever and [to judge the poor with righteousness and with equ]ity, to administer justice to the meek of the earth and to walk blamelessly before Him in all [. . .] ways and to restore His holy covenant with all those who seek Him:
>
> May the Lord exalt thee to an eternal height and (make thee) like a strong tower with a high wall, and [mayest thou smite the people] with the might of thy mouth. With thy rod mayest thou lay waste the earth, and with the breath of thy lips mayest thou slay the wicked, and with a spirit of counsel and eternal might, a spirit of knowledge and the fear of God, and may righteousness be the girdle of thy loins and faithfulness the girdle of thy waist, and may He make thy horns of iron and thy hoofs of brass to gore as a bull [. . .] and that thou mayest trample down the peoples like mud of the streets, for God has established thee as a scepter of rulers [. . . . . . .], and all nations shall serve thee, and with His Holy Name shall He make thee strong. And thou shalt be as a li[on . . .] prey and no one takes it back. . . .

[29] Schubert, "Die Messiaslehre . . . ," *op. cit.*, pp. 184 ff.

That this prince is the messianic king is clear from several observations:

1) He has the gifts which according to the prophecy in Isaiah 11:1-5 belong to the messiah (lines 24-26).

2) The final words clearly allude to Genesis 49:9 and this passage receives a messianic interpretation in the Patriarchal Blessings:

> The ruler shall not depart from the tribe of Judah as long as Israel has dominion, neither shall one who sits on the throne of David be uprooted. For the ruler's staff is the covenant of the kingdom, Israel's thousands are the feet (an explanation of Genesis 49:10: "nor the ruler's staff from between his feet"), until the Anointed One of righteousness, the Branch of David, comes, for to him and his seed has been given the covenant of His people's kingdom for eternal generations. . . .

3) All nations shall serve him (line 28), cf. Numbers 24: 17 f.—there are also reminiscences of Isaiah 60:10-14.

Hence, this messianic king will be of the lineage of David, he will be "a branch (*ṣemaḥ*) of David"—Isaiah 11:1 has a similar expression: "a branch (*nēṣer*) from the roots of Jesse." The same term occurs in the Florilegium in a messianic context: David's booth is fallen, but the branch of David will come to restore it and save Israel. According to CD vii.20 he will annihilate all the rebellious and, as is clear from the context, restore David's kingdom.

A close parallel is afforded by the Testament of Judah 24 in which the Davidic messiah will judge the nations and save those who seek God. Moreover, similar ideas are also encountered in a Commentary on Isaiah from Cave

4, where it says that "the Branch of David, who will arise at the end of days . . . will rule over all the gentiles [. . .], and his sword will judge all nations." This is in line with the War Scroll's program of fighting against all the gentiles and destroying them.

To a certain extent it can be said that it is this messianic figure who most closely is a continuation of the messianic expectations of the Old Testament. But his activity is purely political. The features of a different nature which are found in the messianic prophecies of the Old Testament have disappeared or perhaps rather have been transferred to the priestly messiah.

It has been suggested that it is this double messianic expectation which is the basis of the argumentation of the Epistle to the Hebrews. If two Anointed Ones were expected, then Jesus could not be the fulfillment of the prophecy. Therefore the author of the Epistle strives to show that Jesus was not only the royal Messiah but also the great high priest.[30] The idea is attractive, but it is probably still too soon to give a definitive verdict.

THE TEACHER OF RIGHTEOUSNESS [31]

One of the most difficult questions in the messianology of the Qumran sect concerns the Teacher of Righteousness: is he to be understood as one of the three eschatological figures just mentioned or is he a fourth person? If he is identical with "the unique teacher" in CD xx.1,

[30] Yadin, et al.; see below, p. 248.
[31] Dupont-Sommer has written several works on this subject, among others: The Dead Sea Scrolls, A Preliminary Survey, op. cit.; The Jewish Sect of Qumran, op. cit.; see also, F. F. Bruce, The Teacher of Righteousness in the Qumran Texts (1957).

then it is immediately apparent that he is neither the prophet nor one of the two Anointed Ones. Further, it is clear from $_1$QS ix.11 that these three figures pertain to the future. But the Teacher of Righteousness has already appeared and was perhaps already dead when the Habakkuk Commentary was written. But where then is the Teacher to fit into the eschatological time-table? Or perhaps, rather: what is his role, his function; how was his activity interpreted?

The task of the Teacher is to explain the words of the prophets ($_1$QpHab. ii.8 f.; vii.4 f.); according to the Commentary on Psalm 37 he built a congregation of the elect of God, which presumably means that he founded or at least organized the Qumran community ($_4$QpPs. 37 ii.16).[32] From the same source it appears that he was a priest (line 15). The task of interpreting scriptures is to a certain extent a prophetic task, and he is called the Teacher of Righteousness in order to stress the contrast with lying and false prophets (the man of the lie, the preacher of the lie). The title was chosen in order to show that he fulfills the words of the prophecy, and it was probably interpreted as "the true teacher," "he who teaches correctly and accurately and truthfully."

Dupont-Sommer and others think that the Teacher was called bāḥîr, the "chosen one," and that this title is to be taken as a messianic epithet.[33] In $_1$QpHab. v.4

[32] This is doubted by van der Woude; cf. "Die messianischen Vorstellungen . . . ," op. cit., p. 127.
[33] Dupont-Sommer, in the Acta of the Orientalist Congress in Istanbul, 1951; cf. also Delcor, "L'eschatologie . . . ," op. cit., pp. 363 ff.

f. it is said that God will give the judgment of all the
nations into the hand of "His chosen one" (BḤYRW).
In the same text ix.12 it reads that the wicked priest will
be punished since he has done evil against "His chosen
one" (BḤYRW). The word interprets an expression
which is plural in the Habakkuk Commentary. In the
Ethiopic Book of Enoch the "chosen one" is a messianic
title. Consequently, according to Dupont-Sommer, the
Teacher is a messianic figure.

But in another passage, ₁QpHab. x.13 f. it says that
the followers of the prophet of the lie will be judged
since they have reviled God's chosen ones. The plural
is also found in I Enoch, alluding to the people of God.
In ₁QS viii.6 and ix.14 the congregation is called "the
chosen ones." It is probable that in the two passages in
the Habakkuk Commentary the plural forms also were
intended, although the orthography is not that which
is normal to biblical Hebrew.[34] Hence, the Teacher is
not "the chosen one," neither is he a messiah so described.

The Teacher of Righteousness has died ("been taken
away": CD xx.1); perhaps he suffered martyrdom.[35]
Dupont-Sommer, Rabin and others think that it was
expected that he would return as "one who teaches
righteousness at the end of days" (CD vi.10-11).[36] The
question is: how much can be built upon the similarity
of terminology. It is not explicitly said that it is the

[34] Cf. Mansoor, "Some Linguistic Aspects . . . ," op. cit., p. 49.
[35] This is the opinion of Dupont-Sommer, "Le Maître de Justice
fut-il mis à mort?" VT 1 (1951), 200-215.
[36] See the works of Dupont-Sommer cited above (The Dead
Sea Scrolls, A Preliminary Survey, op. cit., chap. 3; et passim);
Rabin, Qumran Studies (1957), p. 74.

Teacher who is to return; and if this had been a basic
doctrine then it ought also to have found some expression. It is certain that it refers to a figure who is to
come but it could equally well allude to the prophet or
the priestly messiah or to a new Teacher who need not
be identical with the first one.

The passages in the Habakkuk Commentary which
Dupont-Sommer interprets as referring to the return of
the Teacher must certainly be interpreted in some other
way and they do not allude at all to any returning
messiah.[37]

What, then, is the Teacher's task? Precisely to teach,
to instruct, to make known the mysteries of God. According to CD i.11 f., "he leads them in the ways of
God's heart." Is he a savior? According to the Micah
Commentary from Cave 1, he gives saving knowledge so
that the chosen ones, who listen to him, are delivered
from judgment (provided the editors' reconstructions
are fairly correct). According to ₁QpHab. viii.2 f. God
will save from the judgment those who observe the Law
for the sake of their tribulation and their faithfulness
to (or: faith in?) the Teacher of Righteousness. The
passage interprets the prophetic words: "The righteous
shall live by his faith," but it seems probable that the
interpreter has understood the word 'emûnāh in its meaning of "faithfulness," "loyalty." In any event, it says
this: that the stand taken toward the Teacher by the
people in question has meaning for their fate in the

[37] For a more detailed discussion, see: Carmignac, "Le retour du
Docteur de Justice à la fin des jours?" *RQ* 1 (1958-59), 235-248.

judgment; but it can hardly be said that the Teacher delivers those who believe in him.

We could go somewhat further if we could understand the Thanksgiving Psalms as the work of the Teacher and much speaks for this.[38] In that case we could make the following observations:

We need not repeat the numerous passages which treat of the possession of a higher knowledge.[39] But it is important to call attention to the fact that this knowledge is not only for the psalmist himself but it applies to the many: "Through me hast Thou illumined the faces of the many" ($_1$QH iv.27). And his proclamation has a decisive meaning for his hearers:

> I became a snare for the transgressors,
> and healing for those who repent of transgression,
> prudence for the simple
> and a steadfast mind for all the timid. . . .
> But thou hast made me as a banner for the chosen ones
>   of righteousness
> and an interpreter of knowledge concerning the won-
>   drous mysteries
> in order to test [those who seek] truth
> and to put to the test those who love chastisement.
>   —$_1$QH ii.8-9, 13-14 [40]

Hence the stand they take with respect to his proclamation is of decisive meaning to the hearers. He becomes a snare or a healing according to their attitude toward the truth; thus, their true selves are tested through him and his action.

[38] See above, pp. 15 f.
[39] See above, pp. 114 ff.
[40] This section is treated by Michaud, "À propos d'un passage des Hymnes ($_1$Q Hôdâyôt, II, 7-14)," *RQ* 1 (1958/59), 413-416.

The same idea is expressed even more clearly in the following section:

For my lips silence the lips of falsehood,
and all who attack me Thou dost condemn in judgment
in order that through me Thou dost separate righteous
   and wicked. . .
And Thou didst make me as a father for the children of
   grace
and as a foster father for the men of wonder.
—¬QH vii.11-12, 20-21

Hence man's stand with regard to the Teacher determines his place among the righteous or the wicked. The last section is reminiscent of Numbers 11:12 where something similar is said of Moses. Thus the Teacher is in a way a new Moses [41]—as was also the case with the prophet.

An interesting text is the psalm which makes up the major portion of column viii of the Thanksgiving Psalms; it is, unfortunately, rather badly damaged, but on the whole its train of thought can be made out.[42] The whole psalm is obviously a parable or allegory in which two kinds of trees are contrasted with each other: the "trees of life" which form an "eternal plantation" or a "plantation of truth," and "trees by the water" (the phrase is taken from Ezekiel 31:14) which grow high and try to

[41] On this point, see also: Schubert, "Die jüdischen und judenchristlichen Sekten im Lichte des Handschriftenfundes von 'En Fešcha," ZkathTheol 74 (1952), 39 f.; Black, "Servant of the Lord and Son of Man," ScJTh 6 (1953), 7; Wieder, "The 'Law-Interpreter' of the Sect of the Dead Sea Scrolls: The Second Moses," JJS 4 (1953), 158-175.

[42] See Ringgren, "The Branch and the Plantation in the Hodayot," Bibl. Res. 6 (1961), 2-8.

force out the trees of life. The trees of life and the eternal plantation are either Israel or the Qumran community as the true Israel; the trees by the water are the evil world. A number of prophetic passages concerning "streams in the desert" and trees which are planted have been used, and there is also reference to the story of the garden of Eden, the entrance to which is blocked by "flames of a fire which blazes" (a clear allusion to Genesis 3:24)—it seems that the meaning is that those who do not belong do not gain access to the mystery which the "plantation of truth" secretly possesses, i.e., the saving knowledge. In this context and still dependent on the images used in what was said before, the psalmist then speaks of himself:

> But thou, my God, hast put in my mouth as it were early
>   morning rain,
> rain for all the [thirsty? children of men?]
> and a spring of living water that will not fail,
> to open streams that will not cease;
> and they shall become an overflowing river [bursting
>   over the banks] of water,
> and seas without measure;
> suddenly they burst forth, (long) hidden in secret,
> [. . . . . .]
> and turn into waters [sweeping away] every green and
>   dry tree,
> and into a deep for all the living (or: beasts)
> [and the trees by the water shall sink as] lead in the
>   mighty waters,
> [. . . .] and a fire (?) and they will dry up.
> But the plantation of the fruit [of truth . . . .] an ever-
>   lasting spring (?)
> into a glorious delight and a cr[own of beauty].
>   —₁QH viii.16-20

The teaching of the psalmist is as lifegiving rain to men who thirst after salvation, that much is clear; and in what follows he apparently means to say that its effect grows into a flood in which everything except the good plantation is swept away and which finally destroys all the disobedient—but the details remain unclear.

The psalmist continues:

> And it was by my hand that thou didst open their source
> and [their] channels,
> [. . . .] to clear with a true measuring line
> and the plantation of their trees with a "sun level"
> for the [. . .] of its foliage and glorious boughs.
>
> —₁QH viii.20-22

In other words, the psalmist is the gardener who cultivates the soil and waters God's plantation so that it flourishes and bears fruit. The decisive role which his work plays for this plantation appears in the following lines:

> When I move my hand to dig furrows,
> its roots strike even into the flinty rock,
> and they [plant] their stocks [firmly] in the earth,
> and in the time of heat the source retains (water?).
> But if I turn back my hand,
> it becomes like a shrub in the desert
> and its stocks like nettles in a salt-marsh,
> and its furrows yield thorns and thistles,
> it [turns to] briers and brambles,
> [and the trees at] its border become like worthless trees;
> before the heat its leaves fade,
> and its [stock] is not exposed [to the spring].
>
> —₁QH viii.22-26

As long as the psalmist carries out his activity, the roots

of the plantation penetrate deep down and have strength
even to stand the heat and dryness of summer; in other
words the community is in a state of spiritual well being
and can endure in all difficulties; but if he stops his
work, it is handed over to the forces of death and darkness—for it is these which are illustrated with the many
images of the desert's barren growth which the writings
of the prophets have furnished. If the psalmist is identified with the Teacher of Righteousness, it may be concluded that the spiritual weal or woe of the community
are entirely dependent on the activity of the Teacher.
And it is a question as to what other leader in the community could have emerged with such a claim.

The psalmist was chosen for his extraordinary task
already from the womb:

> For Thou didst know me (ever since I came forth)
>   from my father,
> and from the womb [didst Thou . . . me]
> and from my mother's body hast Thou dealt bounti-
>   fully with me,
> and from my mother's breast is Thy mercy toward me,
> and in my nurse's bosom [have I rejoiced in Thy
>   grace?]
> and from my youth hast Thou shone before me with the
>   might of Thy justice,
> and with dependable truth hast Thou sustained me,
> and through Thy holy Spirit hast Thou delighted me,
> and unto this day hast Thou [led] me.
>
> —1QH ix.29-32

To be chosen from the womb is in the ancient Near East
a distinctive attribute of a king; but in the Old Testament the same is also said of a prophet such as Jeremiah

(Jer. 1:5) and of the Servant of the Lord in Isaiah 49:1. In the context here in the Thanksgiving Psalm it is very uncertain as to whether any royal or messianic feature is intended. It is almost more probable that the whole passage is meant to describe the unfailing fulfillment of divine predestination through all stages of the life of the psalmist-teacher: all that has happened to him from his very first beginnings until now stands under the sign of the divine election.

A puzzling section which has played a definite role in discussions concerning messianic ideas is the first half of column iii of the Thanksgiving Psalms.[43] The beginning is damaged, so that the context is not entirely clear. The psalmist first says that the enemies counted him as nothing and set his soul in a ship on the depths of the sea, or, with a slight change of a preposition, made his soul *as* a ship on the deep sea and as a fortress before [the enemies]; then the psalmist continues:

> And I came in anguish
> as a woman who brings forth her first born.
> When (her) birth pangs come
> and horrible pains upon the mouth of her womb
> to give birth to the first born of her who is pregnant.
> For sons come to death's breakers (or: the mouth of
>   the womb),

[43] Chamberlain, "Another Qumran Thanksgiving Psalm," *JNES* 14 (1955), 32-41; Chamberlain, "Further Elucidation of a Messianic Thanksgiving Psalm from Qumran, *ibid.,* pp. 181 f.; Dupont-Sommer, "La mère du Messie et la mère de l'Aspic dans un hymne de Qoumrân," *RHR* 147 (1955), 174-188; Delcor, "Un Psaume messianique de Qumran" in *Mélanges Bibliques . . . A. Robert, op. cit.,* pp. 334-340; Betz, "Die Geburt der Gemeinde durch den Lehrer," *NTS* 3 (1956/57), 314-326; G. Hinson, "Hodayot, III, 6-18: In What Sense Messianic?" *RQ* 2 (1959/60), 183-204.

and she who is pregnant with a man is tormented in her
    birth pangs.
Since through the breakers of death she is delivered of a
    man child,
and through the bands (or: birth pangs) of Sheol he
    bursts forth out of the womb of the pregnant one,
"wonderful counselor," with his strength
and a man is delivered out of the breakers (mouth of
    the womb),
In his mother all the breakers cause pain,
and horrible pains at their birth
and fear to their mothers,
and at his birth come all birth pangs in the womb of the
    pregnant one.

—1QH iii.7-12

The following lines speak of one who is pregnant with
'*ep'ēh* a word which in the Old Testament means "viper,"
but in Qumran seems to have been used in a figurative
sense for evil and wickedness (according to some
scholars it might be the same as '*epa'* or "nothingness,"
which, however, seems less probable). She gives birth,
and it is described how the waves roar and swell and
finally it is said that "the gates of Sheol shall open for
all doings of vipers, and the doors of the grave shall
be closed around her who is pregnant of evil, and eternal
bars around all spirits of vipers" (iii.17-18).

Apparently a contrast is intended between "she who is
pregnant of a man (*geber*)" and "she who is pregnant
of a viper," but who are these two women and who is
"the man"? It has been suggested that *geber* might be
a messianic title and that the woman who gives birth to
the Messiah—and who is reminiscent of the woman in
Revelation 12—might be Israel. In support of this mes-

sianic interpretation the clear allusions to Isaiah 9:6 are further quoted ("Wonderful Counselor, Mighty God"—the word for "mighty" has the same root as the word for "strength" in the psalm). Yet it is still difficult to fit the messianic interpretation to the context of the psalm. If the author is the Teacher-Messiah, why then should he say: "I came in anguish *as* a woman in child-bed," if the one to bear a child gave birth to him, i.e., the Messiah? It appears more suitable to take the whole passage as a description of the Teacher's travail when he founded his community—this is *compared* with the agony of a woman in childbirth (and here Jeremiah 4:31, 6:24 could have served as a pattern); and once the comparison is made, the author continues in true Semitic style to paint his picture without all the details having to have their application in reality.

What makes the psalm so difficult to understand—and still more difficult to translate—is the fact that it uses double meanings of two Hebrew words to put across its imagery: *mišbārîm* "breakers, waves," which also can be read *mašbēr*, "mouth of the womb"; and the other, the construct form *ḥeblê* "bonds, cords" which can also mean "birth pangs"; both words occur in their more usual meaning in descriptions of distress in Psalm 18:5, 6 with its parallel in II Samuel 22:5-6. But these double associations are lost as soon as the psalm is translated into any other language.

Naturally, a special problem is the identification of the second woman who is to give birth. It seems probable that she in some way symbolizes the opponents of the sect; but whether this is the more orthodox form of Judaism or evil in general can hardly be decided. (It may be recalled that John the Baptist called the Pharisees "brood of vipers"). A closer discussion of this question would, however, lead us away from messianism and the position of the Teacher.

The interpretation given of Thanksgiving Psalm iii brings us, however, to a new problem: If the psalm describes the distress which is connected with the formation and origin of the community, how then can the community as such be identified with the Messiah—Wonderful Counselor? This can be answered partly by saying that the interpretation of "Wonderful Counselor" as a messianic title seems to be Christian—in Jewish exegesis the expression alludes to God—and also partly that the community is also elsewhere credited with the functions which more usually would be expected of an individual. One of these cases has to do with messianic expectations and messianic titles.

In the section concerning the plantation and the gardener discussed above, *nēṣer* "branch, shoot" (the same word which is used in the messianic prophecy of the branch from the root of Jesse in Isaiah 11.1 ff.) occurs several times with an allusion which leaves us in uncertainty as to whether it refers to the community or its founder. It says:

> . . . trees of life at a fount of mystery
> hidden among all the trees by the water.
> And they shall put forth a branch for an eternal planta-
> tion,
> striking root before they sprout. . . .
>
> —1QH viii.5-7

And it (allusion unclear) shall become an eternal source,
and all the beasts of the forest shall feed on the branch
    on it,
and its trunk will be trampled by all that pass by,
and every winged bird shall perch on its boughs,
and all the trees by the water shall rise against it.

—₁QH viii.8-9

And he who causes a holy branch (*nēṣer*) to sprout for
    a plantation of truth,
his (or: its) mystery was concealed without being
    accounted and sealed up without being known.[44]

—₁QH viii.10-11

The second of these three texts is perhaps the most
clear: A little plant grows up into a big tree which gives
protection and food to all the beasts and birds of the
earth (cf. Ezek. 31:6; Dan. 4:10; Matt. 13:31 f.)—here
it can hardly be a question of anything but the community, against which "trees by the water"—opponents
—rise up. The first text permits of the same interpretation, if the "trees of life" be Israel (or possibly the pious
in Israel), the branch the small beginnings of the community, and the plantation the community when it has
grown strong. But it also would be possible to consider
that the branch was the founder. Finally, the third text
speaks of one who causes a small plant to grow up into
a plantation—here it would seem natural to let the
founder be he who "causes a branch to sprout" and the
plantation be the result. But it is also possible to trans-

[44] For a note on the translation see: P. Wernberg-Møller in a
review of E. Nielsen and B. Otzen, *Dødehavsteksterne. Skrifter
fra den jødiske menighed i Qumran i oversaettelse og med noter*
(1959), *RQ* 1 (1958/59), 545.

late "*that* which causes a branch to sprout" which could allude to the message of the Teacher, or the saving knowledge.[45]

Thus, in all of these cases it seems that a term which can be messianic has been applied to the community and not to a particular individual. Of the two remaining quotations, vii. 19 is unfortunately so damaged that the context is not at all clear, but it appears as if it is here the "I" of the psalms who has caused a branch to sprout (i.e., the community); and vi.15 uses the image of the plantation but because of damage to the text it is not clear how the sprouting of the branch is related to the "I" of the psalm. Thus here again is a case where an interpretation familiar to Christian and modern exegetes obviously leads them astray if they want to understand the Qumran texts in their own context.

To a considerable extent this is probably also the case with the numerous allusions to the songs about the Servant of the Lord.[46] In ₁QH iv.5 f. it says: "Thou hast illumined my face concerning Thy covenant" (cf. Isaiah 42:6 where both the covenant and a light for the Gentiles occur); ₁QH ix.29-32, a section already discussed, speaks of election from the womb, which is reminiscent of Isaiah 49:1: "Yahweh called me when I was yet in the womb . . ."; moreover, one can find allusions to Isaiah 42:1 ff. (words like "justice," "spirit," "truth—faithfulness")—further, ₁QH viii.26 f. has: "And I was plunged among sicknesses and plagued in my heart

[45] Cf. Ringgren, "The Branch and the Plantation . . . ," *op cit.*, pp. 3-9.

[46] Black, "Servant of the Lord . . . ," *op. cit.*, pp. 6 ff.

by plagues, and I became as one forsaken . . ." (cf. Is. 53:3-5); in vii.10 and viii.35 f. the term "a disciple's tongue" (or: "a tongue with learning") is encountered; in the latter passage with the qualification "to give life to the spirit of the stumbling and to comfort the weary with a word," a clear allusion to Isaiah 50:4 (cf. also Matt. 11:28).

The section of ₁QH viii which speaks of the plantation also is reminiscent of Deutero-Isaiah: the enumeration of the types of trees derives from 41:19, "streams on the dry ground" comes from 44:3, etc. But precisely this—together with the combination of quotations from several other books of the Bible—shows that it is not a question of an application of the Servant Songs as an isolated messianically understood prophecy but of a general use of such scriptural sayings which the author saw as fulfilled in his life and the life of the community. It is also striking that several "messianic" passages have been applied to the community as a whole, an observation which is also applicable to the passages which tell how the whole congregation by its pious life will obtain for the whole land atonement for the guilt of infidelity and of sinful faithlessness (₁QS ix.4; cf. v.6, viii.6-10 *et passim*).[47] Thus, the community has—as does the Servant of the Lord—a vicarious task.

Here is a problem for which a satisfactory solution has not yet been found. It should not be forgotten, however, that according to Jewish tradition the Servant Songs allude to the people, Israel, and not to the Messiah;

[47] *Ibid.,* p. 7. Cf. also Gärtner, "Bakgrunden . . . ," *op. cit.,* pp. 68 ff.

which naturally does not exclude the possibility that these ideas could have been a preparation for the New Testament concept of vicarious suffering.

In any case this much is clear: the Teacher of Righteousness was not understood as a Messiah but rather as a prophetic forerunner to the two Anointed Ones. On the other hand, as representative for the community he had founded and led, he can have appeared as the bearer of those ideals for which the community stands and which to a certain extent are understood as fulfillment of messianic prophecies. Doubtless he is a figure who was considered to have inaugurated or at least prepared for the new, messianic era.

Part Two

ORGANIZATION AND CULT

6

The Community

The organization of the Qumran congregation and to some extent its cult are quite well described in the Manual of Discipline and partly in the Damascus Document. The chronological relationship between these writings cannot, however, be established with full certainty. Consequently some discrepancies bearing on organization cannot be dated and thus the process of development cannot be demonstrated with certainty.

Although the Qumran community only included a small number of adherents, they apparently considered themselves to represent the true Israel. Therefore the texts often give the impression of being directed to the whole people, while they actually only apply to the community and its members. By calling the community "the new covenant," the author of the Damascus Document (xix.35) evidently wants to describe it as the fulfillment of the prophecy of a new covenant in Jeremiah 31:31. Becoming a member of the community is called "entering the covenant" ($_1$QS i.18, etc.) This presupposes willingness (forms of the verb NDB) to do God's statutes ($_1$QS i.7) and to offer "his knowledge, his strength and his wealth to God's congregation" ($_1$QS i.11 f.). Hence it is a question of a real covenant which puts one under obligation and not only a designation for the community as such.

There does not seem to be any fixed terminology with respect to the community. Several different words are used. A term which appears to be specific for Qumran is *yáḥad*, literally "unity, togetherness" which is perhaps best translated by "community." (While it is true that the corresponding verb often means "to unite," "union" does not give the right associations.) Another term is *'ēdāh*, "congregation" an ancient term for Israel's cult-community. Sometimes *'ēṣāh*, "council, counsel" also seems to refer to the whole community (this has, as will be seen below, also a more limited meaning). On the other hand, *qāhāl* "assembly," another term well known from the Old Testament, is only used exceptionally in this technical meaning. From time to time, as we have seen, the community is referred to under the image of a plantation (₁QH vi.15 ff.; viii.4 ff.; ₁QS viii.5)—in connection with the prophetic sayings concerning a new plantation of Israel and the idea of the garden of Eden —or a building:

> For Thou layest a foundation upon a rock
> and the stones of the wall according to the measuring
>   line of justice
> and the plumb-line of truth
> in order to lay tested stones
> to build a [. . . .] of power, which will not tremble,
> and none who enter therein shall falter.
>
> —₁QH vi.25-27

It is difficult not to think in this connection of Jesus' words concerning the church built on a rock (Matt. 16:18). But it should also be remembered that there are in this passage in the Thanksgiving Psalms many allusions to the Old Testament prophecies (e.g., Isa. 28:17: "And I will make justice the line and righteousness the plummet"; the previous verse—interpreted messianically in the New Testament—also mentions a tested stone). How this image was interpreted in Qumran can be understood from a passage in the Manual of Discipline where there is mention of the establishment of a fifteen man council in the congregation:

> When these things come to pass in Israel the council of the community will be established in truth for a holy plantation, a holy house (Temple) for Israel and a foundation for the Holy of Holies for Aaron. . . . This is a tested wall, a precious cornerstone; its foundations will not tremble and they will not stir from their place, a dwelling —the Holy of Holies—for Aaron through the knowledge of all, for a covenant of justice and for an offering of sweet savor and a house of perfection and truth in Israel to establish a covenant with eternal statutes.
>
> —₁QS viii.4-6, 7-10

The congregation or its "council" is, thus, a continuation of the temple, where the priests (Aaron) present sacrifices, but this also has significance for the whole people (Israel): laymen participate in this building to the extent that they practice justice and truth in obedience to God's commandments. The so-called Florilegium is, as a matter of fact, a collection of biblical passages with reference to the temple which have been interpreted as alluding to the congregation as God's living temple-house, a "temple not built by hands." [1] In con-

---

[1] Flusser, "Two Notes on the Midrash . . . ," *op. cit.*, pp. 99 ff. A work by Gärtner on this topic is in preparation.

nection with this there is also mention of the atoning work for "the land" which the community or its council carries out through their existence and activity.[2]

It was clear from the last passage cited from the Manual of Discipline that "Aaron and Israel" appear to be the two main components in the community. The same applies to the phrase "the anointed ones of Aaron and Israel" and in several other cases: evidently Aaron is the representative of the priests and Israel of the laity. The Manual of Discipline sometimes distinguishes between priests, Levites, and "the whole people" (e.g., ii.19-21); in addition, the Damascus Document names proselytes (*gērîm*, literally: "strangers, guests"). In another passage elders are mentioned instead of Levites (₁QS vi.8).

The community seems to have been organized in smaller groups of ten men (or at least ten men as a minimum) with a priest as leader (₁QS vi.3 f.); over and above this the War Scroll in particular speaks of larger units of fifty, one hundred or a thousand men which correspond to Israel's old military organization. But this appears somewhat unrealistic considering that the whole Qumran community has been estimated as comprising only about two hundred people. It seems to be rather an ideal organization for the coming battle than an actual, accomplished order. It is, of course, possible that members could also have lived in places other than Qumran, something which also is assumed by

[2] See pp. 121 f. and 207 f.; see also Chamberlain. "Toward a Qumran Soteriology," *op. cit.*, pp. 309 ff.

the Damascus Document, with its mention of several "camps" or encampments.

Wherever there is a group of ten people there should be a priest as its leader (₁QS vi.3 f.; CD xiii.2). Thus it is the priests who are in charge of leadership of the congregation.[3] The priests, the Sons of Zadok, are "those who keep the covenant" (₁QS v.2, 9); they know the Law and interpret it; likewise according to CD x.6, xiii.2, they give instruction in the book of *Hagu*, a work the identity of which is unknown for the present.[4] At the common meals it is the priests who pronounce the blessing over the bread and the wine (₁QS vi.4-6; cf. ₁QSa ii.17 ff.); and it is they who lead the ceremonies for entrance into the community (₁QS i.18 ff.). In the War Scroll the high priest—the priestly "messiah"—plays an important role, but priests in general also are mentioned as leaders in the battle.

The blessing of "the priests, the sons of Zadok" which is given in ₁QSb iii.22 ff. is of interest. It first says concerning them that "God has chosen them to strengthen the covenant forever and to confirm all His judgments among His people and to instruct them as He has commanded so that they may establish the covenant in truth (faithfulness) and observe all His statutes in righteous-

[3] Cf. Delcor, "Le sacerdoce, les lieux de culte, les rites et les fêtes dans les documents de Khirbet Qumrân," *RHR* 144 (1953) 5-41.

[4] Some scholars consider the Book of *Hagu* to be identical with the Thanksgiving Psalms (*hāgû* means meditation); others interpret the word as a cryptogram for *ṣōrēp*, goldsmith, refiner, cf. Mal. 3:1-3, where the messenger sent to prepare the way of the Lord at the end time is described as a refiner of precious metals. Cf. *MLS*, pp. 206 f. and 325 f.

ness and walk according to that which He has chosen."
Then comes the blessing itself:

> May the Lord bless thee from His holy dwelling and make
> of thee a glorious ornament among the holy ones, and the
> covenant of [the eternal] priesthood may He renew for
> thee, and may He grant thee thy place in the holy
> [dwelling?], and with thy works mayest thou judge the
> princes (hardly: the willing ones, Hebr. n^edîbîm), and
> through that which proceeds from thy lips [the princes]
> of the nations. May He give thee as an inheritance the
> first fruits [. . . .] and may He bless all the counsel of
> flesh through thee . . . . (the continuation is fragmentary).

Here, as in the War Scroll, the question naturally is:
how much of this is reality and how much is a dream
for the future; most of it may well fall in the latter
category. But it clearly shows the significance and importance attached to the priests.

It has been observed that the priests are very often
called "sons of Zadok." The Qumran writings seem to
have been dependent on this point on the tradition from
Ezekiel which maintains that the sons of Zadok are the
only legitimate priests. In this connection a portion of
the Damascus Document (iii.21—iv.4) is of interest. The
author quotes Ezekiel 44:15 and comments:

> . . . as God swore to them through the prophet Ezekiel:
> "the priests and the Levites and the sons of Zadok, who
> kept the charge of My sanctuary when (the rest of) the
> people of Israel strayed from Me, shall offer to Me fat
> and blood." "The priests" are those in Israel who repent
> and go out from the land of Judah and [the Levites are
> those who] join themselves to them. And "the sons of
> Zadok" are the elect of Israel, they who are called by
> name, who shall arise in the end of days.

The quotation is somewhat abbreviated, but the author has in addition, no doubt intentionally, made a little change. He has inserted an "and" before "the Levites" and "the sons of Zadok," so that the three terms come to mean different groups, instead of the single group found in Ezekiel, namely, the Levitical priests who are sons of Zadok. Thus, in the interpretation the author of the Damascus Document appears to have made the "sons of Zadok" allude to the community as a whole, which would mean something of a "priesthood of all believers." But since this is the only witness to this concept, it is hard to draw any general conclusion. Otherwise it is the priests who always play the most important role, and any tendency toward doing away with the division between priests and laity is not appreciable.

But in addition to the priests as leaders, the Manual of Discipline speaks of a "council of the community" consisting of "twelve men and three priests" ($_1$QS viii.1)[5]—whether the three priests are included among the twelve or whether there are fifteen in all is not at all clear, but the latter alternative seems at present to have the most adherents[6] and concerning this council it is said that they shall be "perfect in all that is revealed of the whole Law" and shall lead a good life in order to "preserve faithfulness in the land" and "to atone for

[5] On this point see Sutcliffe, "The First Fifteen Members of the Qumran Community: A Note on $_1$QS 8:1 ff.," *JSS* 4 (1959), 134-138.

[6] CD x.5 mentions ten judges; four from Levi and Aaron and six from "Israel," who are instructed in the Book of *Hagu* and the teachings of the covenant. How this "collegium" of judges is related to the council of fifteen is not clear.

(expiate)[7] iniquity" (viii.1-3). We have previously seen how this atoning role which in itself is, of course, a priestly function is attributed to the community as a whole. But this is clearly something other than a "priesthood of all believers": it is the community or its leading corporate body which in its entirety exercises these functions.

Both in the Manual of Discipline and the Damascus Document an official is mentioned who is called the $m^e baqq\bar{e}r$, inspector or overseer; the same Hebrew word which in Greek is usually translated $epískopos$—our "bishop."[8] As the title indicates, he seems actually to be some sort of overseer or superintendent. According to CD xiii.7 ff. he is supposed to "give 'the many' insight into God's works and teach them to understand His mighty wonders and recount before them that which has come to pass from aforetime ('from eternity') . . . and he shall have mercy upon them as a father upon his children . . . (some undecipherable words) . . . as a shepherd his flock; he shall loose all their bonds so that there is no one oppressed or broken in his congregation." Further, he is to test those who wish to enter into the community (CD xiv.5-11; xiii.11 f.), he is to judge concerning questions of transgression of the commandments of the Law (ix.17 f.; xv.14 f.), he is to supervise the business transactions of the community with

[7] Here the Hebrew word is $r\bar{a}s\bar{a}h;$ on this word see: Chamberlain, "Toward a Qumran Soteriology," $op.$ $cit.,$ pp. 311 f.

[8] Among others, see R. Marcus, "$Mebaqqer$ and $Rabbim$ in the Manual of Discipline vi.11-13," JBL 75 (1956), 298-302; also, W. Eiss, "Das Amt des Gemeindeleiters bei den Essenern und der christliche Episkopat," in WdO II (1954-59), pp. 514-519.

those who are are outside of it (xiii.14 ff.) and administer its common treasury (xiv.13 ff.). He is supposed to be between thirty and fifty years of age and "be master of all the secrets of men and every language according to their families" (xiv.9 f.), but it seems that he is not to be a priest. Nevertheless, he is required in certain difficult cases to be able to instruct the priest concerning the exact meaning of the Law (xiii.5 f.).

In the Manual of Discipline on the other hand, $m^e baqq\bar{e}r$ mainly is in charge of the work and funds of the members and he deals with questions of order ($_1$QS vi.12, 20); along with him there is a $p\bar{a}q\hat{\imath}d$, "overseer" (vi.14) who, for example, examines those seeking entrance to the community—or is the $p\bar{a}q\hat{\imath}d$ simply another name for the $m^e baqq\bar{e}r$? (The term $p\bar{a}q\hat{\imath}d$ also occurs several times in the War Scroll, but his position is entirely different.)

In addition, the Manual of Discipline mentions a $ma\acute{s}k\hat{\imath}l$ "one who has insight" or "who gives insight"; according to iii.13 it is his duty to give instruction concerning the doctrine of the two spirits, in ix.12, 21 it is not quite clear whether this term refers to a particular office or more generally to a wise man. In the Blessings, on the other hand, he clearly has a distinct function: each of the formulae of blessing is said to be designed for this $ma\acute{s}k\hat{\imath}l$, that he may bless the various groups in the community. The so-called Liturgy of the Sabbath offering (Angelic Liturgy) is also introduced with the phrase $l^e ma\acute{s}k\hat{\imath}l$, whereupon this person exhorts the angels to praise God.[9] This is, however, all that is known of

[9] Strugnell, "The Angelic Liturgy . . . ," *op. cit.*, p. 320.

this official; whether he can have anything to do with the priest who, according to CD xiv.7 ff. is "appointed at the head of 'the many'" is highly uncertain. The two occurrences of a *maśkîl* in the Damascus Document (xii.21; xiii.22) give no clue whatsoever.

All who were admitted to membership in the community handed over their property to the community treasury, which was then administered in common ($_1$QS i.11 f.; cf. iii.2; vi.19 f.).[10] On the other hand, CD xiv.13 f. implies that a member was allowed control over his own income, for it is directed that a minimum of two days' wages per month were to be set aside for the common funds. Whether these regulations date from different periods or whether they actually should be reconciled with each other is uncertain.

Admission as a fully qualified member was preceded by two years of probation. He who sought entrance was examined by the overseer (*pāqîd*), as to whether his motives were pure and his life blameless and whether he understood what he was doing ($_1$QS vi.13 ff.). Subsequently a plenary session of the community decided whether or not he should be accepted. After one year a new examination took place but it was only after still another year that the postulant could be accepted into the community as a regular member and that his property would fall to the community ($_1$QS vi.18 ff.).

When one entered into the fellowship of the covenant, he had to take a solemn oath that with all his heart he

[10] Cf. W. R. Farmer, "The Economic Basis of the Qumran Community," *ThZ* 11 (1955), 295-308; *ibid.*, 12 (1956), 56-58; for further discussion see pp. 143 f. above, and Kandler, "Die Bedeutung der Armut . . . ," *op. cit.*

would turn to the Law of Moses and "separate himself from all men of error who walk in the way of wickedness" ($_1$QS v.7-11; cf. i.7-18: "to love all the children of light . . . and hate all the children of darkness . . . not to transgress a single one of all of God's words . . . not to swerve from the statutes of His truth . . . to do according to everything that He has commanded . . ."). In connection with this the priests should "recount God's righteousness" and the Levites "the iniquities of the children of Israel"; and those who enter the covenant recited a confession of sins ($_1$QS i.21-ii.1) whereupon the priests would pronounce a blessing on "those who walk blamelessly in all of God's ways"—this blessing is, in fact, an expansion of the Aaronic benediction "The Lord bless thee and keep thee"—and the Levites would "curse all the men of Belial's lot" with a corresponding curse-formula ($_1$QS ii.1-9). This ceremony seems to have been modeled on Deuteronomy 27 f. There is an obvious reference to it in the hymn $_1$QH xiv.8-22, where mention is made of choosing what God loves and abhorring what he hates (lines 10 f.), of coming near (into the covenant, lines 13 f.), of binding oaths (line 17) and being brought into the covenant. The hymn may or may not have been used at the ceremony.[11]

The fully qualified members are called *rabbîm*,[12] a word which either can be understood as "the many" or as "the great ones." Burrows is reminded of a parallel in the medieval guilds with their "masters" and "ap-

[11] Delcor, in the review of Arens, *Die Psalmen im Gottesdienst des alten Bundes*, in *RQ* 3 (1961/62), 576 f.

[12] Cf. Huppenbauer, "*rbym, rwb, rb* in der Sektenregel," *ThZ* 13 (1957), 136-137.

prentices," and of the use of "rabbi" or "master" as the form of address for a teacher in Jesus' time and elsewhere in Judaism.[13] Consequently, he translates *rabbîm* as "the masters." If, on the other hand, one chooses to translate "the many," it suggests the "many" in the Words of Institution in the Lord's Supper and possibly also the "many" of Isaiah 53:11, whom the Servant of the Lord makes to be accounted righteous. To decide on either "the many" or "the masters" is difficult, and probably the associations to both were present for the members of the Qumran congregation. The main point is that *rabbîm* is the term for the fully initiated members, and it is interesting that they as a whole may be designated with the abstract term *rôb* (so, for example, in ₁QS iv.16), which otherwise is usually translated by "multitude, abundance," (here: the initiated members as a unit).

On various occasions the members (i.e., *rabbîm*) assembled for meetings which are called *môšab hā-rabbîm* "the session of the many (masters)." [14] For such occasions a special order of precedence was fixed for the seating of each: first the priests, then the elders, then the rest of the members, each in his own place in a carefully regulated order, apparently according to the number of years of membership in the community (₁QS vi.8 ff.). The course of the meeting was likewise carefully regulated. Anyone who wanted to speak had to rise and say: "I have something to say to the *rabbîm*." Only after he had received permission of the presiding officer

[13] See *MLS*, pp. 234, 355 ff.

[14] Cf. Sutcliffe, "The General Council of the Qumran Community," *Biblica* 40 (1959), 971-983.

could he speak, and then no other member was allowed to interrupt him (₁QS vi.10 ff.). Improper behavior during the meetings, as for example, idle talk, loud laughter or falling asleep, indeed even spitting on the floor was punished (₁QS vii.1 ff.).

In general there was strict discipline and both the Damascus Document and the Manual of Discipline give directions concerning punishment for various offenses. In this connection it is of interest that there is a precept that erring brothers are to be reproved with humility and love and that one should not speak against a brother before the community unless he had first been rebuked before witnesses (₁QS v.24-vi.1; also CD ix.3 ff.).

7

The Cult

The question of the cult in Qumran [1] may be broken down into two parts: 1) What was the relationship of the Qumran community to the official cult of Judaism? and 2) How was its own cult structured?

The first question is answered in different ways in the Damascus Document and in the Manual of Discipline (as well as in the Thanksgiving Psalms).

The Damascus Document refers to sacrifice as something which is a matter of course and gives detailed directions for various situations involving sacrifice (e.g., ix.14; xi.17 f.; xvi.13); but nowhere does it say whether these sacrifices are offered in Jerusalem or elsewhere. In xi.22 it mentions a "house of prostration, or worship" (*bēt hištaḥ{}^awôt*) into which one may not enter unless he is pure, but what is meant by this is not said.

In the Manual of Discipline there is another attitude toward sacrifices. It is true that sacrifices are not rejected

[1] Cf. p. 205, n. 3 above; for further discussion see: J. M. Baumgarten, "Sacrifice and Worship among the Jewish Sectarians of the Dead Sea (Qumrân) Scrolls," *HTR* 46 (1953), 141-159; Teicher, "Priests and Sacrifices in the Dead Sea Scrolls," *JJS* 5 (1954), 93-99; Carmignac, "L'utilité ou l'inutilité des sacrifices sanglants dans la 'Règle de la Communauté' de Qumrân," *RB* 63 (1956), 524-532; D. Wallace, "The Essenes and Temple Sacrifice," *ThZ* 13 (1957), 335-338.

but it is said that the fulfillment of the program of the community atones for guilt and transgression "better than (or possibly simply: "without"–Hebrew *min*) flesh of burnt offerings and fat of sacrifices"; after that it continues: "offerings (*terûmāh*) of the lips is accounted as a sweet fragrance of righteousness and blamelessness of conduct as an acceptable freewill offering" (₁QS ix.4-5). Similarly the enumeration of the times of prayer in ₁QS ix.26-x.5 speaks of an "offering of the lips" in such a context that it is perfectly clear that it refers to praise and prayer. The verb *kipper* "to atone," which in the Old Testament is especially connected with the acquiring of forgiveness through bloody sacrifices, is used, as has been seen, with reference to the result of the community's existence and activity in general. The righteous life which is led within the community brings atonement to the land (₁QS viii.6, ix.4). The congregation or its council is "a dwelling of the Holy of Holies for Aaron . . . to offer a pleasing fragrance" (₁QS viii.9).

This recalls what Philo says concerning the Essenes *De vita contemplativa* II, 12): they became God's servants (*therapeutai*) not by sacrifices but by making their thoughts worthy of those who have been dedicated to the priesthood. It is reasonable to assume that the enforced exclusion from the temple necessitated a spiritualization of the sacrificial cult.

But at the same time it must be kept in mind that the people of Qumran were not indifferent to the Temple and its sacrifices.[2] The Habakkuk Commentary's accusations against Jerusalem's priests (₁QpHab. viii.8-10;

[2] Cullmann, "A New Approach to the Interpretation of the

ix.4 f.; xii.7-9; xi.4-8) show that there was interest in the purity of the cult and its proper performance. The Damascus Document also often speaks with indignation about the profanation of the temple (CD iv.15-18; v.6-7; xii.1-2; cf. vi.11-14) in a way that by no means witnesses to indifference.

CD xx.21-23 gives in a way a solution to the problem. God will show compassion toward the house of Peleg (= separation) who went out from the holy city and placed their confidence in God in that time when Israel sinned and defiled the temple. Here the founding of the sect is clearly connected with a break with the Jerusalem cult, which is understood as perverted and impure. It is simply concern about the purity of the worship and its proper performance which had forced a break. But this had as a result exclusion from the temple which made it impossible to carry out the sacrificial rites and gradually caused or at least hastened a spiritualization of these.

But for the future, the new age, a new temple was apparently awaited and re-establishment of the sacrificial cult. Column ii of the War Scroll describes the organization of the new sacrificial cult headed by the high priest, with twelve leaders to attend to the daily sacrifice, twenty-six chiefs of the courses, etc.; who each in turn do service and "take their stand beside the burnt offerings and the sacrifices to arrange incense offerings of sweet fragrance to the pleasure of God and to bring

Fourth Gospel," *Exp. Times* 71 (1959), 8-12, 39-43; this is a translation (without a number of footnotes) of "L'opposition contre le temple de Jerusalem, motif commun de la theologie Johannique et du monde ambiant," *NTS* 5 (1958/59), 157-173.

atonement for the whole congregation and to bring fat offerings before Him continuously on the table of glory" (ii.5 f.). Thus, the present order is only provisional. When the new age comes, God will again receive his sacrifices in accordance with the command of the Law.

As will be seen, there is also the concept of a heavenly temple and of a counterpart in heaven to the worship on earth, in which the angels bring God their praise.

Concerning the Qumran congregation's own cult we are incompletely informed. A passage in the Manual of Discipline presents some main features:

> In every place where there are ten men of the community's followers (lit.: council) there shall not be missing among them a priest; each according to his rank shall they sit before him. . . . And when they arrange the table for eating or for drinking, the priest shall first stretch out his hand to bless the first of the bread or wine. And in the place where the ten are there shall not be missing one who searches in the law day and night, continually, in turn (?). And "the many" shall watch together a third of all the nights of the year in order to read in the book and to search in the law, and to give praise together.
>
> —₁QS vi.3-8

Three things should be noted here: 1) the common meal, 2) study of the law, and 3) common praise.

The common meal [3] is mentioned also in other passages, particularly in the so-called Two Column Fragment (₁QSa) where similar instructions are given for the case when the Messiah is present. In conclusion it says there that this statute shall be followed wherever ten men are present. From this the conclusion has been drawn that

[3] K. G. Kuhn, "The Lord's Supper and the Communal Meal

the daily common meal was understood as an anticipation of the great banquet of the messianic age. This is possible but not entirely certain and indeed it rests partly on a comparison with the Christian Lord's Supper. However, it should in this connection be remembered that the Essene meal was, in fact, a sacred meal, but as far as can be judged it was not regarded as a sacrament. Nowhere is it said that the bread and the wine represent or signify something else or mediate specific spiritual gifts.

It is usually assumed that it is these meals which are meant when "the purity of the many," Hebrew, *ṭoh°rat ḥā-rabbîm*, is spoken of. *Ṭoh°rat* in rabbinic literature often means "pure things," or "pure food," and when exclusion for a certain time from "the purity of the many" occurs as a punishment for offenses, it is probable that the term designates something which belongs, so to speak, to the daily routine. According to Huppenbauer, however, the term could be taken to mean the bath through which purity is attained (₁QS vi.16,25; vii.3,16, 19; v.13; viii.17).[4] But ₁QS v.13 shows that the bath of cleansing and "the purity" are two separate things and that the former is a condition for partaking in the latter. It is therefore evident that *ṭoh°rat* designates the meal.

In addition, the expression "the drink of the many"

at Qumran," in *SNT*, pp. 65-93, (a substantial revision and enlargement of "Über den ursprünglichen Sinn des Abendmahls und sein Verhältnis zu den Gemeinschaftsmahlen der Sektenschrift," *EvTh* 10 [1950/51], 508-527); van der Ploeg, "The Meals of the Essenes," *JSS* 2 (1957), 163-175; Sutcliffe, "Sacred Meals at Qumran?" *Heythrop Journal* 1 (1960), 48-65; Gnilka, "Das Gemeinschaftsmahl der Essener," *BZ* 5 (1961), 39-55.

[4] Huppenbauer, "*ṬHR* und *ṬHRH* . . . ," *op. cit.*, pp. 350 f.

occurs twice ($_1$QS vi.20; vii.20), but there is no more specific information as to what it signifies. However, it is clear that entrance to "the purity" is granted after one year's novitiate, but one may not touch "the drink of the many" until after a second year. Either the drink (wine, *tîrôš*, which actually means unfermented grape juice but is often used parallel to and synonymously with *yayin*, wine) is ascribed a special meaning, so that it required a longer preparation; or else *mišqeh* is synonymous with *mišteh*, a similar derivative of another verb for "to drink," which however has received the more general meaning "feast, banquet," so that *mišqeh* could designate an especially solemn form of meal.

The common meal is most nearly to be understood as a transformation of the Jewish family meal where the priest has assumed the place of the head of the household. But another phenomenon also comes to mind which offers certain points of comparison. On Friday afternoon, thus before the beginning of the Sabbath, pious Jews, *ḥᵃbērîm*—"companions, friends"—gathered to meals, *ḥᵃbūrôt;* these ended at dusk with a goblet of wine and a "consecration of the (Sabbath) day" (*qiddûšat hay-yôm*). This custom was later transferred to the synagogue and the blessing of the bread and wine became a part of the rites of the Sabbath eve.[5] Of course there are certain analogies here, but one can hardly speak of identity. Rabin points out an interesting fact: at reception into a Pharisaic *ḥᵃbûrāh*—which in this context connotes the typical "fellowship" of the Pharisees—there

[5] Cf., for example, I. Elbogen, *Der jüdische Gottesdienst in seiner geschichtlichen Entwicklung* (3rd ed., 1931), pp. 107 ff.

also occurred two stages, of which one included the obligation of eating in a condition of Levitical purity, and the other involved the right to attend "the drink." [6] Naturally this does not prove that the Qumran community was Pharisaic, but it shows that such a distinction was not unknown to Judaism in general.

If we have interpreted the texts correctly, a ritual lustration or perhaps rather, a purifying bath was a prerequisite condition for participation in the common meal. But there is not much information apart from this concerning these baths. The Manual of Discipline emphasizes that the water of purification as such does not cleanse from sin and impurity but that repentance and amendment are required for this:

> (He who disdains to enter into God's covenant and walks in the hardness of his heart . . .) he will not be purified by atonement and not become pure by water of purification, he is not sanctified through seas and rivers and he will not be made clean through any water of washing. Unclean, unclean is he, as long as he rejects the statutes of God and does not let himself be disciplined in the community of His counsel. . . . By an upright and humble spirit is his sin atoned for, and by his soul's humiliation under all God's ordinances is his flesh cleansed, so that he may be sprinkled with the water of purification and be sanctified with the water of purity.
>
> —₁QS iii.4-9

Hence it may be concluded that water in itself does not

---

[6] Rabin, *Qumran Studies, op. cit.,* pp. 1-21. Concerning ḥabûrāh, see also: J. Neusner, "The Fellowship (*ḤBWRH*) in the Second Jewish Commonwealth," *HTR* 53 (1960), 125-142. An interesting parallel is offered by T. Levi 8:4, where Levi is anointed and washed and then participates in a meal.

bring about purity, but one must dissociate oneself from
evil and humbly submit to God's commandments in
order that the water of purification will be effective.
This recalls the preaching of John the Baptist, according
to which similarly baptism without repentance was of
no use. The same is said in another passage in the Manual
of Discipline:

> No one shall go into the water to touch the pure (food)
> of the holy men, for one is not cleansed unless he turns
> from his error.

—₁QS v.13-14

The Damascus Document directs that the water of
purification may not be dirty or be of less than the
quantity to cover a man (x.11 f.). Here, as in the other
two passages from the Manual of Discipline, only the
word "water" is used; in the section first quoted there
is the expression *mê niddāh*, water of purification,
actually water against impurity (defilement), a term
which in the Old Testament has a very special meaning:
it is used of the water that is mixed with ashes from a
red heifer and is used for certain purifications (Num.
19; cf. 31:23).[7] The word *niddāh* is used of sexual impurity, and this is perhaps the reason that precisely this
term was adopted in Qumran; for, as is known, sin was
often described in terms taken from this sphere.

Cisterns found within the enclosure of the buildings
of the community seem to provide archeological com-
ment on these literary witnesses. Two of them seem to

[7] J. Bowman, "Did the Qumran Sect Burn the Red Heifer?"
RQ 1 (1958/59), 73-84, maintains that the Qumran sect actually
performed rites which included the burning of the red heifer.

be functionally differentiated from the normal Roman type of cistern in such a fashion that it may be claimed that they were used for at least minor lustrations.[8]

The searching in the Holy Scriptures, especially in the Law, has already been touched upon (see Introduction). A question in dispute is the translation of *'L YFWT 'iš l^erē'ēhû* in ₁QS vi.7. Reicke translates "for the sake of mutual benefit"—which can be defended philologically—but the current consensus among translators is: "in turn, relieving one another" or something similar—which is difficult to justify on purely linguistic grounds but is thought to fit the context.

The common praise is probably also what is referred to in three sections of the texts which are more or less identical: ₁QS x.1-7, ₁QH xii.3-9 and ₁QM xiv.12-14, the last of which is, however, more brief. In all three cases, however, they offer a poetic description of how the life of the believer is at all times full of prayer and adoration rather than a systematic enumeration of prayers and services of worship. Yet it is clear that the times for prayer and praise are fixed by the course of the sun (₁QH xii.5) and that certain festivals are particular occasions for the praise of God, fixed in God's established ordering of the world. It is evidently difficult to construct an exact comparison with the Jewish hours of prayer [9] based on this type of material, but certain interesting observations can however be made.

---

[8] Cf. de Vaux, *L'archéologie et les manuscrits de la Mer Morte* (*The Schweich Lectures of the British Academy, 1959*) (1961), p. 99.

[9] S. Talmon, "The 'Manual of Benedictions' of the Sect of the Judaean Desert," *RQ* 2 (1959/60), 475-500. (A translation with

First of all there are obviously three daily hours of prayer:

$_1$QS	$_1$QH
Morning Prayer:	
"at the beginning of the dominion of light"	"when the light comes from its dwelling"
Midday Prayer:	
"at its 'circuit' "	"at the 'circuits' of the day"
Evening Prayer:	
"at its gathering to its ordained dwelling"	"when evening sets in and the light departs"

Prayer three times daily is mentioned in Daniel 6:10 and Psalm 55:16 f. Next there seems to be a question of a corresponding division of the night:

a) "at the beginning of the watches of darkness"	"at the beginning of the dominion of darkness"
b) "at its circuit"	"at the appointed time of night at its circuit"
c) "at its ingathering before the light"	

A division of the night into three parts is perhaps assumed in $_1$QS vi.7 f. where there is mention of nightly vigils for the study of the Law (see above p. 9).

What follows apparently refers to holy days, but it is difficult to identify them. In any case the festival of

some alterations of "The Order of Prayers of the Sect from the Judaean Desert," [in Hebrew], *Tarbiz* 29 [1959], 1-20); A. Arens, *Die Psalmen im Gottesdienst des alten Bundes. Eine Untersuchung zur Vorgeschichte des christlichen Psalmengesanges* (1961), pp. 152-159. Concerning new theories concerning the Day of Atonement, see: M. R. Lehmann, " 'Yom Kippur' in Qumran," *RQ* 3 (1961/62), 116-124.

the new moon is mentioned (₁QS x.3: "when the festivals occur according to the days of the new moon"; ₁QH xii.8: "the beginnings of time") and festivals which are fixed by the circuit of the sun (the Manual of Discipline: "their 'circuit' [i.e., the circuit of the festivals]"; Thanksgiving Psalms: "the 'circuit' of festivals"). In addition, the Manual of Discipline has a series of expressions which do not have any counterpart in the Thanksgiving Psalms, but they are too general to permit specific identification.

The idea that times for prayer and religious festivals are fixed by the courses of the heavenly bodies and are thereby a part of God's world plan is central to the point of view in Qumran. It appears that the Qumran community used a solar calendar according to which the length of the year was 364 days or fifty-two weeks, as distinguished from orthodox Judaism's lunar calendar with twelve months of twenty-nine or thirty days each and an intercalated month every third year.[10] This explains why the priests in the War Scroll are divided into twenty-six groups (half of fifty-two). It probably also explains the passage in the Habakkuk Commentary where it says that the wicked priest wanted to lead the faithful astray and make them to stumble on the Day of Atonement (xi.6 f.): in Qumran the Day of Atonement occurred on a different day than within orthodox

[10] A. Jaubert, "Le calendrier des Jubilés et de la secte de Qumrân. Ses origines bibliques," *VT* 3 (1953), 250-264; Jaubert, "Le calendrier des Jubilés et les jours liturgiques de la semaine," *VT* 7 (1957), 35-61; J. Morgenstern, "The Calendar of the Book of Jubilees, Its Origin and Its Character," *VT* 5 (1955), 34-76; J. Obermann, "Calendaric Elements in the Dead Sea Scrolls," *JBL* 75 (1956), 285-297.

Judaism. On the other hand, it is not entirely clear that the prohibition against hastening or delaying God's established times in ₁QS i.14 f. actually has to do with the calendar; it can also refer to submission to God's predestination in general. In any case, it is clear that the Qumran community had its own calendar, the same as the one the Book of Jubilees advocates; and lists have been found which are designed to coordinate the two calendars with their festivals and to indicate the duties of the priests according to the two systems.[11]

The longer texts from Cave 1 mention festivals only in passing: the Sabbath, the New Moon, New Year's Day and the Day of Atonement; while the great festivals, Passover, the Feast of Weeks (Pentecost) and the Feast of Tabernacles are not mentioned. The texts from Cave 4, however, produce the whole series of festivals with the addition of a second Passover, a month after the first—which elsewhere in Judaism is permitted only for certain special cases—and an agricultural feast of oil in the autumn which does not occur in the biblical calendar of festivals.[12]

A high point in the liturgical year was apparently the feast at which the covenant was renewed and new members were admitted.[13] A similar rite seems to be mentioned in Jubilees 6:17: "For this reason it is ordained and written on the heavenly tablets, that they shall celebrate the Feast of Weeks . . . to renew the covenant

[11] Milik, "Le travail d'édition . . ." op. cit., pp. 24 f.

[12] See: MLS, p. 377.

[13] M. Weise, Kultzeiten und kultischer Bundesschluss in der "Ordensregel" vom Toten Meer (1961).

every year." As a certain affinity exists between the Book of Jubilees and the Qumran writings, one could therefore assume that the Qumran community celebrated its covenant renewal at the Feast of Weeks, seven weeks after Passover. On the other hand the confession of sin included in the covenant-renewal celebration is otherwise connected with the Day of Atonement. This leads Talmon [14] to the hypothesis that these ceremonies took place on the Day of Atonement. This is indicated also by certain similarities in the vocabulary and train of thought between ₁QS i.19 ff. and a fragment of a "prayer for the Day of Atonement" from Cave 1 (₁Q 34 bis.). According to Talmon this could also explain the stress which is placed on the Day of Atonement in ₁QpHab. xi.6 f. However, an unpublished fragment of the Damascus Document places the covenant renewal in the third month, which is the month of the Feast of Weeks.[15]

The essential components in this festival have already been mentioned in connection with the rites of entrance into the community: praising of the God of salvation (₁QS i.19), proclamation of God's righteousness and mighty acts and of the sins of the children of Israel (i.21-23), a confession of sin (i.24-ii.1) and finally formulas of blessing and curse (ii.2-9). It should be noted that the praise and blessing are entrusted to the priests, while the proclamation of sins and curses falls

[14] Talmon, "The 'Manual of Benediction' . . . ," op. cit., pp. 498 f.

[15] Milik, Ten Years of Discovery . . . ," op. cit., p. 117; cf. Delcor's review of Arens, Die Psalmen . . . , in RQ 3 (1961/62), 575.

to the Levites. Baltzer [16] observes that this is a good example of the old formula for making a covenant and for covenant renewal with a confession of sin as a new element.

From the point of view of the history of liturgy the confession of sins which is included in the ceremony is interesting. This confession occurs in CD xx.28 f. in a shorter form than that found in the Manual of Discipline: "We have done evil, we have transgressed, we have sinned, we have been wicked, we and our fathers" (₁QS i.25 ff.). This confession of sin is based on Leviticus 16:21 and Psalm 106:6 ("We have sinned as did our fathers, we have done evil, we have been wicked"), and the sequence of the different verbs for "to sin" is the same as in the high priest's confession on the Day of Atonement according to Mishnah Yoma iii.8: *'āwāh, pāša', ḥātā',* (plus *rāšā'*). In the second century A.D. the order was changed to *ḥātā', 'āwāh, pāša'.* Thus, Qumran has followed the old order which was in use during the period of the Second Temple.[17]

A special problem is presented by the so-called Angelic Liturgy or, as it was called in the original: the songs of the Sabbath sacrifice. For each Sabbath during the year it is stated which angel shall pronounce the blessing formulas and praise God in different ways. Up to now

[16] K. Baltzer, *Das Bundesformular* ("Wissenschaftliche Monographien zum Alten und Neuen Testament, 4") (1960), pp. 58 f., 171 ff.

[17] See: Baumgarten, "Sacrifice and Worship among the Jewish Sectarians of the Dead Sea (Qumrân) Scrolls," *HTR* 46 (1953), 158 f.

only a couple of sample texts are available. One of these reads:

> The seventh among the chief princes will bless in His holy Name all the holy ones among those who establish knowledge, with seven words of His wondrous holiness; and he will bless all those who exalt His judgments with seven words of wonder, which will be for them strong shields; and he will bless all those appointed for righteousness and praise his glorious kingdom [. . .] eternity, with seven words of wonder which will be to them for eternal peace.
>
> And all the wondrous chief princes will bless (i.e., praise) the God of the godly ones in His [. . .] Name [. . .].[18]

At present there is no consensus as to whether these songs were sung at particular sacrifices which were performed at Qumran—though scarcely probable—or whether they were intended to replace sacrifices. It is important, however, that here there is a reference to worship, apparently here on earth, in which angels are exhorted to take part. Perhaps it is a matter of a program for the final time of fulfillment. Or is the earthly worship understood as a copy of such worship in heaven?

There are texts where heavenly worship before the throne of God is actually described. In this case, too, only a sample is available:

> . . . they who serve before the face (i.e., presence) of the Glory in the tabernacle of the godly (angels) of knowledge. Before Him fall the cherubim and bless (i.e., praise) as the still voice of the godly ones is lifted up on

[18] Strugnell, "The Angelic Liturgy . . . ," *op. cit.*, pp. 322 f.

high and there is tumult of jubilation as their wings lift up the still voice of the godly ones.[19]

Then there follows a description of the throne of God which is strongly reminiscent of the vision of the call of Ezekiel, after which the text continues with a description of the jubilation of the angels and a "still voice" (*qôl dᵉmāmāh*, the same words which in I Kings 19:12 are rendered as "a still small voice"), which blesses after the jubilation has become silent.

This is apparently a preliminary stage to the later Jewish *Hêkālôt* literature's descriptions of the heavenly throne and temple. The nature of the relationship of this heavenly worship to the actual service of worship at Qumran can hardly be decided on the basis of the texts thus far made known.

[19] *Ibid.*, pp. 336 f.

Part Three

PLACE WITHIN THE HISTORY OF RELIGION

8

Identification

After this description of the beliefs and cult of the Qumran community, an attempt to place it in the history of the Jewish religion remains to be made. As has been seen, there are many points of comparison with other Jewish movements and with some of the pseudepigraphic writings.[1] There has been occasion several times to call attention to similarities to the Testaments of the Twelve Patriarchs and to the Book of Jubilees, and affinities to what is known from other sources about the Jewish "party" known under the name of Essenes have been mentioned. But identification of the Qumran community with any of these movements within Judaism or with any other has been deliberately avoided.

It has been pointed out that the Qumran sect has certain points of contact with the Pharisees, and in a detailed study Rabin has tried to prove that this sect is simply a preliminary stage of Pharisaism.[2] His study, however,

[1] Concerning the relation of the Qumran community to the Book of Wisdom, see: Philonenko, "Le Maître de justice et la Sagesse de Salomon," *ThZ* 14 (1958), 81–88; and Dubarle, "Une source du livre de la Sagesse?" *RSPhTh* 37 (1953), 425–442. For the relation to Sirach, see: Winter, "Ben Sira and the Teaching of 'Two Ways,'" *VT* 5 (1955), 315–318.

[2] Rabin, *Qumran Studies.*

deals mainly with scattered traits such as the period of probation and the acceptance in stages into membership in the community, certain details of organization and the application of some legal enactments. But a similarity as to the total picture cannot be spoken of. Nor is Rabin able to produce convincing evidence in the Qumran writings for a detail as the Pharisees' belief in the resurrection of the dead (Acts 23:6, Josephus *Antiquities* XIII, 5.9).[3]

Teicher has attempted to prove that the Qumran community simply was a group of Jewish-Christian Ebionites, and that Jesus is the Teacher of Righteousness and Paul the false prophet.[4] But it is difficult to get this theory to fit in with the historical facts and it has not gained any supporters.

The identification which at the present time is held by most scholars is that which was proposed right from the start by Dupont-Sommer:[5] the Qumran people were Essenes. This thesis will not be examined in detail here;[6] but a brief study will be made of what ancient writers

[3] *Ibid.*, pp. 73 f.
[4] See the literature listed on p. 141, note 61.
[5] See the literature listed on p. 183, note 31.
[6] Among others, see: Brownlee, "A Comparison of the Covenanters of the Dead Sea Scrolls with Pre-Christian Jewish Sects," *BA* 13 (1950), 55 f.; Goossens, "Encore la Nouvelle Alliance et les Esséniens," (Rapports des Séances de la Societé 'Théonoé')," *Nouvelle Clio* 5 (1953), 190–234; M. H. Goshen-Gottstein "Anti-Essene Traits in the Dead Sea Scrolls," *VT* 4 (1954), 141–147; B. J. Roberts, "The Qumran Scrolls and the Essenes," *NTS* 3 (1956/57), 58–65; and the discussion in *MLS*, chap. 23—"Essenes? Christians? Zealots?" pp. 263–274. Concerning the relationship of the Qumran community to other Jewish movements, see Brownlee, "A Comparison . . . ," cited in this note, and Marcus, "The Qumran Scrolls and Early Judaism," *Bibl. Res.* 1 (1956), 9–47.

have to say concerning the Essenes,[7] and to what extent this agrees with the testimony of the Dead Sea writings.

The oldest information which exists concerning the Essenes comes from the Jewish theologian, Philo of Alexandria, who in his book *Quod omnis probus liber sit* (75-91) gives the following general picture:

The Essenes were a Jewish sect more than 4000 in number who lived in Syria and Palestine. They were called Essenes because of their holiness and piety, since "Essene" is equal to *hósios*, "holy." [8] They did not offer sacrifices since they considered that a God-fearing spirit was the only proper sacrifice. They lived in villages and avoided city life in order to avoid its bad influences. They carried on farming and peaceful handicraft but they despised weapons and trade and had no slaves, since they considered all men to be brothers.

Nothing in this is so particular that it could serve as

[7] Among others, see: del Medico, "Les Esséniens dans l'oeuvre de Flavius Josèphe," *Byzantinoslavica* 13 (1952/53), 1-45 and 189-226; Black, "The Account of the Essenes in Hippolytus and Josephus," in *The Background of the New Testament and Its Eschatology (Dodd Festschrift)*, ed. W. D. Davies and D. Daube (1956), pp. 172-175; F. M. Braun, "Essénisme et Hermétisme," *Revue Thomiste* 54 (1954), 523-558; Molin, "Qumrân-Apokalyptik-Essenismus. Eine Unterströmung im sogenannten Spätjudentum," *Saeculum* 6 (1955), 244-281; D. Wieluck, "Zwei 'neue' Antike Zeugen über Essener," *VT* 7 (1957), 418-419. For texts, see: A. A. Adam (ed.), *Antike Berichte über die Essener* (1961); and *EWQ*, pp. 21-38.

[8] The word "Essene" is generally derived from the Aramaic $h^a sayyā'$, "the pious ones." Vermès, "The Etymology of 'Essenes,' " *RQ* 2 (1959/60), 427-443, pleads the case for '*assayyā*', "those who heal, physicians," with reference to mention of "healing" as a reward of the good, and of a cure by the laying on of hands which is mentioned in the Genesis Apocryphon (xx.28 f.).

an identification with the Qumran sect; neither does it exclude such. Philo continues:

They avoided philosophy in so far as it did not serve an ethical life. They only studied natural philosophy in so far as it taught that there is a God who made everything and watches over his creation. Their primary interest was in moral teachings and their life was regulated by their own laws. These they studied particularly on the seventh day which they held holy in that they put aside all work and met in their synagogues. There they took their places according to rank, the older before the younger. Then one of them read aloud from the Bible and another who was learned in these passages explained that which was hard to understand. They were taught piety, holiness, justice and knowledge of that which is truly good and bad.

Here, too, the language is mostly rather general. What is said concerning the synagogue services could apply to the Jewish sabbath service in general, possibly with the exception of the information that they sat in order of rank, which in any case tallies with the Qumran writings.

Philo goes on to relate that the Essenes avoided oaths and falsehood and believed in a good providence. They were indifferent to money and pleasures. They had no private property but shared everything with each other. They had supplies, expenses, and clothes in common and together they ate the food of the community.

The Dead Sea Scrolls do not know of a prohibition against oaths—on the contrary, the members had to swear an oath upon entrance into the community, and the

Damascus Document contains directions for the oath of a woman (xvi.10-13).[9] Community of goods and the common meals agree, on the other hand, and it is very possible that the Essenes could have refused to take oaths before the authorities of official Judaism and still have permitted a proper oath within the community.

From a chronological point of view Pliny the Elder comes next. In his *Naturalis historia* v.17 (ca. A.D. 70) there is mention of the Essenes as a Jewish community which lived in the vicinity of the Dead Sea "above" 'Ain Geddi. They renounced all love of women and lived in celibacy. They avoided money. There is nothing in this account which cannot apply to the Qumran community, with the possible exception of the statement that no women were to be found among them—since female skeletons have been found in the graves at Qumran. But to all appearances there seem to have been two movements among the Essenes, one of which did not keep this prohibition so strictly.

The latest and at the same time the most extensive account of the Essenes is found in Josephus. He mentions them both in the *Jewish War* and in the *Antiquities*. He states that he himself had belonged to their circle for a while, but judging from his age and from what is known about his career he could not have

---

[9] Cf. on this point: O. Michel, "Der Schwur der Essener, *TLZ* 81 (1956), cols. 189-190; E. Kutsch, "Der Eid der Essener: Ein Beitrag zu dem Problem des Textes von Josephus bell. jud. 2, 8, 7 (§142)," *ibid.*, cols. 495-498; E. Gross, "Noch einmal: Der Essenereid bei Josephus," *ibid.* 82 (1957), cols. 73 f.; see also J. Baumgarten, "On the Testimony of Women in 1QSa," *JBL* 76 (1957), 266-269.

reached more than the novice stage, and it can thus not be assumed that everything he says is entirely exact.

In the *Jewish War* II, 8.2-13, Josephus presents the Essenes as one of three philosophical schools among the Jews: Sadducees, Pharisees and Essenes. The Essenes, he says, scorn pleasure as an evil and esteem continence highly. They disdain marriage—there is, however, one movement that permits marriage—but they adopt children and bring them up in their teaching. They despise wealth and have everything in common, appointing special stewards to handle their affairs. They have no one city but live spread out in most cities—this would agree with the Dead Sea texts if the reference to various "camps" is to Essenes outside of Qumran.

Before the rising of the sun they do not speak a word about profane things but they offer up ancient prayers, as if they were beseeching the sun to arise—this has often been understood as sun worship but strictly speaking it is only a question of prayers at sunrise, something also mentioned in the Dead Sea texts. Thereafter, Josephus says, they are sent out to their work by their overseers. Later they assemble again, put on white clothes and bathe in cold water and enter their refectory, to which no nonmember has access, and they sit down quietly. The food is served, a priest says a prayer and no one may touch the food until the prayer is said. After the meal the priest recites another prayer. Then they return to work, and in the evening the same procedure is repeated. This agrees quite well with the testimony of the Qumran writings with the exception of the fact that there nothing is said of a prayer after the meal.

Josephus states further that they never have shouting or disturbance in their houses but speak in turn; that they are loyal, peaceful and truthful and do not take oaths. They study the writings of the ancients and choose among them those which are of use to them. That they speak in turn is in agreement. The question of oaths has already been discussed. If the writings of the ancients are the Bible then everything fits in well.

After this Josephus describes the procedure for entrance into the sect. He who wishes to become a member has to live the life of the community on probation for one year, and if he then proves worthy he may have access to the water of purification. Only after a further two years can he be accepted as a fully qualified member. Here there seems to be a certain difference. Josephus reckons a novitiate of three years, the Manual of Discipline, two. Neither do the details completely agree unless the water of purification is identical with what the Manual of Discipline calls "the purity of the many" and which has been assumed here to be the common meals. Josephus continues: And before he may touch the common food, he must swear a solemn oath to practice piety toward God, and exercise justice toward men, to hate the wicked and assist the righteous, constantly to love the truth, not to reveal the teachings of the sect to outsiders and, finally, to preserve the books of the sect and the names of the angels. Here there is clearly the oath of entrance from the Manual of Discipline; the discrepancies are not greater than what can be explained as lack of accuracy or slips of memory. It should be noted that Josephus himself has just said that the Essenes refused to take oaths—and here those seeking entrance are enjoined to do so. This agrees with the comments made above.

Further it says in Josephus that those who commit any grave sin are expelled from the sect—again this agrees well with the rules in the Manual of Discipline. They consider it good to obey the elders and the majority. Therefore, when ten men are together, no one speaks without the consent of the others. Here the number ten and the necessity of asking for permission before speaking occur as they are found in the Manual of Discipline. They refrain from spitting when they are together, says Josephus, and thereby gives still another detail which agrees with the Manual of Discipline. He goes on to report that they observe the Sabbath more strictly than other Jews which is in good agreement with the Sabbath rules of the Damascus Document, which even forbid a man to lift a sheep out of a pit on the Sabbath (cf. Matt. 12:11, which shows that this was generally considered permissible).

Josephus reports further that the Essenes teach that the body is corruptible but the soul is immortal and that the soul dwells in the body as in a prison.[10] This is a real difficulty but it should be noted first that Josephus here makes an extensive comparison with Greek thought and possibly wished to adapt his presentation to the Greek way of thinking; and second, that differences

[10] On this point, see P. Grelot, "L'eschatologie des Esséniens et le Livre d'Hénoch," RQ 1 (1958/59), 113-131.

could have existed within the community so that some could have believed in immortality or at least resurrection, while others did not.[11]

In the *Antiquities* it is further learned that the Essenes believed that fate directs everything and that nothing befalls man which is not in accordance with its decree (*Ant.* XIII, 5, 9). This deterministic point of view is again recognized from Qumran, but the word "fate" may well be ascribed to Josephus: it was apparently easier for his Greco-Roman readers to speak of fate than an almighty God. In another place Josephus states that it is true that the Essenes send gifts to the temple but since they do not have access to it they offer their own sacrifices and do not participate in the regular temple sacrifices. Here reference should be made to what has already been said concerning the Qumran community's attitude toward sacrifice.

The conclusion of this discussion must be either that the people of Qumran are Essenes or that they are very close to the Essenes. But is it actually probable that two communities which were as similar as the Essenes of Josephus and the Qumran community had lived so close to each other without having had anything to do with each other? Hardly. The differences which still exist however must be explained on the basis that our sources were not sufficiently well informed or on the assumption of various movements within the Essenes' own circle—it should be noted that the three informants do not entirely agree with each other.

[11] The text was abridged and rendered freely here, but nothing of importance for the argument has been intentionally omitted.

An important observation concerning the Qumran sect's place in the history of the Jewish religion has been made by Stauffer, when he maintains that the sect arose out of what he calls priestly tradition [12]—traditions rooted in the Priestly document of the Pentateuch, I and II Chronicles, and Ezekiel. Hereby the unique position of the priests receives its explanation, as does the emphasis on the Zadokite character of the priesthood. The latter is furthermore connected to an opposition to the Hasmonaeans who were not descendants of Zadok, and therefore did not conform to the standards laid down by Ezekiel.

[12] Stauffer, "Probleme der Priestertradition," *TLZ* 81 (1956) cols. 135-150 and 255.

9

Relationship With Other Forms Of Religion

In conclusion brief reference will be made to the question of how the Essenes are related to a number of other religious movements which are later in time than Qumran: Jewish movements, Christianity and Gnosticism.

First there is John the Baptist with his disciples.[1] He was active in an area which was not far from Qumran. The Gospels apply the same saying from Isaiah 40:3 to him ("In the wilderness prepare the way of the Lord") which the Manual of Discipline viii.14 understands as a prophecy concerning the Qumran community. He preached a baptism of purification, which was not effective unless accompanied by repentance, precisely as was taught at Qumran. He called the Pharisees a "brood of vipers" and as has been seen, one

---

[1] Reicke, "Nytt ljus över Johannes döparens förkunnelse," *Religion och Bibel* 11 (1952), 5-18; Brownlee, "John the Baptist in the New Light of Ancient Scrolls," in *SNT*, pp. 33-53 (a revision of the article first published in *Interpretation* 9 [1955], 71-90); J. A. T. Robinson, "The Baptism of John and the Qumran Community," *HTR* 50 (1957), 175-191; Rowley, "The Baptism of John and the Qumran Sect," in *New Testament Essays; Studies in Memory of T. W. Manson*, A. J. B. Higgins (ed.), (1959), pp. 218-229.

of the Thanksgiving Psalms uses a word as a symbol for evil which in any case *can* mean "viper."[2] Perhaps John's austere way of life can also recall the references to the Essenes' simple and ascetic life. Of less significance is the observation that certain phrases in Zechariah's *Benedictus* (Luke 1:68–79) are reminiscent of expressions in the Thanksgiving Psalms, for since the same can be said about Mary's *Magnificat* in Luke 1, it could not be considered typical only of the traditions around John the Baptist.

Most interest for obvious reasons has centered around the relationship to early Christianity, and here there are also the greatest differences of opinion. Many rash conclusions built on insufficient or misinterpreted evidence can now be left aside. But for a careful analysis of the ideas of the New Testament and its Jewish background, the Qumran material will always retain its remarkable significance.[3] For a detailed presentation of these problems, reference must be made to specialized studies.[4] Here only a few of the most important points will be briefly touched upon.

The idea that the Teacher of Righteousness with his life and death and his expected return is to a considerable

[2] Betz, "Die Proselytentaufe der Qumransekte und die Taufe im Neuen Testament," *RQ* 1 (1958/59), 223.

[3] See the discussion in *MLS*, chaps. 3–11.

[4] See the collection of papers on this subject edited by Stendahl, *The Scrolls and the New Testament* (= *SNT*) (1957), including Stendahl, "The Scrolls and the New Testament: An Introduction and a Perspective," pp. 1–17. See also: Black, "The Gospels and the Scrolls," in *Studia Evangelica (International Congress on the Gospels at Oxford, 1957)*, K. Aland, F. L. Cross, *et al.* (eds.) *Texte und Untersuchungen* 73 (1959), 565–579.

extent an anticipation of Jesus must be considered to be in error, according to what is now known concerning the Teacher. For a study of the messianic interpretation of certain biblical passages and therefore also perhaps of Jesus' messianic self-consciousness, however, a careful analysis of the Qumran literature appears to provide valuable contributions.

The common meal of the Essenes exhibits certain similarities to the Christian celebration of the Lord's Supper: bread and wine, the blessing and perhaps even an eschatological significance.[5] There is however, an important difference; that which makes the Christian celebration of the Lord's Supper what it is, the interpretation of the elements as the body and blood of Christ, is entirely missing in Qumran. It is a sacral but not a sacramental meal, but as such it sheds light on aspects of the Jewish meal which previously were little known, and hence indirectly on the first celebrations of the Lord's Supper.

The similarities between the lustrations of the Essenes and Christian baptism are less pronounced.[6] For it is fairly clear that in Qumran the washing was not an unrepeatable occurrence, which marked admission into the fellowship, but was a daily routine. Neither is there any counterpart to baptism in the name of Jesus.

Much more significant are similarities in style, vocabulary and to some extent in the thought of the Qumran

[5] See especially K. G. Kuhn, "The Lord's Supper and the Communal Meal at Qumran," in *SNT*, pp. 65-93; cf. also p. 218 above, note 3.

[6] See Betz, "Die Proselytentaufe der Qumransekte . . . ," *op. cit.*, pp. 218 ff.

documents and the Johannine writings in the New Testament.[7] The opposition between light and truth on the one hand and darkness and error on the other runs through both of these groups of writings. This means more than a few literal agreements in expression and phrase. It is the whole concept of the world and religious reality that is similar in character; the atmosphere itself, so to speak. It is not difficult to point out differences on many points. Yet these common attitudes must signify that the Dead Sea Scrolls and the Johannine writings in some way have a common background. To determine what this is requires thorough investigations. Perhaps it is not without significance that the Gospel according to St. John contains two pericopes that have no counterpart in the Synoptic Gospels (John 1:19 ff., 3:25 ff.), the point of which is to show that Jesus is superior to John the Baptist. Did the author of the Gospel come out of the milieu of the Baptist? Or is it

[7] L. Mowry, "The Dead Sea Scrolls and the Background of the Gospel of John," *BA* 17 (1954), 78-97 F.-M. Braun, "L'arrière-fond judaïque du quatrième évangile et la Communauté de l'Alliance," *RB* 62 (1955), 5-44; Brown, "The Qumran Scrolls and the Johannine Gospel and Epistles," in *SNT*, pp. 183-207 (originally published in *CBQ* 17 [1955], 403-419, 559-574); F.-M. Braun, "Où en est l'étude du quatrième évangile?" *EphThLov* 32 (1956), 535-546; W. F. Albright, "Recent Discoveries in Palestine and the Gospel of John," in *The Background of the New Testament* . . . (*Dodd Festschrift*), *op. cit.*, pp. 153-171; Cullmann, "A New Approach to the Interpretation of the Fourth Gospel," *op. cit.*; G. Baumbach, *Qumran und das Johannesevangelium. Eine vergleichende Untersuchung der dualistischen Aussagen der Ordensregel von Qumran und des Johannesevangeliums mit besonderer Berücksichtigung der spätjüdischen Apokalypsen* (1958); cf. also: R. Schnackenburg, "Logos-Hymnus und johanneischer Prolog," *BZ* 1 (1957), 69-109.

addressed to disciples of John the Baptist or to former
Essenes from Qumran?

For the understanding of Paul, the Qumran writings
also have a great deal to offer.[8] Paul's view of man is
certainly understood better against the background of
what Qumran teaches concerning the concepts of flesh,
spirit, etc. Many have also observed that the Thanksgiving Psalms in particular teach that man does not have
any righteousness of his own but is made righteous
through God's grace, which at least on the surface seems
to be a purely Pauline idea.[9] It should be noted, however,
that when the Habakkuk Commentary interprets the passage which Paul quotes in the Epistle to the Romans
(Rom. 1:17) "The righteous shall live by faith," the saying is made to refer to the "doers of the Law" (1QpHab.
viii.1); thus, the exact opposite to what Paul finds in
the same prophecy.[10] Another Pauline thought that is
reminiscent of Qumran is the concept of the mystery
of salvation which has been hidden but now is revealed
(Rom. 16:25 f.; I Cor. 2:7-10; Eph. 3:3-9).[11] The Epistle
to the Ephesians and the Epistle to the Colossians, which
because of their "Gnostic" tendency were long con-

[8] H. Braun, "Römer 7, 7-25 und das Selbstverständnis des Qumran-Frommen," *ZThK* 56 (1959), 1-18; S. Schulz, "Zur Rechtfertigung aus Gnaden in Qumran und bei Paulus," *ibid.*, pp. 155-185;
H. J. Cadbury, "A Qumran Parallel to Paul," *HTR* 51 (1958),
1-2.

[9] W. Grundmann, "Der Lehrer der Gerechtigkeit von Qumran
und die Frage nach der Glaubensgerechtigkeit in der Theologie
des Apostels Paulus," *RQ* 2 (1959/60), 237-259.

[10] J. A. Sanders, "Habakkuk in Qumran, Paul and the Old
Testament," *JR* 39 (1959), 232-244.

[11] Cf. p. 63 above; and Allegro, *The Dead Sea Scrolls, op. cit.*,
pp. 130 ff.

sidered as occupying a unique position among the Pauline letters, constitute a special problem.[12] In style and phraseology they are strongly reminiscent of Qumran, which also in its way has "Gnostic tendencies" (see further below).

The possibility has already been mentioned in passing that the Epistle to the Hebrews could have been directed to Jewish Christians who expected two messianic figures and therefore found it difficult to accept Jesus who neither was a priest nor had the appearance of a king. The author of the Epistle to the Hebrews therefore wished to show that Jesus is precisely the messianic high priest.[13]

The Dead Sea sect's interpretation of Scripture is also of great interest for New Testament research. Its use of biblical citations even if in altered form, and the combination of sayings from different books provide valuable material for the understanding of Old Testament quotations in the New Testament.[14]

In addition there are a series of details which either agree with or in various ways give the background to passages in the New Testament, "The sons of his good

[12] Cf. K. G. Kuhn, "Der Epheserbrief im Lichte der Qumrantexte," *NTS* 7 (1960/61), 334-346.

[13] Yadin, "The Dead Sea Scrolls and the Epistle to the Hebrews," *Scripta Hierosolymitana* 4 (1958), 36-55; C. Spicq, "L'épitre aux Hébreux, Apollos, Jean-Baptiste, les Hellénistes et Qumran," *RQ* 1 (1958/59), 365-390; H. Kosmala, *Hebräer-Essener-Christen. Studien zur Vorgeschichte der frühchristlichen Verkündigung* ("Studia Post-Biblica, I") (1959).

[14] Compare concerning this point: Stendahl, *The School of St. Matthew* (1954); B. Gärtner, "The Habakkuk Commentary (DSH) and the Gospel of Matthew," *StTh* 8 (1954), 1-24; Bruce, *Biblical Exegesis in the Qumran Texts* (1959).

pleasure," *bᶜnê rᶜṣônô* (₁QH iv.32 f.; xi.9), i.e., the chosen ones, perhaps is the key to the expression in the song of the angels ". . . men with whom He is pleased," *ánthrōpoi eudokías* (lit.: men of [God's] good pleasure), in Luke 2:14.[15] The oath upon entering the community with its ". . . love all the children of light and hate all the children of darkness," comes as close to "You shall love your neighbor and hate your enemy" (Matt. 5:43) as could be. Jesus' hymn of praise to his Father in Matthew 11:25 f., "I thank (praise) Thee, Father, Lord of heaven and earth . . ." begins exactly like a Thanksgiving Psalm. The instructions concerning behavior toward erring brothers in Matthew 18:15 ff. is quite reminiscent of ₁QS v.24-vi.1. The community of goods among the early Christians and their *epískopos* seem also in some respects to have had their antecedents in Qumran. Paul's catalogs of virtues and vices are reminiscent of the enumeration of the fruits of the good and the evil spirit in ₁QS iv.3 f., 9 f.[16] The expression "because of the angels" in I Corinthians 11:10 as the explanation for women keeping their heads veiled could be understood on the basis of the idea found in the War Scroll that the angels fight together with the hosts of the faithful.[17] Hence, out of respect for the presence of the angels women must cover their heads, lest the uncovered head

[15] Vogt, " 'Peace Among Men of God's Good Pleasure' Lk. 2:14," in *SNT*, pp. 114-117; see also: Hunzinger, "Neues Licht auf Lc. 2,14 *ánthrōpoi eudokías*," *ZNW* 44 (1952/53), 85-90.

[16] Wibbing, *Die Tugend- und Lasterkataloge im Neuen Testament . . .* (1959).

[17] Fitzmyer, "A Feature of Qumran Angelology and the Angels of I Cor. XI. 10," *NTS* 4 (1957/58), 48-58; cf. p. 217, above.

be considered as a bodily defect and cause exclusion from such an assembly.

Such parallels in details are of less significance, however, than the fact that taken together they contribute to a better knowledge of the milieu and atmosphere in which the New Testament took form. Thus, their primary import is the help they provide in understanding its modes of expression.

The relationship to Gnosticism [18] presents a special problem. It has been pointed out that knowledge in Qumran as in Gnosticism can be described as man's knowledge of himself and of his nature as revealed by God, and also knowledge of God as Savior and of the way to salvation. But salvation in Qumran is not as it is in Gnosticism an ascent to the divine and deification, but it is salvation under the conditions of earthly life. And the dualism of the Qumran congregation is not a metaphysical-cosmic dualism but a religious-ethical dualism. Thus it becomes rather a question of definition as to whether the Essenes in Qumran should be called Gnostics or not. One must apparently take into account

[18] Among works in this area, the following should be mentioned: Schubert, "Der gegenwärtige Stand der Erforschung der in Palästina neu gefundenen hebräischen Handschriften . . . ," *TLZ* 78 (1953), cols. 495-506; G. Quispel, "Christliche Gnosis und jüdische Heterodoxie," *EvTh* 14 (1954), 474-484; Davies, "'Knowledge' in the Dead Sea Scrolls and Matthew 11:25-30," in *Christian Origins and Judaism, op. cit.,* pp. 119-144; Reicke, "Traces of Gnosticism in the Dead Sea Scrolls?" *NTS* 1 (1954), 137-141; R. McL. Wilson, "Gnostic Origins," *VigChr* 9 (1955), 193-211; Wilson, "Simon, Dositheus and the Dead Sea Scrolls," *ZRGG* 9 (1957), 21-30; H. J. Schoeps, *Urgemeinde, Judentum, Gnosis* (1956); Ringgren, "Gnosis i Qumrantexterna," *SEÅ* 24 (1959), 41-53.

a whole series of gradations, of shades of meaning between Gnostic and non-Gnostic movements. Qumran
lies somewhere in the middle of the scale. Viewed from
a historical point of view, perhaps it should be a question
of a preliminary stage of Gnosticism, a proto- or pre-
Gnosticism.

There is a rather firm tradition in the early Church
to the effect that Gnosticism originates with Simon
Magus (Acts 8:9 ff.). And as a matter of fact there is
no Gnosticism known to be earlier than the time of
Simon. This Simon is supposed to have been a disciple
of a certain Dositheus, and he was said to have been a
son of Zadok—this could indicate some sort of connection with Qumran. He was supposed to have kept the
Sabbath very carefully, he was an ascetic and is reported
to have known John the Baptist. Further, he applied
to himself Deuteronomy 18:18, the prophecy concerning
the prophet who would be raised up in the last day. All
of these associations constitute, of course, a very weak
basis for the assumption of a historical connection, but
there is the possibility that behind this partly legendary
information there could still be a kernel of truth. In
that case, it would have to be assumed that the Hellen-
ization of Gnosticism occurred with Simon, who actually
lived in a Hellenistic environment.[19]

Another side of the problem concerns early Jewish
mysticism, which is often called Jewish gnosis and which
has received its literary expression in the so-called

[19] Cf. Wilson's articles in note 17, above; for further discussion
see: Black, "The Patristic Account of Jewish Sectarianism,"
BJRL 41 (1958/59), 285-303.

Hêkālôt literature and III Enoch, i.e., descriptions of heavenly visions of God's majesty, in keeping with Ezekiel 1-3.[20] Schubert called attention at an early point to the fact that many of the terms and ideas at Qumran recur in these "Gnostic" documents.[21] At this time the texts of the Angelic Liturgy provisionally published by Strugnell have also shown that a very real depiction of the heavenly temple with God's throne existed already in Qumran.[22] Thus it would seem to be proven that there is a connection between Qumran and early Jewish mysticism. Now these associations may be by no means more direct than in the question of Gnosticism. It is probably necessary to see that in Judaism in the time of Jesus there were not only the three "parties" which Josephus reports but also a series of various gradations and intermediary forms. It could be any one of these forms of Judaism related to Qumran which is the direct precursor of the *Hêkālôt* tradition. The so-called Therapeutae in Egypt about which Philo reports may have constituted such a group.[23] (There would seem to be no cause to doubt their historicity.)

In connection with Gnosticism the Mandaeans should finally also be mentioned.[24] There is considerable infor-

[20] G. Scholem, *Major Trends in Jewish Mysticism* (1941).

[21] Schubert, "Der gegenwärtige Stand . . . ," *op. cit.*, cols. 495 ff.

[22] Strugnell, "The Angelic Liturgy at Qumran . . . ," *VT Suppl.* 7 (1960), 343 f.

[23] Reicke puts this information from Philo to use in his "Remarques sur l'histoire de la forme (Formgeschichte) des Textes de Qumran," in *Les Manuscrits de la Mer Morte* (Colloque de Strasbourg) (1957), pp. 37-44.

[24] Reicke, "Nytt ljus . . . ," *op. cit.*, pp. 17 f.; F.-M. Braun, "Le mandéisme et la Secte Essénienne de Qumrân," in *L'Ancien*

mation about them which is reminiscent of Qumran: lustrations, dualism between light and darkness, etc. One detail is the term "plantation" for the community.[25] John the Baptist plays a special role in the mythology of the Mandaeans. Mandaean studies seem increasingly to tend toward the view that the sect actually originated in the West, in Palestine or Syria.[26] Once again it is difficult to prove a direct connection. It is more a question of general similarities in attitudes and modes of expression. But the problem concerning the relationship of the Johannine writings to the Mandaean writings must perhaps be taken up once again from new points of departure, since the similarities of both to the Qumran literature has been established.

Finally some points of contact with other Jewish movements may be mentioned. Bowman thinks that in several points he can demonstrate a certain similarity with the Samaritans.[27] Wieder and Golb have called attention to connections with the Karaites, a Jewish sect otherwise better known in later times, approximately in the eighth century.[28] It should be pointed out that it was in a Karaite synagogue that the Damascus Document was discovered. Wieder points to the following facts: the expression t^emîmê derek "those who are perfect in

Testament et l'Orient (Études présentées aux VIe Journées Bibliques de Louvain) (1954), pp. 193-230.

[25] B. Gärtner, "Die Rätselhaften Termini Nazoräer und Iskariot (Horae Soederblomianae, 4) (1957), pp. 26 ff.

[26] R. Macuch, "Alter und Heimat des Mandäismus nach neuer schlossenen Quellen," TLZ 82 (1957), cols. 401-408.

[27] Bowman, "Contact Between Samaritan Sects and Qumran?" VT 7 (1957), 184-189.

[28] Wieder, "The Qumran Sectaries and the Karaites," JQR 47

(the way =) conduct" occurs among the Karaites and is very common in Qumran (twenty-three times in ₁QS, six times in CD). The same holds for *šābê peša'* "they who turn away from sin," with the concept of the remnant, and with the designation *'ebyônîm* "the poor." Golb points to several other details and Wieder notes that the Karaite view also envisaged two messianic figures—one Messiah a son of David, and one a *mᵉšiaḥ kᵉhunnāh* or "priestly anointed one"; the latter is identified with Elijah. This teaching is partly based on Zechariah 4:14 concerning the two who are anointed with oil. Apparently within Judaism there existed a rich variation in messianic expectations, and Qumran represents only one of the many possible combinations.

(1956/57), 97-113, 269-292; Wieder, "The Doctrine of the Two Messiahs among the Karaites," *JJS* 6 (1955), 14-25; N. Golb, "Literary and Doctrinal Aspects of the Damascus Covenant in the Light of Karaite Literature," *JQR* 47 (1956/57), 354-374; Golb, "The Dietary Laws of the Damascus Covenant in Relation to Those of the Karaites," *JJS* 8 (1957), 51-69; see further: P. Kahle, "The Karaites and the Manuscripts from the Cave," *VT* 3 (1953), 82-84; Szyszman, "A propos du Karaïsme et des textes de la Mer Morte," *VT* 2 (1952), 343-348; Szyszman, "La communauté de la Nouvelle Alliance et le Karaïsme," *Institut International de Sociologie XVIème Congrès, Beaune, Fasc. III*, Sep. 19-26, 1954, 189-202; Szyszman, "Note sur la structure sociale des Karaïtes dans les Pays Arabes," *ibid.*, 183-187; Szyszman, "Ascèse et Pauvreté dans la Doctrine Karaïte," *ZRGG* 11 (1959), 373-380.

Bibliography

TEXTS

Background:

Charles, R. H. (ed.). *The Apocrypha and Pseudepigrapha of the Old Testament in English.* I-II. Oxford: Clarendon Press, 1913.

Adam, A. A. (ed.). *Antike Berichte über die Essener.* ("Kleine Texte für Vorlesungen und Übungen, 182.") Berlin: Walter de Gruyter, 1961.

Editions of Texts:

Burrows, M. (ed.). *The Dead Sea Scrolls of St. Mark's Monastery.* Vol. I. *The Isaiah Manuscript and the Habakkuk Commentary.* New Haven, Conn.: American Schools of Oriental Research, 1950.

——. *Ibid.* Vol. II., Fasc. 2. *Plates and Transcription of the Manual of Discipline.* New Haven, Conn.: American Schools of Oriental Research, 1951.

Sukenik, E. L. and Avigad, N. (eds.). *The Dead Sea Scrolls of the Hebrew University.* Jerusalem: Hebrew University, Magnes Press, 1955.

Barthélemy, D. and Milik, J. T., *et al.* (eds.). *Qumrân Cave I, Discoveries in the Judaean Desert I.* Oxford: Clarendon, 1955.

Collections of English Translations of the Scrolls:
Gaster, T. H. *The Dead Sea Scriptures.* Garden City,
N. Y.: Doubleday (Anchor), 1957.
Dupont-Sommer, A. Translated by G. Vermes. *The
Essene Writings from Qumran.* Oxford: Basil Black-
well, 1961; New York: World (Meridian), 1962.
(Translation of *Les Ecrits esséniens découverts près
de la Mer Morte.* 2nd. ed.; Paris: Payot, 1961.)
Vermes, G. *The Dead Sea Scrolls in English.* Baltimore,
Md.: Penguin, 1962.

The Manual of Discipline:
Brownlee, W. H. *The Dead Sea Manual of Discipline.*
Translation and Notes. ("*BASOR* Suppl. Studies 10-
12.") New Haven, Conn.: American Schools of
Oriental Research, 1951.
Wernberg-Møller, P. *The Manual of Discipline.* Trans-
lated and Annotated with an Introduction. (*Studies
on the Texts of the Desert of Judah;* Vol. I.) Leiden:
Brill, 1957; Grand Rapids, Mich.: Eerdmans, 1957.

The Damascus Document:
Schechter, S. *Fragments of a Zadokite Work.* ("Docu-
ments of Jewish Sectaries, I.") Cambridge: University
Press, 1910.
Rost, L. *Die Damaskusschrift.* ("Kleine Texte, 167.")
Berlin: de Gruyter, 1933.
Rabin, C. R. *The Zadokite Documents.* 2nd ed.; Ox-
ford: Clarendon Press, 1958.

The Habakkuk Commentary:
Brownlee, W. H. "The Jerusalem Habakkuk Scroll,"
BASOR 112 (1948), 8-18.

————. "Further Light on Habakkuk," *ibid.* 114 (1949), 9-10.

Elliger, K. *Studien zum Habakuk-Kommentar vom Toten Meer.* ("Beiträge zur historischen Theologie, 15.") Tübingen: J. C. B. Mohr, 1953.

The Genesis Apocryphon:

Avigad, N. and Yadin, Y. *A Genesis Apocryphon.* Jerusalem: The Magnes Press of the Hebrew University and Hekhal ha-Sefer, 1956.

The Thanksgiving Psalms:

Licht, J. *Megillat hahôdāyôt (The Thanksgiving Scroll).* [Hebrew] Jerusalem: Bialik Institute, 1957.

Holm-Nielsen, S. *Hodayot, Psalms from Qumran.* Aarhus: Universitetsforlaget, 1960.

Mansoor, M. *The Thanksgiving Hymns.* (*Studies on the Texts of the Desert of Judah;* Vol. III.) Leiden: Brill, 1961; Grand Rapids, Mich.: Eerdmans, 1961.

The War Scroll:

Carmignac, J. *La règle de la guerre des fils de lumière contre des fils de ténèbres.* Paris: Letouzey et Ané, 1958.

Ploeg, J. van der. *Le Rouleau de la Guerre.* (*Studies on the Texts of the Desert of Judah;* Vol. II.) Leiden: Brill, 1959.

Yadin, Y. *The Scroll of the War of the Sons of Light against the Sons of Darkness.* Translated by B. and C. Rabin. London: Oxford University Press, 1962. (A revised edition of the Hebrew original, 1955.)

LITERATURE

Adam, A. A. (ed.). *Antike Berichte über die Essener.* See under Texts.

Albright, W. F. "Recent Discoveries in Palestine and the Gospel of John," in *The Background of the New Testament and its Eschatology*, W. D. Davies and D. Daube (eds.), in honour of C. H. Dodd. Cambridge: University Press, 1956: pp. 153-171.

Allegro, J. M. "A Newly-Discovered Fragment of a Commentary on Psalm XXXVII from Qumran," *PEQ* 86 (1954), 69-75.

_____. *The Dead Sea Scrolls.* Baltimore, Md.: Penguin Books Inc., 1956.

_____. "Further Light on the History of the Qumran Sect," *JBL* 75 (1956), 89-95.

_____. "Further Messianic References in Qumran Literature," *JBL* 75 (1956), 174-187.

_____. "Fragments of a Qumran Scroll of Eschatological Midrāšîm," *JBL* 77 (1958), 350-354.

_____. "More Isaiah Commentaries from Qumran's Fourth Cave," *JBL* 77 (1958), 215-221.

_____. "A Recently Discovered Fragment of a Commentary on Hosea from Qumran's Fourth Cave," *JBL* (1959), 142-147.

_____. *The Treasure of the Copper Scroll.* Garden City, N. Y.: Doubleday, 1960.

Arens, A. *Die Psalmen im Gottesdienst des alten Bundes. Eine Untersuchung zur Vorgeschichte des christlichen Psalmengesanges.* ("Trierer Theologische Studien, 11"). Trier: Paulinus-Verlag, 1961.

Atkinson, K. M. T. "The Historical Setting of the 'War

of the Sons of Light and the Sons of Darkness,' " *BJRL* 40 (1957/58), 272-297.

Audet, J.-P. "Affinités littéraires et doctrinales du 'Manuel de Discipline,' " *RB* 59 (1952), 219-238; 60 (1953), 41-82.

Avigad, N. and Yadin, Y. *A Genesis Apocryphon. See under* Texts.

Avi-Yonah, M. "The 'War of the Sons of Light and the Sons of Darkness' and Maccabean Warfare," *IEJ* 2 (1952), 1-5.

Baillet, M. "Fragments Araméens de Qumrân 2—Déscription de la Jérusalem nouvelle," *RB* 62 (1955), 222-245.

———. "Fragments du Document de Damas. Qumrân, Grotte 6" *RB* 63 (1956), 514-523.

———. "Un recueil liturgique de Qumrân, Grotte 4: 'Les paroles des luminaires,' " *RB* 68 (1961), 195-250.

Baltzer, K. *Das Bundesformular.* ("Wissenschaftliche Monographien zum Alten und Neuen Testament, 4.") Neukirchen: Neukirchener Verlag, 1960.

Bardtke, H. "Considérations sur les cantiques de Qumrân," *RB* 63 (1956), 220-233.

———. "Das Ich des Meisters in den Hodajoth von Qumrân," *Wissenschaftliche Zeitschrift der Karl-Marx-Universität Leipzig* 6 (1956/57), 93-104.

Barnard, L. W. "The Problem of the Epistle of Barnabas," *CQR* 159 (1958), 211-230.

Barthélemy, D. "Le Grand Rouleau d'Isaïe trouvé près de la Mer Morte," *RB* 57 (1950), 530-549.

——— and Milik, J. T., *et al. Qumran Cave I, Discoveries in the Judean Desert. See under* Texts.

Baumbach G. *Qumran und das Johannesevangelium.*

Eine vergleichende Untersuchung der dualistischen Aussagen der Ordensregel von Qumran und des Johannesevangeliums mit besonderer Berücksichtigung der spätjüdischen Apokalypsen. (*Aufsätze und Vorträge zur Theologie und Religionswissenschaft, 6.*) Berlin: Evangelische Verlagsanstalt, [1957].

Baumgarten, J. M. "Sacrifice and Worship among the Jewish Sectarians of the Dead Sea (Qumrân) Scrolls," *HTR* 46 (1953), 141-159.

————. "On the Testimony of Women in ₁QSa," *JBL* 76 (1957), 266-269.

Beijer, E. *Kristologi och etik i Jesu bergspredikan.* Stockholm: Svenska Kyrkans Diakonistyrelses Bokförlag, 1960.

Benoit, P., *et al.* Translated by J. L. Moreau. "Editing the Manuscript Fragments from Qumran," *BA* 19 (1956), 75-96. (A translation of "Le travail d'édition des fragments manuscrits de Qumrân," *RB* 63 [1956], 49-67).

Betz, O. "Die Geburt der Gemeinde durch den Lehrer," *NTS* 3 (1956/57), 314-326.

————. "Die Proselytentaufe der Qumransekte und die Taufe im Neuen Testament," *RQ* 1 (1958/59), 213-234.

————. *Offenbarung und Schriftforschung in der Qumransekte.* ("Wissenschaftliche Untersuchungen zum Neuen Testament, 6.") Tübingen: J. C. B. Mohr, 1960.

Black, M. "Servant of the Lord and Son of Man," *ScJTh* 6 (1953), 1-11.

————. "The Account of the Essenes in Hippolytus and Josephus," in *The Background of the New Testa-*

ment and its Eschatology. W. D. Davies and D. Daube (eds.), in honour of C. H. Dodd. Cambridge: University Press, 1956: pp. 172-175.

————. "The Patristic Account of Jewish Sectarianism," *BJRL* 41 (1958/59), 285-303.

————. "The Gospels and the Scrolls," in *Studia Evangelica (International Congress on the Gospels at Oxford, 1957)*, K. Aland, F. L. Cross, *et al.* (eds.), *Texte und Untersuchungen* 73 (1959), 565-579.

Boccaccio, P. "I manoscritti del Mar Morto e i Nomi di Dio *YHWH*, *'EL*," *Biblica* 32 (1951), 90-96.

Bousset, W. and Gressmann, H. *Die Religion des Judentums im späthellenistischen Zeitalter.* 3rd ed.; Tübingen: J. C. B. Mohr, 1926.

Bowman, J. "Contact Between Samaritan Sects and Qumran?" *VT* 7 (1957), 184-189.

————. "Did the Qumran Sect Burn the Red Heifer?" *RQ* 1 (1958/59), 73-84.

Braun, F.-M. "Essénisme et Hermétisme," *Revue Thomiste* 54 (1954), 523-558.

————. "Le mandéisme et la Secte Essénienne de Qumrân," in *L'Ancien Testament et l'Orient (Études présentées aux VIᵉ Journées Bibliques de Louvain).* Louvain: Publications Universitaires, 1954: pp. 193-230.

————. "L'arrière-fond judaïque du quatrième évangile et la Communauté de l'Alliance," *RB* 62 (1955), 5-44.

————. "Où en est l'étude du quatrième évangile?" *EphThLov* 32 (1956), 535-546.

Braun, H. " 'Umkehr' in spätjüdisch-häretischer und in frühchristlicher Sicht," *ZThK* 50 (1953), 243-258.

————. *Spätjüdisch-häretischer und frühchristlicher*

Radikalismus. ("Beiträge zur historischen Theologie, 24.") Tübingen: J. C. B. Mohr (Paul Siebeck), 1957.

—————. "Römer 7, 7-25 und das Selbstverständnis des Qumran-Frommen," *ZThK* 56 (1959), 1-18.

Brown, R. E. "The Qumran Scrolls and the Johannine Gospel and Epistles," in *SNT*, pp. 183-207. (Originally published in *CBQ* 17 [1955], 403-419, 559-574.)

—————. "The Messianism of Qumran," *CBQ* 19 (1957), 53-82.

—————. "The Pre-Christian Semitic Concept of 'Mystery,'" *CBQ* 20 (1958), 417-443.

—————. "The Semitic Background of the New Testament *Mysterion*," *Biblica* 39 (1958), 426-448; 40 (1959), 70-87.

Brownlee, W. H. "The Jerusalem Habakkuk Scroll," *BASOR* 112 (1948), 8-18.

—————. "Further Light on Habakkuk," *ibid.* 114 (1949), 9-10.

—————. "A Comparison of the Covenanters of the Dead Sea Scrolls with Pre-Christian Jewish Sects," *BA* 13 (1950), 50-72.

—————. *The Dead Sea Manual of Discipline. See under* Texts.

—————. "The Habakkuk Midrash and the Targum of Jonathan," *JJS* 7 (1956), 169-186.

—————. "Messianic Motifs of Qumran and the New Testament," *NTS* 3 (1956/57), 12-30, 195-210.

—————. "John the Baptist in the New Light of Ancient Scrolls," in *SNT*, pp. 33-53. (A revision of the article first published in *Interpretation* 9 [1955], 71-90.)

————, and Reider, J. "On *MŠḤTY* in the Qumran Scrolls," *BASOR* 134 (1954), 27-28.

Bruce, F. F. *The Teacher of Righteousness in the Qumran Texts.* ("The Tyndale Lecture in Biblical Archaeology, 1956.") London: Tyndale Press, 1957.

————. *Biblical Exegesis in the Qumran Texts.* Grand Rapids, Mich.: Eerdmans, 1959.

————. *Second Thoughts on the Dead Sea Scrolls.* 2nd. ed.; Grand Rapids, Mich.: Eerdmans, 1961.

Burrows, M. (ed.). *The Dead Sea Scrolls of St. Mark's Monastery,* I. The Isaiah Manuscript and the Habakkuk Commentary. (1950). *See under* Texts.

————. *The Dead Sea Scrolls of St. Mark's Monastery,* II. Plates and transcription of the Manual of Discipline. *See under* Texts.

————. *The Dead Sea Scrolls.* New York: Viking Press, 1955.

————. *More Light on the Dead Sea Scrolls.* New York: Viking Press, 1958.

Cadbury, H. J. "A Qumran Parallel to Paul," *HTR* 51 (1958), 1-2.

Caevel, J. de. "La connaissance religieuse dans les hymnes d'action de grâces de Qumran," *EphThLov* 38 (1962), 435-460.

Carmignac, J. "Les Kittim dans la 'Guerre des fils de lumière contre les fils de ténèbres,' " *NRTh* 77 (1955), 737-748.

————. "Les citations de l'Ancien Testament dans 'La Guerre des fils de lumière contre les fils de ténèbres,' " *RB* 63 (1956), 234-260, 375-390.

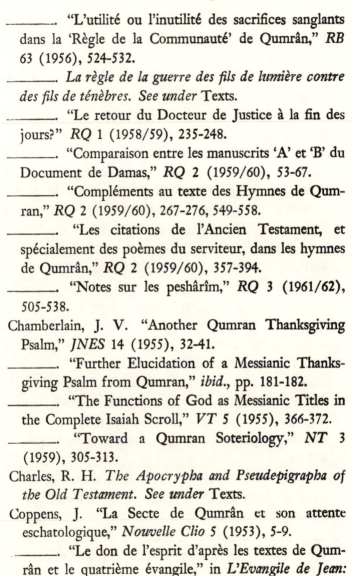

————. "L'utilité ou l'inutilité des sacrifices sanglants dans la 'Règle de la Communauté' de Qumrân," *RB* 63 (1956), 524-532.

————. *La règle de la guerre des fils de lumière contre des fils de ténèbres.* See *under* Texts.

————. "Le retour du Docteur de Justice à la fin des jours?" *RQ* 1 (1958/59), 235-248.

————. "Comparaison entre les manuscrits 'A' et 'B' du Document de Damas," *RQ* 2 (1959/60), 53-67.

————. "Compléments au texte des Hymnes de Qumran," *RQ* 2 (1959/60), 267-276, 549-558.

————. "Les citations de l'Ancien Testament, et spécialement des poèmes du serviteur, dans les hymnes de Qumrân," *RQ* 2 (1959/60), 357-394.

————. "Notes sur les peshârîm," *RQ* 3 (1961/62), 505-538.

Chamberlain, J. V. "Another Qumran Thanksgiving Psalm," *JNES* 14 (1955), 32-41.

————. "Further Elucidation of a Messianic Thanksgiving Psalm from Qumran," *ibid.*, pp. 181-182.

————. "The Functions of God as Messianic Titles in the Complete Isaiah Scroll," *VT* 5 (1955), 366-372.

————. "Toward a Qumran Soteriology," *NT* 3 (1959), 305-313.

Charles, R. H. *The Apocrypha and Pseudepigrapha of the Old Testament.* See *under* Texts.

Coppens, J. "La Secte de Qumrân et son attente eschatologique," *Nouvelle Clio* 5 (1953), 5-9.

————. "Le don de l'esprit d'après les textes de Qumrân et le quatrième évangile," in *L'Evangile de Jean:*

Études et Problèmes (Recherches Bibliques, III). Louvain: Desclée de Brouwer, 1958: pp. 209-223.

————. "La Piété des Psalmistes à Qumrân," in *La Secte de Qumrân et les Origines du Christianisme (Recherches Bibliques, IV).* Louvain: Desclée de Brouwer, 1959: pp. 149-161.

Couard, L. *Die religiösen und sittlichen Anschauungen der alttestamentlichen Apokryphen und Pseudepigraphen.* Gütersloh, 1907.

Cross, F. M., Jr. *The Ancient Library of Qumran and Modern Biblical Studies* ("The Haskell Lectures, 1956-1957"). 2nd ed.; New York: Doubleday (Anchor), 1961.

Cullmann, O. "The Significance of the Qumran Texts for Research into the Beginnings of Christianity," in *SNT*, pp. 18-32. (First published in *JBL* 74 [1955], 213-226.)

————. "A New Approach to the Interpretation of the Fourth Gospel," *Exp. Times* 71 (1959/60), 8-12 and 39-43. (A translation [without a number of footnotes] of "L'opposition contre le temple de Jerusalem, motif commun de la theologie Johannique et du monde ambiant," *NTS* 5 [1958/59], 157-173.)

Daniélou, J. "La communauté de Qumrân et l'organisation de l'Eglise ancienne," *RHPhR* 35 (1955), 104-115.

————. "Eschatologie sadocide et eschatologie chrétienne," in *Les Manuscrits de la Mer Morte* (Colloque de Strasbourg, 1955). Paris: Universitaires de France, 1957: pp. 111-125.

————. *The Dead Sea Scrolls and Primitive Christianity*. Translated by S. Attanasio. Baltimore, Md.: Helicon, 1958. (Translation of *Les manuscrits de la Mer Morte et les origines du Christianisme*. Paris: Editions de l'Orante, 1957.)

Davies, W. D. " 'Knowledge' in the Dead Sea Scrolls and Matthew 11:25-30," in *Christian Origins and Judaism*. Philadelphia: Westminster, 1962, pp. 119-144. (First published in *HTR* 46 [1953], 113-139.)

————. "Paul and the Dead Sea Scrolls: Flesh and Spirit," in *SNT*, pp. 157-182.

de Jonge, M. "Christian Influence in the Testaments of the Twelve Patriarchs," *NT* 4 (1960), 182-235.

Delcor, M. "L'eschatologie des documents de Khirbet Qumran," *RScRel* 26 (1952), 363-386.

————. "Le sacerdoce, les lieux de culte, les rites et les fêtes dans les documents de Khirbet Qumrân," *RHR* 144 (1953), 5-41.

————. "Contribution a l'étude de la législation des sectaires de Damas et de Qumrân," *RB* 61 (1954), 533-553; 62 (1955), 60-75.

————. "L'immortalité de l'âme dans le livre de la Sagesse et dans les documents de Qumrân,"*NRTh* 77 (1955), 614-630.

————. "Des diverses manières d'écrire le tétragramme sacré dans les anciens documents hébraïques," *RHR* 147 (1955), 145-173.

————. "Un Psaume messianique de Qumrân," in *Mélange bibliques rédigés en l'honneur de André Robert*. ("Travaux de l'Institute Catholique de Paris, 4.") Paris: Bloud and Gay, [1957]: pp. 334-340.

————. Review of A. Arens, *Die Psalmen im Gottesdienst des alten Bundes*, in *RQ* 3 (1961/62), 574-578.

Dubarle, A.-M. "Une Source du livre de la Sagesse?" *RSPhTh* 37 (1953), 425-442.

Duchesne-Guillemin, J. "Le Zervanisme et les manuscrits de la Mer Morte," *Indo-Iranian Journal* 1 (1957), 96-99.

Dupont-Sommer, A. *The Dead Sea Scrolls, A Preliminary Survey*. Translated by E. M. Rowley. New York: Macmillan, 1952. (A translation of *Aperçus preliminaires sur les manuscrits de la Mer Morte*. 1950.)

————. "Le Maître de Justice fut-il mis à mort?" *VT* 1 (1951), 200-215.

————. "La sainteté du signe 'noun' dans le Manuel de Discipline," in *Bulletin de l'Académie royale de Belgique, Classe des Lettres* (1952): pp. 184-193.

————. *The Jewish Sect of Qumran and the Essenes: New Studies on the Dead Sea Scrolls*. Translated by R. D. Barnett. London: Vallentine, Mitchell and Co.; 1954. (A translation of *Nouveaux Aperçus sur les manuscrits de la Mer Morte*, 1953.)

————. "Les Manuscrits de la Mer Morte; leur importance pour l'histoire des religions," *Numen* 2 (1955), 168-189.

————. "La mère du Messie et la mère de l'Aspic dans un hymne de Qoumrân," *RHR* 147 (1955), 174-188.

————. *The Essene Writings from Qumran*. See under Texts.

Edlund, C. *Das Auge der Einfalt, Eine Untersuchung zu Matt. 6, 22-23 und Luk. 11, 34-35*. ("Acta Seminarii

Neotestamentici Upsaliensis, XIX.") Lund: Gleerups, 1952.

Ehrlich, E. L. "Ein Beitrag zur Messiaslehre der Qumransekte," *ZAW* 68 (1956), 234-343.

Eiss, W. "Das Amt des Gemeindeleiters bei den Essenern und der christliche Episkopat," in *WdO* 2 (1954-59), pp. 514-519.

Eissfeldt, O. *Einleitung in das Alte Testament*. 2nd ed.; Tübingen: J. C. B. Mohr (Paul Siebeck), 1956.

Elbogen, I. *Der jüdische Gottesdienst in seiner geschichtlichen Entwicklung*. 3rd ed.; Frankfurt am Main: J. Kauffmann, 1931.

Elliger, K. *Studien zum Habakuk-Kommentar von Toten Meer*. See under Texts.

Eppel, R. *Le piétisme juif dans les Testaments des douze Patriarches*. ("Études d'Histoire et de Philosophie Religieuses, 22" [Strasbourg].) Paris: Alcan, 1930.

Farmer, W. R. "The Economic Basis of the Qumran Community," *ThZ* 11 (1955), 295-308; 12 (1956), 56-58.

Festugière, A. J. "Cadre de la mystique hellénistique," in *Aux Sources de la Tradition Chrétienne. Mélange offerts à M. Maurice Goguel* (Bibliothèque Théologique.) Paris: Delachaux & Niestlé, 1950; pp. 74-85.

Février, J. G. "Tactique hellénistique dans un texte de 'Ayin Fashkha," *Semitica* 3 (1950), 53-59.

Fitzmyer, J. A. "A Feature of Qumrân Angelology and the Angels of I Cor. XI.10," *NTS* 4 (1957/58), 48-58.

Flusser, D. "The Dualism of 'Flesh and Spirit' in the Dead Sea Scrolls and the New Testament," *Tarbiz* 27

(1957/58), 158-165. (Article in Hebrew; English summary, p. v.)

————. "Two Notes on the Midrash on 2 Sam. vii," *IEJ* 9 (1959), 99-109.

Friedrich, G. "Beobachtungen zur messianischen Hohenpriestererwartung in den Synoptikern," *ZThK* 53 (1956), 265-311.

Gärtner, B. "The Habakkuk Commentary (DSH) and the Gospel of Matthew," *StTh* 8 (1954), 1-24.

————. *Die Rätselhaften Termini Nazoräer und Iskariot* (*Horae Soederblomianae*, 4) [Uppsala]. Lund: Gleerup, 1957.

————. "Bakgrunden till Qumranförsamlingens krig," *RoB* 19 (1960), 35-72.

Gaster, T. H. *The Dead Sea Scriptures. See under* Texts.

Giblet, J. "Prophétisme et attente d'un Messie prophète dans l'ancien Judaïsme," in *L'Attente du Messie* (*Coppens Festschrift*). Paris, 1954; pp. 85-130.

Gnilka, J. "Die Erwartung des messianischen Hohenpriesters in den Schriften von Qumran und im Neuen Testament," *RQ* 2 (1959/60), 395-426.

————. "Das Gemeinschaftsmahl der Essener," *BZ* 5 (1961), 39-55.

Golb, N. "Literary and Doctrinal Aspects of the Damascus Covenant in the Light of Karaite Literature," *JQR* 47 (1956/57), 354-374.

————. "The Dietary Laws of the Damascus Covenant in Relation to Those of the Karaites," *JJS* 8 (1957), 51-69.

Goossens, R. "Encore la Nouvelle Alliance et les

Esséniens," (Rapports des Séances de la Societé 'Théonoé')," *Nouvelle Clio* 5 (1953), 190-234.

―――――. "L'énigme du signe *nun* dans le Manuel de Discipline," *Nouvelle Clio* 6 (1954), 5-39.

Goshen-Gottstein, M. H. "Anti-Essene Traits in the Dead Sea Scrolls," *VT* 4 (1954), 141-147.

―――――. "Philologische Miszellen zu den Qumrantexten," *RQ* 2 (1959/60), 43-51.

Greenfield, J. C. "The Root '*GBL*' in Mishnaic Hebrew and in the Hymnic Literature from Qumran," *RQ* 2 (1959/60), 155-162.

Grelot, P. "L'eschatologie des Esséniens et le Livre d'Hénoch," *RQ* 1 (1958/59), 113-131.

Gross, E. "Noch einmal: Der Essenereid bei Josephus," *TLZ* 82 (1957), cols. 73-74.

Grundmann, W. "Der Lehrer der Gerechtigkeit von Qumran und die Frage nach der Glaubensgerechtigkeit in der Theologie des Apostels Paulus," *RQ* 2 (1959/60), 237-259.

Guilbert, P. "Le Plan de la 'Règle de la Communauté'," *RQ* 1 (1958/59), 323-344.

Handbuch der Orientalistik I, Aegyptologie. Leiden: Brill, 1952.

Hinson, G. "Hodayot, III, 6-18: In What Sense Messianic?" *RQ* (1959/60), 183-204.

Holm-Nielsen, S. *Hodayot. Psalms from Qumran. See under* Texts.

Hunzinger, C. H. "Neues Licht auf Lc. 2, 14 *ánthrōpoi eudokías*," *ZNW* 44 (1952/53), 85-90.

―――――. "Fragmente einer älteren Fassung des Buches

Milḥamā aus Höhle 4 von Qumran," *ZAW* 69 (1957), 131-151.

Huppenbauer, H. W. "*rbym, rwb, rb* in der Sektenregel," *ThZ* 13 (1957), 136-137.

————. "*BŚR* 'Fleisch' in den Texten von Qumran (Höhle 1)," *ThZ* 13 (1957), 298-300.

————. "*ṬHR* und *ṬHRH* in der Sektenregel von Qumran," *ThZ* 13 (1957), 350-351.

————. "Belial in den Qumrantexten," *ThZ* 15 (1959), 81-89.

————. *Der Mensch zwischen zwei Welten. Der Dualismus der Texte von Qumran (Höhle I) und der Damaskusfragmente. Ein Beitrag zur Vorgeschichte des Evangeliums.* ("Abhandlungen zur Theologie des Alten und Neuen Testaments, 34".) Zürich: Zwingli Verlag, 1959.

Hyatt, J. P. "The View of Man in the Qumran 'Hodayot,'" *NTS* 2 (1955/56), 276-284.

Jaubert, A. "Le calendrier des Jubilés et de la secte de Qumrân. Ses origines bibliques," *VT* 3 (1953), 250-264.

————. "Le calendrier des Jubilés et les jours liturgiques de la semaine," *VT* 7 (1957), 35-61.

Jeremias, J. "Hēl(e)ías," in *Theol. Wörterb. z. N.T.*, G. Kittel (ed.), II, 930-943.

Johnson, S. E. "The Dead Sea Manual of Discipline and the Jerusalem Church of Acts," in *SNT*, pp. 129-142. (First published in *ZAW* 66 [1954], 106-120.)

Kahle, P. "The Karaites and the Manuscripts from the Cave," *VT* 3 (1953), 82-84.

Kandler, H. J. "Die Bedeutung der Armut im Schrifttum von Chirbet Qumran," *Judaica* 13 (1957), 193-209.

Kosmala, H. *Hebräer-Essener-Christen: Studien zur Vorgeschichte der frühchristlichen Verkündigung.* ("Studia Post-Biblica, I"). Leiden: Brill, 1959.

Kraft, C. F. "Poetic Structure in the Qumran Thanksgiving Psalms," *Bibl. Res.* 2 (1957), 1-18.

Kuhn, H. W. "Die beiden Messias in den Qumrantexten und die Messiasvorstellung in der rabbinischen Literatur," *ZAW* 70 (1958), 200-208.

Kuhn, K. G. "Die Sektenschrift und die iranische Religion," *ZThK* 49 (1952), 296-316.

————. "The Lord's Supper and the Communal Meal at Qumran," in *SNT*, pp. 65-93. (A substantial revision of "Über den ursprünglichen Sinn des Abendmahls und sein Verhältnis zu den Gemeinschaftsmahlen der Seckenschrift," *EvT* 10 [1950/51], 508-527.)

————. "New Light on Temptation, Sin and Flesh in the New Testament," in *SNT*, pp. 94-113. (A translation with some revisions of *"Peirasmós-hamartía-sárx* im Neuen Testament und die damit zusammenhängenden Vorstellungen," *ZThK* 49 [1952], 200-222.)

————. "The Two Messiahs of Aaron and Israel," in *SNT*, pp. 54-64. (A revision of "Die beiden Messias Aarons und Israels," *NTS* 1 [1954/55], 168-180.)

————. "Der Epheserbrief im Lichte der Qumrantexte," *NTS* 7 (1960/61), 334-346.

Kutsch, E. "Der Eid der Essener: Ein Beitrag zu dem Problem des Textes von Josephus bell. jud. 2, 8, 7 (§ 142)," *TLZ* 81 (1956), cols. 495-498.

Kutscher, E. Y. "The Language of the Genesis Apocryphon: A Preliminary Study," *Scripta Hierosolymitana* 4 (1958), 1-35.

Larsson, E. "Qumranlitteraturen och De tolv patriarkernas testamenten," *SEÅ* 25 (1960), 109-118.

Laurin, R. B. "The Question of Immortality in the Qumran Hodayot," *JSS* 3 (1958), 344-355.

Légasse, S. "Les pauvres en esprit et les 'Volontaires' de Qumran," *NTS* 8 (1961/62), 336-344.

Lehmann, M. R. "'Yom Kippur' in Qumran," *RQ* 3 (1961/62), 116-124.

Licht, J. *Megillat hahôdāyôt* (The Thanksgiving Scroll). [Hebrew] *See under* Texts.

————. "The Doctrine of the Thanksgiving Scroll," *IEJ* 6 (1956), 1-13, 89-101.

————. "An Analysis of the Treatise of the Two Spirits in DSD," *Scripta Hierosolymitana* 4 (1958), 88-100.

Liver, J. "The Doctrine of the Two Messiahs in Sectarian Literature in the Time of the Second Commonwealth," *HTR* 52 (1959), 149-185.

Ludin-Jansen, H. *Die spätjüdische Psalmendichtung, ihr Entstehungskreis und ihr "Sitz im Leben."* Oslo: Jacob Dybwad, 1937.

Lyonnet, S. "De notione expiationis," *VD* 37 (1959), 336-352.

Macuch, R. "Alter und Heimat des Mandäismus nach neuerschlossenen Quellen," *TLZ* 82 (1957), cols. 401-408.

Mansoor, M. "Some Linguistic Aspects of the Qumran Texts," *JSS* 3 (1958), 40-54.

————. *The Thanksgiving Hymns. See under* Texts.

Marcus, R. "*Mebaqqer* and *Rabbim* in the Manual of Discipline vi. 11-13," *JBL* 75 (1956), 298-302.

————. "The Qumran Scrolls and Early Judaism," *Bibl. Res.* 1 (1956), 9-47.

Medico, H. E. del. "Les Esséniens dans l'oeuvre de Flavius Josèphe," *Byzantinoslavica* 13 (1952/53), 1-45.

————. *L'énigme des manuscrits de la Mer Morte.* Paris: Plon, 1957.

Menasce, J. P. de. "Un Mot Iranien dans les hymnes," *RQ* 1 (1958/59), 133-134.

Michaud, H. "Un mythe zervanite dans un des manuscrits de Qumrân," *VT* 5 (1955), 137-147.

————. "A propos d'un passage des Hymnes ($_1$Q Hôdayôt, II, 7-14)," *RQ* 1 (1958/59), 413-416.

Michel, O. "Der Schwur der Essener," *TLZ* 81 (1956), cols. 189-190.

Milik, J. T. "Fragments d'un Midrash de Michée dans les Manuscrits de Qumrân," *RB* 59 (1952), 412-418.

————. "Le Testament de Lévi en Araméen," *RB* 62 (1955), 398-406.

————. "Prière de Nabonide et autres écrits d'un cycle de Daniel—Fragments Araméens de Qumrân 4," *RB* 63 (1956), 407-415.

————. "Le travail d'édition des manuscrits du Désert de Juda," in *Volume du Congrès, Strasbourg 1956, VT Suppl.* 4 (1957), 17-26.

————. *Ten Years of Discovery in the Wilderness of Judaea.* Translated by J. Strugnell. ("Studies in Biblical Theology, 26.") London: SCM, 1959. (A translation of *Dix ans de Découvertes dans le Désert de Juda* [1957].)

————. "Le Rouleau de Cuivre de Qumrân (₃Q 15)," *RB* 66 (1959), 321-357.

Molin, G. *Die Söhne des Lichtes.* Wien: Herold, 1954.

————. "Qumrân-Apokalyptik-Essenismus. Eine Unterströmung im sogenannten Spätjudentum," *Saeculum* 6 (1955), 244-281.

————. "Die Hymnen von Chirbet Qumran (₁QT)," in *Festschrift für Prof. Dr. Viktor Christian. Vorderasiatische Studien.* Vienna, 1956; pp. 74-82.

Morgenstern, J. "The Calendar of the Book of Jubilees, Its Origin and Its Character," *VT* 5 (1955), 34-76.

Mowry, L. "The Dead Sea Scrolls and the Background of the Gospel of John," *BA* 17 (1954), 78-97.

Munch, P. A. "The Spirits in the Testaments of the Twelve Patriarchs," *Acta Orientalia* 13 (1935), 257-263.

Murphy, R. E. *"Yēṣer* in the Qumran Literature," *Biblica* 39 (1958), 334-344.

————. *"BŚR* in the Qumran Literature and *SARKS* in the Epistle to the Romans," *Sacra Pagina* (1959), II, pp. 60-76. (Miscellanea biblica Congressus internationalis catholici de re biblica, J. Coppens, *et al.* [eds.]. Bibliotheca *EphThLov,* Paris: Gabalda, 1959.)

Mussner, F. "Einige Parallelen aus den Qumrântexten zur Areopagrede (Apg. 17, 22-31)," *BZ* 1 (1957), 125-130.

Neusner, J. "The Fellowship (*ḤBWRH*) in the Second Jewish Commonwealth," *HTR* 53 (1960), 125-142.

Nielsen, E. *Håndskriftfundene i Juda ørken.* Copenhagen: G. E. C. Gad, 1956.

North, R. "The Damascus of Qumran Geography," *PEQ* 87 (1955), 34-48.

————. " 'Kittim' War or 'Sectarian' Liturgy?" *Biblica* 39 (1958), 84-93.

Nötscher, F. *Zur theologischen Terminologie der Qumran Texte*. ("Bonner Biblische Beiträge, 10.") Bonn: Peter Hanstein, 1956.

————. "Geist und Geister in den Texten von Qumran," in *Mélanges bibliques rédigés en l'honneur de André Robert*. ("Travaux de l'Institut Catholique de Paris, 4.") Paris: Bloud & Gay, [1957]; pp. 305-315.

————. "Himmlische Bücher und Schicksalsglaube in Qumran," *RQ* 1 (1958/59), 405-411.

————. "Schicksalsglaube in Qumrân und Umwelt," *BZ* 3 (1959), 204-234; 4 (1960), 98-121.

————. "Heiligkeit in den Qumranschriften," *RQ* 2 (1959/60), 315-344.

Obermann, J. "Calendaric Elements in the Dead Sea Scrolls," *JBL* 75 (1956), 285-297.

Otzen, B. "Die neugefundenen hebräischen Sektenschriften und die Testamente der zwölf Patriarchen," *StTh* 7 (1953), 125-157.

————. "Some Text-problems in $_1$QS," *StTh* 11 (1957), 89-98.

Philonenko, M. "Le Maître de justice et la Sagesse de Salomon," *ThZ* 14 (1958), 81-88.

————. *Les interpolations chrétiennes des Testaments des douze patriarches et les manuscrits de Qoumran*. ("Cahiers de la Revue d'histoire et de philosophie religieuses, 35.") Paris: Presses universitaires de France, 1960.

Piper, O. A. "The 'Book of Mysteries' (Qumran I 27) A Study in Eschatology," *JR* 38 (1958), 95-106.

Ploeg, J. van der. "Le Rouleau d'Habacuc de la Grotte de 'Ain Fešḥa," *Bibl. Orient.* 8 (1951), 2-11.

———. "L'immortalité de l'homme d'après les textes de la Mer Morte," *VT* 2 (1952), 171-175.

———. "L'usage du parfait et de l'imparfait comme moyen de datation dans le commentaire d'Habacuc," in *Les Manuscrits de la Mer Morte* (Colloque de Strasbourg, 1955). Paris: Presses Universitaires de France, 1957.

———. *The Excavations at Qumran: A Survey of the Judean Brotherhood and its Ideas.* Translated by K. Smyth. New York: Longmans, Green and Co., 1958. (A translation of *Vondsten i de Woestijn van Juda* [1957.])

———. "The Meals of the Essenes," *JSS* 2 (1957), 163-175.

———. *Le Rouleau de la Guerre. See under* Texts.

———. "The Belief in Immortality in the Writings of Qumran," *Bibl. Orient.* 18 (1961), 118-124.

Quispel, G. "Christliche Gnosis und jüdische Heterodoxie," *EvTh* 14 (1954), 474-484.

Rabin, C. "Notes on the Habakkuk Scroll and the Zadokite Documents," *VT* 5 (1955), 148-162.

———. *Qumran Studies. (Scripta Judaica, II.)* London: Oxford University Press, 1957.

———. *The Zadokite Documents. See under* Texts.

———. "Literary Structure of the War Scroll," in *Essays on the Dead Sea Scrolls in Memory of E. L. Sukenik.* C. Rabin and Y. Yadin (eds.), assisted by J. Licht. Jerusalem: Hekhal ha-Sefer, 1961. (In Hebrew.)

Reicke, B. "Nytt ljus över Johannes döparens förkunnelse," *Religion och Bibel* 11 (1952), 5-18.

————. "Traces of Gnosticism in the Dead Sea
Scrolls?" *NTS* 1 (1954), 137-141.

————. "Remarques sur l'histoire de la forme
(Formgeschichte) des Textes de Qumran," in *Les
Manuscrits de la Mer Morte* (Colloque de Strasbourg,
1955). Paris: Presses Universitaires de France, 1957;
pp. 37-44.

Ringgren, H. *Handskrifterna från Qumran IV-V*.
("Symbolae Biblicae Upsalienses, 15.") Uppsala:
Wretmans, 1956.

————. "Gnosis i Qumrantexterna," *SEÅ* 24 (1959),
41-53.

————. "The Branch and the Plantation in the
Hodayot," *Bibl. Res.* 6 (1961), 3-9.

Roberts, B. J. "The Qumran Scrolls and the Essenes,"
NTS 3 (1956/57), 58-65.

Robinson, J. A. T. "The Baptism of John and the Qum-
ran Community," *HTR* 50 (1957), 175-191. (Also in
Twelve New Testament Studies. ["Studies in Biblical
Theology, 34."] Naperville, Ill.: Allenson, 1962.)

Rost, L. *Die Damaskusschrift. See under* Texts.

Roth, C. "A Solution to the Mystery of the Scrolls,"
Commentary 24 (1957), 317-324.

Rowley, H. H. *The Zadokite Fragments and the Dead
Sea Scrolls*. Oxford: Basil Blackwell, 1952.

————. "The Internal Dating of the Dead Sea Scrolls,"
EphThLov 28 (1952), 257-276.

————. "The Covenanters of Damascus and the Dead
Sea Scrolls," *BJRL* 35 (1952/53), 111-154.

————. "The Teacher of Righteousness and the Dead Sea Scrolls," *BJRL* 40 (1957/58), 114-146.

————. "Some Traces of the History of the Qumran Sect," *ThZ* 13 (1957), 530-540.

————. "The Baptism of John and the Qumran Sect," in *New Testament Essays; Studies in Memory of T. W. Manson*. Edited by A. J. B. Higgins. Manchester: University Press, 1959; pp. 218-229.

Rylaarsdam, J. C. *Revelation in Jewish Wisdom Literature*. Chicago: The University of Chicago Press, 1946.

Sanders, J. A. "Habakkuk in Qumran, Paul and the Old Testament," *JR* 39 (1959), 232-244.

Schechter, S. *Fragments of a Zadokite Work*. See under Texts.

Schnackenburg, R. "Logos-Hymnus und johanneischer Prolog," *BZ* 1 (1957), 69-109.

Schoeps, H. J. *Urgemeinde, Judentum, Gnosis*. Tübingen: J. C. B. Mohr (Paul Siebeck), 1956.

Scholem, G. *Major Trends in Jewish Mysticism*. Jerusalem: Schocken Publishing House, 1941.

Schubert, K. "Die jüdischen und judenchristlichen Sekten im Lichte des Handschriftenfundes von 'En Fešcha," *ZkathTheol* 74 (1952), 1-62.

————. "Der gegenwärtige Stand der Erforschung der in Palästina neu gefundenen hebräischen Handscriften, 25. Der Sektenkanon von En Feshcha und die Anfänge der jüdischen Gnosis," *TLZ* 78 (1953), cols. 495-506.

————. "Zwei Messiasse aus dem Regelbuch von Chirbet Qumran," *Judaica* 11 (1955), 216-235.

————. "Der alttestamentliche Hintergrund der Vorstellung von den beiden Messiassen im Schrifttum von Chirbet Qumran," *ibid.* 12 (1956), 24-28.

————. "Die Messiaslehre in den Texten von Chirbet Qumran," *BZ* 1 (1957), 177-197.

————. "Testament Juda 24 im Lichte der Texte von Chirbet Qumran," *WZKM* 53 (1957), 227-236.

————. *The Dead Sea Community: Its Origin and Teachings.* Translated by J. W. Doberstein. London: Adam and Charles Black, 1959. (A translation of *Die Gemeinde vom Totem Meer* [1958.])

Schulz, S. "Zur Rechtfertigung aus Gnaden in Qumran und bei Paulus," *ZThK* 56 (1959), 155-185.

Schweizer, E. "Röm. 1,3 f. und der Gegensatz von Fleisch und Geist vor und bei Paulus," *EvTh* 15 (1955), 563-571.

Seeligmann, I. L. "Voraussetzungen der Midraschexegese," in *Congress Volume, Copenhagen, 1953. VT Suppl. 1* (1953), 150-181.

Segal, M. H. "The Qumran War Scroll and the Date of its Composition," *Scripta Hierosolymitana* 4 (1958), 138-143.

Seitz, O. J. F. "Two Spirits in Man: An Essay in Biblical Exegesis," *NTS* 6 (1959/60), 82-95.

Silberman, L. H. "Unriddling the Riddle. A Study in the Structure and Language of the Habakkuk Pesher," *RQ* 3 (1961/62), 323-364.

Sjöberg, E. "Wiedergeburt und Neuschöpfung im palästinischen Judentum," *StTh* 4 (1950), 44-85.

————. "Neuschöpfung in den Toten-Meer-Rollen," *StTh* 9 (1955), 131-136.

Smith, M. " 'God's Begetting the Messiah' in ₁QSa,"
NTS 5 (1958/59), 218-224.

――――. "What is Implied by the Variety of Messianic
Figures?" *JBL* 78 (1959), 66-72.

Spicq, C. "L'Épitre aux Hébreux, Apollos, Jean-Baptiste,
les Hellénistes et Qumran," *RQ* 1 (1958/59), 365-390.

Stauffer, E. "Probleme der Priestertradition," *TLZ* 81
(1956), cols. 135-150 and 255.

――――. *Jerusalem und Rom im Zeitalter Jesu Christi.*
Bern: Francke (Dalp), 1957.

Stendahl, K. *The School of St. Matthew and Its Use of
the Old Testament.* ("Acta Seminarii Neotestamentici
Upsaliensis, XX.") Lund: Gleerup, 1954.

――――. (ed.) *The Scrolls and the New Testament.*
New York: Harper and Brothers, 1957.

――――. "The Scrolls and the New Testament: An Introduction and a Perspective," in *SNT*, pp. 1-17.

――――. "Hate, Non-Retaliation, and Love," *HTR* 55
(1962), 343-355.

Strack, H. L. and Billerbeck, P. *Kommentar zum Neuen
Testament aus Talmud und Midrasch: Exkurse zu
Einzelnen Stellen des Neuen Testaments,* Vol. IV.
München: Beck, 1928 (reprinted 1956).

Strugnell, J. "The Angelic Liturgy at Qumrân—₄Q
Serek Šîrôt 'ôlat Haššabbāt," in *Congress Volume,
Oxford, 1959. VT. Suppl.* 7 (1960), pp. 318-345.

Sukenik, E. L. and Avigad, N. *The Dead Sea Scrolls of
the Hebrew University. See under* Texts.

Sutcliffe, E. F. "The First Fifteen Members of the Qumran Community: A Note on ₁QS 8:1 ff.," *JSS* 4 (1959),
134-138.

————. "The General Council of the Qumran Community," *Biblica* 40 (1959), 971-983.

————. "Hatred at Qumran," *RQ* 2 (1959/60), 345-355.

————. "Sacred Meals at Qumran?" *Heythrop Journal* 1 (1960), 48-65.

Szyszman, S. "À propos du Karaïsme et des textes de la Mer Morte," *VT* 2 (1952), 343-348.

————. "La communauté de la Nouvelle Alliance et le Karaïsme," *Institut International de Sociologie XVI ème Congrès, Beaune, Fasc. III*, Sep. 19-26, 1954, pp. 189-202.

————. "Note sur la structure sociale des Karaïtes dans les Pays Arabes," *ibid.*, pp. 183-187.

————. "Ascèse et Pauvreté dans la Doctrine Karaïte," *ZRGG* 11 (1959), 373-380.

Talmon, S. "The 'Manual of Benedictions' of the Sect of the Judaean Desert," *RQ* 2 (1959/60), 475-500. (A translation with some alterations of "The Order of Prayers of the Sect from the Judaean Desert," [in Hebrew], *Tarbiz* 29 [1959], 1-20.)

Teicher, J. L. "The Dead Sea Scrolls—Documents of the Jewish-Christian Sect of Ebionites," *JJS* 2 (1950/51), 67-99.

————. "The Damascus Fragments and the Origin of the Jewish Christian Sect," *ibid.*, 115-143.

————. "The Teaching of the Pre-Pauline Church in the Dead Sea Scrolls," *ibid.*, 3 (1952), 111-118, 139-150; 4 (1953), 1-13, 49-58, 93-103, 139-153.

————. "Priests and Sacrifices in the Dead Sea Scrolls," *JJS* 5 (1954), 93-99.

Treves, M. "The Two Spirits of the Rule of the Community," *RQ* 3 (1961/62), 449-452.

de Vaux, R. "Fouilles de Khirbet Qumrân, Rapport préliminaire sur les 3e, 4e, et 5e campagnes," *RB* 63 (1956), 532-577.

―――――. *L'archéologie et les manuscrits de la Mer Morte.* (*The Schweich Lectures of the British Academy, 1959.*) London: Oxford University Press, 1961.

Vermès, G. "À propos des Commentaires bibliques découverts à Qumrân," *RHPhR* 35 (1955), 95-102.

―――――. "The Etymology of 'Essenes,'" *RQ* 2 (1959/60), 427-443.

―――――. *The Dead Sea Scrolls in English. See under* Texts.

Vogt, E. "'Mysteria' in textibus Qumrān," *Biblica* 37 (1956), 247-257.

―――――. "'Peace Among Men of God's Good Pleasure' Lk. 2:14," in *SNT*, pp. 114-117. (A translation with some revisions from "'Pax hominibus bonae voluntatis' Lc. 2,14," *Biblica* 34 [1953], 427-429.)

Wallace, D. "The Essenes and Temple Sacrifice," *ThZ* 13 (1957), 335-338.

Wallenstein, M. "Some Lexical Material in the Judean Scrolls," *VT* 4 (1954), 211-214.

―――――. "A Hymn from the Scrolls," *VT* 5 (1955), 277-283.

Weise, M. *Kultzeiten und kultischer Bundesschluss in der "Ordensregel" vom Toten Meer.* ("Studia Post-Biblica, 3.") Leiden: Brill, 1961.

Wernberg-Møller, P. *The Manual of Discipline.* See *under* Texts.

————. In a review of E. Nielsen and B. Otzen, *Dødehavsteksterne. Skrifter fra den jødiske menighed i Qumran i oversaettelse og med noter* (1959), *RQ* 1 (1958/59), 545.

————. "A Reconsideration of the Two Spirits in the Rule of the Community," *RQ* 3 (1961/62), 413-441.

Wibbing, S. *Die Tugend- und Lasterkataloge im Neuen Testament, und ihre Traditionsgeschichte unter besondere Berücksichtigung der Qumran-Texte. (Beiheft ZNW,* 25.) Berlin: Töpelmann, 1959.

Wieder, N. "The 'Law-Interpreter' of the Sect of the Dead Sea Scrolls: The Second Moses," *JJS* 4 (1953), 158-175.

————. "The Habakkuk Scroll and the Targum," *JJS* 4 (1953), 14-18.

————. "The Term *QŠ* in the Dead Sea Scrolls and in Hebrew Liturgical Poetry," *JJS* 5 (1954), 22-31.

————. "The Doctrine of the Two Messiahs Among the Karaites," *JJS* 6 (1955), 14-25.

————. "The Qumran Sectaries and the Karaites," *JQR* 47 (1956/57), 97-113, 269-292.

Wieluck, D. "Zwei 'neue' Antike Zeugen über Essener," *VT* 7 (1957), 418-419.

Wiesenberg, E. "Chronological Data in the Zadokite Fragments," *VT* 5 (1955), 284-308.

Wilson, R. McL. "Gnostic Origins," *VigChr* 9 (1955), 193-211.

————. "Simon, Dositheus and the Dead Sea Scrolls," *ZRGG* 9 (1957), 21-30.

Winter, P. "Ben Sira and the Teaching of 'Two Ways,' "
VT 5 (1955), 315-318.

――――. "The Holy Messiah," *ZNW* 50 (1959), 275.

van der Woude, A. S. *Die messianischen Vorstellungen
der Gemeinde von Qumran*. ("Studien Semitica
Neerlandica, 3.") Aasen: Van Gorcum, 1957.

Yadin, Y. *The Scroll of the War of the Sons of Light
against the Sons of Darkness. See under* Texts.

――――. "A note on DSD IV 20," *JBL* 74 (1955), 40-
43.

――――. "Three Notes on the Dead Sea Scrolls," *IEJ* 6
(1956), 158-162.

――――. "The Dead Sea Scrolls and the Epistle to the
Hebrews," *Scripta Hierosolymitana* 4 (1958), 36-55.

――――. "A Midrash on 2 Sam. vii and Ps. i-ii ($_4$Q
Florilegium)," *IEJ* 9 (1959), 95-98.

――――. "A Crucial Passage in the Dead Sea Scrolls.
$_1$QSa ii.11-17," *JBL* 78 (1959), 238-241.

Theologies at Qumran: Selected and Annotated Bibliography

James H. Charlesworth with Henry W. L. Rietz

This bibliography is an annotated selection of major publications on the theologies at Qumran. Emphasis is placed on books that postdate 1980. The annotations are by Charlesworth. They are intended to help guide the scholar and the student, and to stimulate more discussion of the theological importance of the Dead Sea Scrolls. In addition to the books listed below and on pages 255–85, attention is drawn to the theological comments found in the series titled Discoveries in the Judaean Desert, and to the articles appearing in periodicals, especially the following:

Catholic Biblical Quarterly

Dead Sea Discoveries: A Journal of Current Research on the Scrolls and Related Literature

Bible Review

Biblical Archaeologist

Biblical Archaeology Review

Folia Orientalia

Journal of Biblical Literature

Journal for Jewish Studies

Journal for the Study of Judaism

Journal for the Study of the Pseudepigrapha and Related Literature [see the special fascicle on Qumran]

Revue de Qumran

Revue biblique

Tarbiz

Assaf, D., ed. *Proceedings of the Ninth World Congress of Jewish Studies.* Division A: The Period of the Bible. Jerusalem: World Union of Jewish Studies, 1986. [See the discussions on religious change by W. O. McCready, Qumran liturgy by L. H. Schiffman, and the "evil woman" by L. Archer (which can be enriched by including the Qumranic Dame Folly and Lady Wisdom [4Q184]).]

Bammel, E. *Judaica.* Wissenschaftliche Untersuchungen zum Neuen Testament 37; Tübingen: J. C. B. Mohr (Paul Siebeck), 1986. [See esp. pp. 95–126.]

Becker, J. *Das Heil Gottes: Heils-und Sündenbegriffe in den Qumrantexten und im Neuen Testament.* Studien zur Umwelt des Neuen Testaments 3; Göttingen: Vandenhoeck & Ruprecht, 1964. [A brilliant study of holiness and sin at Qumran.]

Ben-Tor, A., J. C. Greenfield, and A. Malamat, eds. *Eretz-Israel: Archaeological, Historical and Geographical Studies [Yigael Yadin Memorial Volume].* Eretz Israel 20; Jerusalem: Israel Exploration Society, 1989. [Examine the discussions on Qumran's sacred meal (E. Lipinski), hymns (H. Ringgren), offerings (L. H. Schiffman), and biblical interpretation (G. Vermes).]

Betz, O. and R. Riesner. *Jesus, Qumran und der Vatikan: Klarstellungen.* Giessen and Basel: Brunnen Verlag, 1993. [Although responding to sensational claims made about the Dead Sea Scrolls during the past five years, Betz and Riesner present many valuable theological insights, esp. regarding the Zadokites, the calendar, Sabbath observance, and messianism.]

Black, M. *The Scrolls and Christian Origins.* Chico, Calif.; Scholars Press, 1983. [Dated but significant reflections on Qumran theology by a pioneer and a revered international expert.]

———— ed. *The Scrolls and Christianity: Historical and Theologial Significance.* S. P. C. K. Theological Collections 11; London: S. P. C. K., 1969. [Eight studies, see esp. those on the sect (Albright and Mann) rites and customs (Harrison), the Righteous Teacher and messianism (Brown), eschatology (Pryke), and dualism (Wilcox).]

Braun, H. *Qumran und das Neue Testament,* 2 vols. Tübingen: J. C. B. Mohr (Paul Siebeck), 1966. [A major survey which draws attention to theological concepts of the Qumran Community]

Brooke, G. J. *Exegesis at Qumran: 4QFlorilegium in its Jewish Context.* Journal for the Study of the Old Testament Supplement Series 29; Sheffield: JSOT Press, 1985. [This is a major study of 4Q Florilegium and other scrolls; Brooke correctly stresses that biblical exegesis at Qumran depended on certain principles, and that scholars must seek to understand the method of composition of each scroll.]

Broshi, M. "Introduction," in *The Dead Sea Scrolls.* Tokyo: Kodansha, 1979; pp. 12–20. [The curator of the Shrine of the Book in Jerusalem rightly emphasizes the following: "Perhaps the most important theological point differentiating the sectarians from the rest of Judaism was their belief in predestination, coupled with a dualistic view of the world (praedestinatio duplex)" (p. 15).]

Brown, R. E., P. Perkins, and A. J. Saldarini. "Dead Sea Scrolls," in *The New Jerome Biblical Commentary,* ed. R. E. Brown, J. A. Fitzmyer, R. E. Murphy. Englewood Cliffs, N.J.: Prentice Hall, 1990; pp. 1068–82. [A solid survey focused on 1QS, 1QSa, 1QSb, 1QH, CD, 1QM, the Pesherim, 4Q Testimonia, 4Q Florilegium, 1QapGen, 3Q15, 11Q Temple, and the history and features of Qumran life and thought.]

Burgmann, H. *Weitere Lösbarre Qumran Problem.* Qumranica Mogilanensia 9; Cracow: Enigma Press, 1992. [Interspersed are frequent theological contributions]

Caquot, A. and M. Philonenko, "Introduction générale," in *La Bible: Écrits intertestamentaires.* [Paris]: Gallimard, 1987. [See esp. pp. xxxiv–lix.]

Casciaro-Ramírez, J.M. *Qumrān y el Nuevo Testamento.* Ediciones Universidad de Navarra 29; Pamplona: Ediciones Universidad de Navarra, 1982. [A study of the theologies of community and salvation at Qumran]

Caserta, N. *Gli Esseni e le Origini del Cristianesimo.* Naples: La Nuova Cultura Editrice, 1978. [Contains numerous reflections on Qumran life, ethics, doctrines, asceticism, liturgy, messianism, knowledge, and eschatology]

Charlesworth, J. H., ed. *The Dead Sea Scrolls: Hebrew, Aramaic, and Greek Texts with English Translations,* 12 vols. The Princeton Theological Seminary Dead Sea Scrolls Project; Tübingen: J.C.B. Mohr (Paul Siebeck) and Louisville: Westminster/John Knox Press, 1993–. [This collection of the Dead Sea Scrolls is the comprehensive and critical edition of all the Scrolls that are not copies of books in the Hebrew Bible.]

————— ed. *Jesus and the Dead Sea Scrolls.* Anchor Bible Reference Library; New York: Doubleday, 1992. [See the first chapter, which focuses on the theologies at Qumran (J. H. Charlesworth); the Temple Scroll (O. Betz); the covenant at Qumran (H. C. Kee); Qumran opposition to the Temple (C. A. Evans); Qumran meals (J. D. G. Dunn); and Qumran angelic mediator figures (A. F. Segal).]

————— ed. *John and the Dead Sea Scrolls.* Christian Origins Library; New York: Crossroad, 1990. [See esp. the chap-

ters on Qumran theology (J. L. Price), Qumran pneumatology (A. R. C. Leaney), the Qumran calendar (A.
Jaubert), and Qumran dualism (J. H. Charlesworth).]

_____ ed. *The Messiah: Developments in Earliest Judaism and
Christianity*. Minneapolis: Fortress, 1992. [See esp. the
studies by S. Talmon, L. H. Schiffman, and J. Priest.]

_____ ed. *The Old Testament Pseudepigrapha*, 2 vols. New
York: Doubleday, 1983, 1985. [This collection of the Old
Testament Pseudepigrapha is the most extensive.]

Collins, J. J. *The Apocalyptic Imagination: An Introduction to
the Jewish Matrix of Christianity*. New York: Crossroad,
1988. [See esp. his study of Qumran apocalyptic theology
on pp. 115–41.]

_____ "The Dead Sea Scrolls," *Anchor Bible Dictionary*
(1992) 2.85–101. [A major survey with special attention
to apocalyptic thought.]

_____ "Patterns of Eschatology at Qumran," in *Traditions
in Transformation*, ed. J. D. Levenson and B. Halpern.
Winona Lake: Eisenbrauns, 1981; pp. 351–75. [Rightly
points to the diverse eschatological conceptions at
Qumran.]

Cross, F. M. "The Early History of the Apocalyptic Community at Qumran," in *Canaanite Myth and Hebrew Epic:
Essays in the History of the Religion of Israel*. Cambridge,
Mass.: Harvard University Press, 1973; pp. 326–46. [A
significant study of the priestly apocalyptists at Qumran.]

Davidson, M. J. *Angels at Qumran: A Comparative Study of 1
Enoch 1–36, 72–108 and Sectarian Writings from Qumran*.
Journal for the Study of the Pseudepigrapha Supplement
Series 11; Sheffield: JSOT Press, 1992. [A study of ange-
lology in the following scrolls: 1QS, CD, 1QH, 1QM,
ShirShab, and numerous fragmentary works.]

Davies, P. R. *Behind the Essenes: History and Ideology in the Dead Sea Scrolls*. Brown Judaic Studies 94; Atlanta: Scholars Press, 1987. [A solid and informative presentation of Qumran theologies.]

———— "Damascus Rule (CD)," *Anchor Bible Dictionary* (1992) 2.8–10. [See esp. "Organization and Ideology."]

———— "Halakah at Qumran," in *A Tribute to Geza Vermes: Essays on Jewish and Christian Literature and History*, ed. P. R. Davies and R. T. White. Journal for the Study of the Old Testament Supplement Series 100; Sheffield: Sheffield Academic Press, 1990. [Responds to and adds to Shiffman's study.]

———— *Qumran*. Cities of the Biblical World; Grand Rapids, Mich.: William B. Eerdmans, 1982. [A well written introduction that brings out many of the theological features of the Qumran sect.]

———— "War Rule (1QM)," *Anchor Bible Dictionary* (1992) 6.875–76. [A short survey that includes theological comments.]

Delcor, M., ed. *Qumrân: Sa piété, sa théologie et son milieu*. Bibliotheca Ephemeridum Theologicarum Lovaniensium 46; Louvain: Leuven University Press and Paris: Gembloux, 1978. [Numerous theological studies by leading Qumran specialists.]

———— *Religion d'Israël et proche orient ancien: Des Phéniciens aux Esséniens*. Leiden: E. J. Brill, 1976. [This leading expert shares his reflections on the Qumran theological concept of covenant, the horoscopes, cultic meals, hymns, mysticism, and initiation (most need to be updated now).]

———— and F. García-Martínez. *Introduccion a la literatura esenia de Qumran*. Madrid: Ediciones Cristiandad, 1982. [See esp. the final section of Essene doctrines on pp. 285–314.]

Denis, A. – M. *Les thèmes de connaissance dans le Document de Damas.* Studia Hellenistica 15; Louvain: Publications Universitaires, 1967. [This is a major study of knowledge in CD by a world class authority; the study needs to be extended to other Scrolls in the search for what is unique to Qumran.]

Dimant, D. "Pesherim, Qumran," *Anchor Bible Dictionary* (1992) 5:244–51. [An informative survey of exegesis at Qumran.]

————— "Qumran Sectarian Literature," in *Jewish Writings of the Second Temple Period: Apocrypha, Pseudepigrapha, Qumran Sectarian Writings, Philo, Josephus,* ed. M. E. Stone. Compendia Rerum Iudaicarum ad Novum Testamentum 2; Assen: Van Gorcum and Philadelphia: Fortress Press, 1984; pp. 483–550. [This Israeli Qumran specialist presents a reliable introduction to most of the Qumran Scrolls, with an emphasis on theological contents.]

————— and U. Rappaport, eds. *The Dead Sea Scrolls: Forty Years of Research.* Studies on the Texts of the Desert of Judah 10; Leiden: E. J. Brill and Jerusalem: The Magnes Press, 1992. [See esp. the reflections on criteria for discerning sectarian composition by E. G. Chazon, and the study of the following Qumran concepts: the exodus and conquest traditions (C. A. Newsom), hymnology (B. Nitzan), influence of Ezekiel (B. Z. Wacholder), purification (J. M. Baumgarten), halakot (L. H. Schiffman), law and truth (D. R. Schwartz), and liturgy (M. Weinfeld).]

Dombrowski, B. W. W. *An Annotated Translation of Miqsāt Ma'śēh ha-Tôrâ (4QMMT).* Cracow: Weezen, 1993. [Contains numerous theological insights into the meaning of this major work.]

Driver, G. R. *The Judaean Scrolls: The Problem and a Solution.* Oxford: Basil Blackwell, 1965. [See esp. the final two chapters on doctrines, customs, covenant, and dualism.]

Duhaime, J. "Dualistic Reworking in the Scrolls from Qumran," *Catholic Biblical Quarterly* 49 (1987) 32–56. [A careful study of dualism at Qumran by an expert.]

————— "L'instruction sur les deux esprits et les interpolations dualistes à Qumran (1QS iii, 13-iv, 26)," *Revue biblique* 84 (1977) 566–94. [A study of interpolations in the major passage on dualism in the Dead Sea Scrolls.]

————— "La rédaction de 1QM xiii et l'évolution du dualisme à Qumran," *Revue biblique* 84 (1977) 210–38. [A focused study of dualism in 1QM 13.]

Evans, C. A. and W. F. Stinespring, eds. *Early Jewish and Christian Exegesis: Studies in Memory of William Hugh Brownlee.* Scholars Press Homage Series; Atlanta: Scholars Press, 1987. [See the chapters on Qumran by G. J. Brooke, J. C. Trever, W. S. LaSor, and J. H. Charlesworth.]

Fabry, H.J. *Die Wurzel Šûb in der Qumran-Literatur: Zur Semantik eines Grundbegriffes.* Bonner Biblische Beiträge 46; Köln-Bonn: Peter Hanstein Verlag, 1975. [A semantic and theological study of "return," with a clarification of its ethical meaning at Qumran.]

Fishbane, M. "Use, Authority and Interpretation of Mikra at Qumran," in *Mikra: Text, Translation, Reading and Interpretation of the Hebrew Bible in Ancient Judaism and Early Christianity,* ed. M. J. Mulder. Compendia Rerum Iudaicarum ad Novum Testamentum 2.1; Assen/Maastricht: Van Gorcum and Philadelphia: Fortress Press, 1988; pp. 339–77. [A study by a leading expert on Jewish interpretation of scripture.]

Fitzmyer, J. A. *Essays on the Semitic Background of the New Testament*. Society of Biblical Literature Society for Biblical Study 5; Missoula, MT: Scholars Press, 1974. [Contains numerous reflections on the theological thoughts in the Dead Sea Scrolls by one of the Qumran experts in the United States.]

————— *Responses to 101 Questions on the Dead Sea Scrolls*. New York and Mahwah, N.J.: Paulist Press, 1992. [Numerous questions answered by this leading Qumran scholar concern theological issues.]

————— *A Wandering Aramean: Collected Aramaic Essays*. Society of Biblical Literature Monograph Series 25; Missoula, MT: Scholars Press, 1979. [Some insights regarding Qumran theological ideas are scattered throughout this book.]

Flusser, D. *Judaism and the Origins of Christianity*. Jerusalem: The Magnes Press, The Hebrew University, 1988. [The 41 chapters often contain major insights into the theologies at Qumran; esp. see chapters 1–16.]

Garnet, P. *Salvation and Atonement in the Qumran Scrolls*. Wissenschaftliche Untersuchungen zum Neuen Testament 2.3; Tübingen: J.C.B. Mohr (Paul Siebeck), 1977. [Focuses primarily on 1 QS, but also on CD, 1QSa, 1QSb, 4Q Testimonia, 1QM, and 1QpHab.]

Gärtner, B. *The Temple and the Community in Qumran and the New Testament*. Society for New Testament Studies Monograph Series 1; Cambridge: Cambridge University Press, 1965. [Discusses the Temple symbolism at Qumran.]

Grözinger, K. E., et al., eds. *Qumran*. Wege der Forschung 410; Darmstadt: Wissenschaftliche Buchgesellschaft, 1981. [Numerous major studies, esp. on the Yahad

(J. Maier), guilt and ritual cleansing at Qumran (A. Dupont-Somner), the Qumran theology of suffering (J. Carmignac), and messianism (K. Schubert).]

Hayes, J. J. and F. Prussner. "Early Judaism and Old Testament Theology," in *Old Testament Theology: Its History & Development*. Atlanta: John Knox Press, 1985; pp. 276–790. [This short passage is the only one about early Jewish theology that appears in major studies of Old Testament Theology, and it makes the point that biblical theologians—especially Eichrodt and von Rad—tend to portray developments subsequent to the Old Testament as degenerations. This is at once true, lamentable, and an indefensible side of Christian apologetics (and perhaps polemics).]

Hellholm, D., ed. *Apocalypticism in the Mediterranean World and the Near East: Proceedings of the International Colloquium on Apocalypticism; Uppsala, August 12–17, 1979*. Tübingen: J. C. B. Mohr (Paul Siebeck), 1983. [See esp. the chapters by M. Philonenko and H. Stegemann on Qumran apocalyptic theology.]

Hengel, M. and A. M. Schwemer, eds. *Königsherrschaft Gottes und himmlischer Kult im Judentum, Urchristentum und in der hellenistischen Welt*. Wissenschaftliche Untersuchungen zum Neuen Testament 55; Tübingen: J. C. B. Mohr (Paul Siebeck), 1991. [See esp. A. M. Schwemer's study of God as king and his kingship in the Qumran ShirShirot.]

Jeremias, G. *Der Lehrer der Gerechtigkeit*. Studien zur Umwelt des Neuen Testaments 2; Göttingen: Vandenhoeck & Ruprecht, 1963. [A classic study which points to the sections in 1QH that were probably written by the Righteous Teacher, and a study of his self-understanding.]

Jeremias, J. *Die theologische Bedeutung der Funde am Toten Meer*. Göttingen: Vandenhoeck & Ruprecht, 1962. (English translation in *Corcordia Theological Monthly* 39 [1968] 557–71). [This world renowned New Testament expert stressed the foundational nature of Qumran dualism for Qumran theology.]

Kapper, C. et al. *Apocalypses et voyages dans l'au-delà.* Paris: Les Éditions du Cerf, 1987. [See esp. the study of Qumran apocalypticism by F. García-Martínez, pp. 201–35.]

Kittel, B. *The Hymns of Qumran: Translation and Commentary.* Society of Biblical Literature Dissertation Series 50; Chico, Calif.: Scholars Press, 1981. [See esp. "Theology and Poetry" on pp. 173–79.]

Klinzing, G. *Die Umdeutung des Kultus in der qumrangemeinde und im Neuen Testament.* Studien zur Umwelt des Neuen Testaments 7; Göttingen: Vandenhoeck & Ruprecht, 1971. [An important study of the Qumran cult as a Temple.]

Kobelski, P. J. *Melchizedek and Melchireša^c.* The Catholic Biblical Monograph Series 10; Washington, D. C.: Catholic Biblical Association of America, 1981. [See esp. pp. 49 until the end.]

Kuhn, H.-W. *Enderwartung und gegenwärtiges Heil: Untersuchungen zu den Gemeindeliedern von Qumran.* Studien zur Umwelt des Neuen Testaments 4; Göttingen: Vandenhoeck & Ruprecht, 1966. [A major study of the eschatological ideas at Qumran.]

Laperrousaz, E.-M. *L'Attente du Messie en Palestine à la veille et au début l'ère chrétienne.* Collection Empreinte; Paris: Picard, 1982. [An important study of Qumran messianism, read in light of the studies published in *The Messiah*, ed. Charlesworth.]

——— *Les Esséniens selon leur témoignage direct.* Religions et culture; Paris: Desclée, 1982. [This study draws attention to Qumran organization, ritual, doctrine, and meals.]

LaSor, W. S. *The Dead Sea Scrolls and the New Testament.* Grand Rapids, Mich.: William B. Erdmans Publishing Company, 1972. [An introduction which discusses many of the theological concerns of the Qumran sect.]

Leaney, A. R. C. *The Rule of the Community.* New Testament Library; London: SCM Press, 1966. [One of the best studies of "Qumran Theology" is found in "The Teaching of Qumran" on pp. 31–107.]

Lichtenberger, H. *Studien zum Menschenbild in Texten der Qumrangemeinde.* Studien zur Umwelt des Neuen Testaments 15; Göttingen: Vandenhoeck & Ruprecht, 1980. [This Qumran expert shows that Qumran concepts of the human are diverse.]

Lohfink, N. *Lobgesänge der Armen: Studien zum Magnifikat, den Hodajot von Qumran und einigen späten Psalmen.* Stuttgarter Bibelstudien 143; Stuttgart: Verlag Katholisches Bibelwerk, 1990. [A distinguished Old Testament specialist publishes his insights regarding the concept of "the Poor" at Qumran, esp. in 1QH.]

MacDonald, J., ed. *Dead Sea Scrolls Studies 1969.* The Annual of Leeds University Oriental Society 6; Leiden; E. J. Brill, 1969. [See esp. the studies of the Holy Spirit at Qumran by F. F. Bruce, the nature of the Yahad by P. Wernberg-Møller, and two studies on the Qumran interpretations of scripture by G. Vermes and by S. Lowy.]

Menzies, R. P. *The Development of Early Christian Pneumatology with Special Reference to Luke-Acts.* Journal for the Study of the New Testament Supplement Series 54;

Sheffield: Sheffield Academic Press, 1991. [See esp. his study of the Qumran theological concepts of Spirits, Wisdom, and prophetic inspiration on pp. 77–90.]

Merrill, E. H. *Qumran and Predestination: A Theological Study of the Thanksgiving Hymns.* Studies on the Texts of the Desert of Judah 8; Leiden; E.J. Brill, 1975. [This study of predestination in 1QH needs to be expanded into a major monograph which will include all the significant predestinarian passages in the scrolls, esp. in 1QS and 4Q186.]

Milgrom, J. "The Qumran Cult: Its Exegetical Principles," in *Temple Scroll Studies: Papers Presented at the International Symposium on the Temple Scroll,* ed. G. J. Brooke. Journal for the Study of the Pseudepigrapha Supplement Series 7; Sheffield: Sheffield Academic Press, 1989; pp. 165–180. [This leading Qumran expert shows that while the Qumranites shared with their fellow Jews many principles of interpreting scripture, they differed from other Jews by their exegetical technique of homogenization. Also, while the rabbis tolerated divergent scriptural exegesis, the Qumranites found them intolerable.]

Moraldi, L. *Il Maestro di Giustizia: "L'innominato" dei manoscritti di Qumrân.* Maestri di Spiritualità; [Milan]: Editrice Esperienze, 1971. [Important reflections on the Righteous Teacher and history, messianism, and Jesus.]

Moraldi, L., ed. *I Manoscritti di Qumrân,* 2nd ed. Classici delle Religioni; Turin: Unione Tipografico-Editrice Torinese, 1986. [One of the major modern collections; on Qumran theological ideas see pp. 24–89.

Muñoz León, D., ed. *Salvacion en la palabra: Targum, Derash, Berith: En memoria del professor Alejandro Diez Macho.* Madrid: Ediciones Cristiandad, 1986. [See esp. the discussion of the theological concepts of the New Jerusalem and the Temple at Qumran by F. García-Martínez on pp. 563–90.]

Murphy-O'Connor, J. "Community, Rule of the (1QS)," *Anchor Bible Dictionary* (1992) 1.1110–1112. [A concise review.]

———— "The Judaean Desert," in *Early Judaism and its Modern Interpreters*, ed. R. A. Kraft and G. W. E. Nickelsburg. Philadelphia: Fortress Press and Atlanta: Scholars Press, 1989; pp. 119–56. [Warns that "wide-ranging syntheses can no longer be taken for granted" (p. 143.]

———— "Qumran and the New Testament," in *The New Testament and its Modern Interpreters*, ed. E. J. Epp and G. W. MacRae. Philadelphia: Fortress Press and Atlanta: Scholars Press, 1989; pp. 55–71. [Though focused on the New Testament, this study isolates many major features of the theologies at Qumran.]

———— and J. H. Charlesworth, eds. *Paul and the Dead Sea Scrolls.* Christian Origins Library; New York: Crossroad, 1990. [See esp. the studies on the following Qumran concepts: angelology (J. A. Fitzmyer), judicial organization (M. Delcor), justification (W. Grundmann), mystery (J. Coppens), and truth (J. Murphy-O'Connor).]

Neusner, J., W. S. Green, and E. Frerichs, eds. *Judaisms and their Messiahs at the Turn of the Christian Era.* Cambridge: Cambridge University Press, 1987. [See the discussions of Qumran messianism by S. Talmon and Jewish messianology by J. H. Charlesworth.]

Newsom, C. *Songs of the Sabbath Sacrifice: A Critical Edition.* Harvard Semitic Studies 27; Atlanta: Scholars Press, 1985. [An important study of a major document; see esp. her discussions of "Angelology" and "The Heavenly Temple."]

Nötscher, F. *Vom Alten zum Neuen Testament: Gesammelte Aufsätze.* Bonner Biblische Beiträge 17; Bonn: Peter Hanstein Verlag, 1962. [Though dated, this collection of essays is focused on some major theological concerns at Qumran by a leading expert.]

Nickelsburg, G. W. E. and M. E. Stone, eds. *Faith and Piety in Early Judaism: Texts and Documents.* Philadelphia: Trinity Press International, 1991. [These leading experts on Early Judaism make available in a convenient format many texts, including the Dead Sea Scrolls; see esp. their theological understanding of Temple, cult, the community as Temple (1QS 8.4-10, 1QH 6.22-31), the way of the Spirit of Truth, God's judgment, the presence of eternal life (1QH 11.3-14), expectations, messianism, Melchizedek, and Wisdom.]

Osten-Sacken, P. von der. *Gott und Belial: Traditionsgeschichtliche Untersuchungen zum Dualismus in den Texten aus Qumran.* Studien zur Umwelt des Neuen Testaments 6; Göttingen: Vandenhoeck & Ruprecht, 1969. [An important study of Qumran dualism.]

[Philonenko, M. and A. Caquot]. *La littérature intertestamentaire.* Bibliothèque des centres d'études supérieures spécialisés; Paris: Presses Universitaires, 1985. [See the preface by A. Caquot and the discussion of Qumran messianism by E.-M. Laperrousaz.]

Räisänen, H. *Beyond New Testament Theology: A Story and Programme.* London: SCM and Philadelphia: Trinity Press International, 1990. [A major appeal to go beyond the canonical myopia that has blinded most studies of biblical theology; attractive are the arguments that we must study so-called New Testament theology in light of the developments in Early Judaism and elsewhere (see p. 113).]

Rowland, C. C. "The Second Temple: Focus of Ideological Struggle?" in *Templum Amicitiae: Essays on the Second Temple presented to Ernst Bammel*, ed. W. Horbury. Journal for the Study of the New Testament Supplement Series 48; Sheffield: Sheffield Academic Press, 1991; pp. 175–98. [This leading expert on apocalypticism writes a major study on anti-Temple polemic in Early Judaism with only brief allusions to the Dead Sea Scrolls, but he calls for a detailed study of this theme at Qumran; cf. Evans' publication in *Jesus and the Dead Sea Scrolls.*]

Sanders, E. P. *Jesus and Judaism*. Philadelphia: Fortress Press, 1985. [See esp. the discussions of the New Temple and restoration eschatology on pp. 77–119.]

_____ *Judaism: Practice and Belief 63 BCE-66 CE*. London: SCM Press and Philadelphia: Trinity Press International, 1992. [See esp. this leading authority's discussion of Qumran membership, organization, practices, and beliefs, pp. 341–79.]

_____ *Paul and Palestinian Judaism*. Philadelphia: Fortress Press, 1977. [Scattered throughout this work are major insights into Qumran theology.]

_____ *Paul, the Law, and the Jewish People*. Philadelphia: Fortress Press, 1983. [See the section on Qumran.]

Schiffman, L. H. *The Eschatological Community of the Dead Sea Scrolls: A Study of the Rule of the Community*. Society of Biblical Literature Monograph Series 38; Atlanta: Scholars Press, 1989. [A study on an important messianic Dead Sea Scroll.]

_____ *Reclaiming the Dead Sea Scrolls: The History of Judaism, the Background of Christianity, the Lost Library of Qumran*. Philadelphia and Jerusalem: The Jewish Publication Society, 1994. [See esp. Part V "Mysticism, Messianism, and the End of Days."]

_____ Sectarian Law in the Dead Sea Scrolls: Courts, Testimony and the Penal Code. Brown Judaic Studies 33; Chico, Calif.: Scholars Press, 1983. [A major study of so-called halakoth at Qumran.]

Schubert, K. "Lebensbild der Gemeinde," in Die Qumran-Essener: Texte der Schriftrollen und Lebensbild der Gemeinde, ed. J. Maier and K. Schubert. Uni-Taschenbücher 224; München/Basel: Ernst Reinhardt Verlag, 1982; pp. 9–105. [A study of the priestly and non-priestly groups at Qumran, the Righteous Teacher, and Qumran eschatology.]

Schwartz, D. R. Studies in the Jewish Background of Christianity. Wissenschaftliche Untersuchungen zum Neuen Tetsament 60; Tübingen: J. C. B. Mohr (Paul Siebeck), 1992. [Esp. significant is Schwartz' judicious appeal to refer to the Qumran Community, not as a Temple, but as "a functional substitute for the Temple" (p. 38).]

Sekki, A. E. The Meaning of Ruah at Qumran. Society of Biblical Literature Dissertation Series 110; Atlanta: Scholars Press, 1989. [A study of "spirit" at Qumran, divided into the spirit of God, of humans, of angels, and of demons, and spirit as wind and breath.]

Shinan, A., ed. Proceedings of the Sixth World Congress of Jewish Studies. Division C: Jewish Thought. Jerusalem: World Union of Jewish Studies, 1977. [See the contribution on Qumran wisdom by Y. Amir.]

Shozo, F. The Temple Theology of the Qumran Sect and the Book of Ezekiel: Their Relationship to Jewish Literature of the Last Two Centuries B.C. Princeton Th.D. 1970. [Shozo argues that the Qumranites considered themselves "as a symbolic temple" (p. 316), and that right interpretation of Torah along with its strict observance "had precedence over sacrificial ritual" (p. 320).]

Stanley, C. D. *Paul and the Language of Scripture: Citation Technique in the Pauline Epistles and Contemporary Literature.* Society for New Testament Studies Monograph Series 69; Cambridge: Cambridge University Press, 1992. [This careful philological study includes a section on Qumran technique of citing scripture.]

Stegemann, H. "Der Land in der Tempelrolle und in anderen Texten aus den Qumranfunde," in *Das Land israel in biblischer Zeit: Jerusalem-Symposium 1981 der Hebräischen Universität und der Georg-August-Universität,* ed. G. Strecker. Göttinger Theologische Arbeiten 25; Göttingen: Vandenhoeck & Ruprecht, 1983; pp. 154–71.

Stendahl, K., ed., with H. H. Charlesworth. *The Scrolls and the New Testament,* Christian Origins Library; New York: Crossroad, 1992. [An anthology which contains important studies on Qumran messianology, the communal meal, temptation, sin and flesh (all by K. G. Kuhn), flesh and spirit (by W. D. Davies), dualism (by R. E. Brown), and other related issues.]

Talmon, S. *The World of Qumran from Within: Collected Studies.* Jerusalem: The Magnes Press, The Hebrew University and Leiden: E. J. Brill, 1989. [This brilliant scholar of Qumran theologies focuses on prayer, messianism, millenarianism, the calendar, the Community, and covenant.]

Thyen, H. *Studien zue Sündenvergebung im Neuen Testament und seinen alttestamentlichen und jüdischen Voraussetzungen.* Forschungen zur Religion und Literatur des Alten und Neuen Testaments 96; Göttingen: Vandenhoeck & Ruprecht, 1970. [See esp. "Sünde und Vergebund in der Gemeinde von Qumran," pp. 77–98.]

Trebolle-Barrera, J. and L. Vegas-Montaner, eds. *The Madrid Qumran Congress: Proceedings of the International Con-*

gress on the Dead Sea Scrolls Madrid 18–21 March, 1991, 2 vols. Studies on the Texts of the Desert of Judah 9.1; Leiden: E. J. Brill, 1992. [See esp. E. Qimron's study of celibacy at Qumran, J. Maier's work on the style and calendar of the ShirShirot, J. Milgrom's insights on ablutions at Qumran, M. Kister's reflections on Qumran halakot, and G. W. E. Nickelsburg's research on the cosmological and eschatological thoughts in 1QH.]

VanderKam, J. *The Dead Sea Scrolls Today.* Grand Rapids, Mich.: William B. Eerdmans, 1994. [An excellent introduction; see esp. "A Sketch of Qumran Thought and Practice," pp. 108–19.]

Vermes, G. *The Dead Sea Scrolls in English*, 3rd ed. London: Penguin, 1987. [See esp. "The Religious Ideas of the Community" pp. 36–57.]

———— *The Dead Sea Scrolls: Qumran in Perspective.* Cleveland: Collins World, 1978. [See esp. "The Religious Ideas and Ideals of the Community" pp. 163–97; this is an early version of the preceding essay.]

———— "Qumran," in *Post-biblical Studies.* Studies in Judaism in Late Antiquity 8; Leiden: Brill, 1975; pp. 3–56. [One of the leading experts on Qumran at Oxford examines, *inter alia*, Early Judaism in light of the scrolls, the etymology of "Essenes," Qumran interpretation of scripture, and sectarian halakah in CD.]

————, F. Millar, M. Goodman, *et al.*, eds. "The Writings of the Qumran Community," in *The History of the Jewish People in the Age of Jesus Christ (175 B.C.–A.D. 135*, by E. Schürer. Edinburgh: T.&T. Clark, 1986; vol. 3.1, pp. 380–469. [A major reference work focused on what was thought to be Qumran literary creations; usually incorporates publications only up to 1983.]

Violette, J.-C. *Les Esséniens de Quomrân*. Les Portes del l'Étrange; Paris: Éditions Robert Laffont, 1983. [See esp. "Les croyances de Quomrân" on pp. 148–218.]

Waltschanow, S. *The Old Testament Pseudepigrapha Texts, Qumran, and the Old Slavonic Pseudepigrapha*. Annuaire de l'academie de theologie "St. Clement d'Orchrida" 23 (49); Sophia, 1976. [In Russian. This article contains important reflections on the theological meaning of paradise and angels at Qumran.]

Weinfeld, M. *The Organizational Pattern and the Penal Code of the Qumran Sect: A Comparison with Guilds and Religious Associations of the Hellenistic-Roman Period*. Novum Testamentum et Orbis Antiquus 2; Göttingen: Éditions Universitaires Fribourg Suisse and Vandenhoeck & Ruprecht, 1986. [A careful study of Qumran's high regard for organization and social stratification.]

Yadin, Y. *The Temple Scroll: The Hidden Law of the Dead Sea Sect*. London: Weidenfeld and Nicolson, 1985. [Yadin concluded that 11Q Temple was composed at Qumran; see esp. his insightful study of numerous concepts, the New Fruits Festival, Temple, purity, and kingship.]

Index of Passages

APOCRYPHA AND PSEUDEPIGRAPHA OF THE OLD TESTAMENT

QUMRAN

RABBINICA

PHILO

PLINY THE ELDER

JOSEPHUS

NEW TESTAMENT

Index of Authors

Index of Subjects